Traditionalism and the Ascendancy of the Malay Ruling Class in Colonial Malaya

The **Strategic Information and Research Development Centre (SIRD)** is an independent publishing house founded in January 2000 in Petaling Jaya, Malaysia. The SIRD list focuses on Malaysian and Southeast Asian studies, economics, gender studies, social sciences, politics and international relations. Our books address the scholarly community, students, the NGO and development communities, policymakers, activists and the wider public. SIRD also distributes titles (via its sister organisation, **GB Gerakbudaya Enterprise Sdn Bhd**) published by scholarly and institutional presses, NGOs and other independent publishers. We also organise seminars, forums and group discussions. All this, we believe, is conducive to the development and consolidation of the notions of civil liberty and democracy.

*****

Operating as the publishing arm of the National University of Singapore, **NUS Press** produces around 50 publications per year, some of them in association with academic publishers in North America, Europe, Japan, China, Hong Kong, Indonesia and the Philippines. The Press maintains a regional focus on Southeast Asia and a disciplinary focus on publications in the humanities and social sciences.

Traditionalism and the Ascendancy of the Malay Ruling Class in Colonial Malaya

Donna J. Amoroso

Strategic Information and Research Development Centre
Malaysia

NUS PRESS
SINGAPORE

First published in Malaysia in 2014 by:

Strategic Information and Research Development Centre
No. 11 Lorong 11/4E, 46200 Petaling Jaya, Selangor, Malaysia
Fax: (60) 3 7954 9202
Email: gerak@gerakbudaya.com
Website: www.gerakbudaya.com
ISBN: 978-967-0630-16-8 (pbk.)
ISBN: 978-967-0630-18-2 (hbk.)

and

First published in Singapore in 2014 by:

NUS Press
National University of Singapore, AS3-01-02
3 Arts Link, Singapore 117569
Fax: (65) 6774 0652
Email: nusbooks@nus.edu.sg
Website: www.nus.edu.sg/nuspress
ISBN: 978-9971-69-814-0 (NUS Press pbk.)

National Library Board, Singapore / Cataloguing-in-Publication Data
Data available

Perpustakaan Negara Malaysia / Cataloguing-in-Publication Data
Data available

Copy-editing by Gareth Richards
Cover design and layout by Janice Cheong

Printed by Vinlin Press Sdn Bhd
2 Jalan Meranti Permai 1
Meranti Permai Industrial Park
Batu 15, Jalan Puchong
47100 Puchong, Selangor, Malaysia

To
Dominic Amoroso
with love and respect

Contents

Table and Map

Table

Map

Abbreviations and Acronyms

AMCJA	All-Malaya Council of Joint Action
ANM	Arkib Negara Malaysia (National Archives of Malaysia)
API	Angkatan Pemuda Insaf (Movement of Aware Youth)
BMA	British Military Administration
CCAO	chief civil affairs officer
CO	Colonial Office
CPM	Communist Party of Malaya
CSEAS	Center for Southeast Asian Studies (Kyoto University)
DCCAO	deputy chief civil affairs officer
FMS	Federated Malay States
GRIPS	National Graduate Institute for Policy Studies
KMM	Kesatuan Melayu Muda (Young Malays Union)
KMT	Kuomintang
MCKK	Malay College Kuala Kangsar
MPAJA	Malayan People's Anti-Japanese Army
MSS	Malayan Security Service
NEP	New Economic Policy
Pekida	Pertubuhan Kebajikan dan Dakwah Islamiah Malaysia
Perkasa	Pertubuhan Pribumi Perkasa Malaysia (Malaysian Organisation for the Strengthening of the Sons of the Soil)
PIJ	Political Intelligence Journal
PKMM	Partai Kebangsaan Melayu Malaya (Malay Nationalist Party of Malaya)
PUTERA	Pusat Tenaga Rakyat (Centre of People's Power)
SCAO	senior civil affairs officer
UMNO	United Malays National Organisation
WIR	Weekly Intelligence Review

Foreword I

Audrey R. Kahin

Malaysia's path to independence stands apart from that of the other Southeast Asian nations, most notably Indonesia and Vietnam, where independent states emerged from armed struggles against their colonial governments. In sharp contrast, the political order that prevailed in Malaya for more than a decade following the Second World War remained critically dependent on a continued British presence that could protect the position of the traditional Malay elite against competing forces within the country. The present work sheds a fresh light on the contest for power in the mid-1940s that brought about this outcome. Originating from Donna Amoroso's PhD dissertation,[1] and published over three years after her untimely death in January 2011, *Traditionalism and the Ascendancy of the Malay Ruling Class in Colonial Malaya* provides a glimpse not only of Donna's particular acuity of analysis and her scholarly abilities but also of the precise reasoning and beautiful prose that characterised all her writing.

The study focuses on the role played by the Malay aristocracy in determining the outcome of the postwar struggle on the Malay peninsula and in shaping the character of the Federation of Malaya that eventually emerged in 1957. It shows how during these early postwar years the Malay elite established their claim to a preeminent position in the federation long before it achieved its full independence, an outcome that has influenced the character of the Malaysian polity up to the present day.

In this original and perceptive work Donna shows how the success of the upper segment of Malay society in the aftermath of the Second World War

[1] Cornell University, 1996.

was to a large extent based on the character of British rule over the previous half century, during which the colonial power had reconstructed Malay tradition for its own ends. She illustrates how earlier British manipulations of the political and social order became a vital component in the Malay elite's ability in 1946 to pressure the government in London to abandon its plan to transfer power to a Malayan Union where all citizens, including non-Malays, had equal rights and the position of the Malay sultans was to be largely ceremonial. Instead, the Malay states and their rulers emerged as 'free and sovereign territories under British protection', and the elites were given time to consolidate their position so that they could eventually replace the British at the helm of the independent state, with political power firmly in the hands of the Malay ruling class.

An original feature of the work is the concept of 'traditionalism', a term that the author employs to describe the conscious use by the British of traditional elements of the earlier Malay kingdoms to consolidate their own administration. The colonial rulers developed a structure of government where the old idioms and rituals were reshaped to provide 'a modern version of an ancient Malay culture' that would not impede the system of government they were trying to impose. These new rituals of state safeguarded the Malay rulers' privileged position while at the same time shielding their subjects from the reality of colonial rule, for the common people in the peninsula's component states were still able to see themselves as living within their previous Malay sultanates. Thus the British helped fashion a Malay culture that was compatible with colonial rule, freezing it in an invented past and separating its leaders from exercising any real power, while creating and centralising a system of government that accorded with the needs of the metropole. While maintaining and reshaping the positions of the Malay rulers as the titular heads of their states and safeguarding the positions of the village heads (*penghulu*) at the lowest level of government, the British undercut the powers of the aristocracy or chiefs (descendants of former rulers), assigning them to largely powerless positions on state councils or eventually training their sons to become bureaucrats within the Malay administrative service. In the positions of real authority were the European district officers, who formed a new layer of state administration. Donna describes the result of this manipulation in the following terms: 'Now both the top stratum of government (the ruler) and the bottom stratum (the *penghulu*) remained Malay. The middle ranges, formerly the province of the powerful district chiefs, were replaced by British officers'. From these positions the British officials could be the driving force in implementing colonial administrative policies.

After 1945 the 'traditionalism' pursued over the previous decades played a new role, protecting the rulers from being ousted from their positions and turning them instead into a weapon the Malay aristocracy could employ to combat both the British plans for a Malayan Union and the anticolonial nationalism that was sweeping other former colonial countries of Southeast Asia. This new force was based on national sovereignty and the political rights of all the people, and its major exponent in Malaya was the Kesatuan Melayu Muda (KMM, Young Malays Union), an organisation founded on radical democratic principles, which took as its model the nationalist movement in Indonesia. As it turned out, adherence to the earlier traditionalism protected not only the sultans' positions but also those of the bureaucratic aristocracy against this nationalist threat from below.

The outcome of the struggle was not a foregone conclusion, for the British returned in 1945 'without the pro-Malay attitude which had defined prewar colonialism'. Both the Malay elite and members of the KMM had collaborated with the Japanese during the occupation. Disillusioned by their protégés' 'betrayal', the British sought to replace the old Malay order with a 'Malayan Union' within which the Malay rulers would lose most of their privileges and a 'Malayan public' would replace the prewar Malay, Chinese and Indian communities. These British plans roused fears among Malay conservatives, who saw the Malayan Union as a threat to the Malay race (*bangsa Melayu*), rendering them merely one group (*kaum*) within their own country.

In tracing the course of the ensuing struggle, Donna portrays Dato Onn bin Jaafar as the prime mover in pressuring the Malay sultans to take a stand against the Malayan Union, so that they could become its major impediment and at the same time serve as symbols of an emerging Malay nation that embraced the whole peninsula. She also highlights Onn's role in shaping the opposition to British plans into a political movement, the United Malays National Organisation (UMNO), which developed into a mainstream political party personifying an 'acceptable Malay nationalism', and able to appropriate 'the powerful tools of nationalist symbolism and practice'. At the same time UMNO provided an opportunity for a resurgence of aristocratic power at the expense of both the rulers and the radicals. From 1948 this led to a wholesale suppression of progressive politics, including both Malay radicalism and, during the Emergency, Chinese and Indian participation.

As Donna points out, the history of this period has shaped the character of the Malayan and later Malaysian Federation. The hijacking of the nationalist movement by the Malay aristocratic forces prevented a restructuring of society where all citizens would enjoy equal access to benefits of nationhood. Because the aristocrats had used the 'legitimising power of the rulers to deflect radical criticism', it was difficult for them later to move decisively against the royal office holders, and the rulers retained their ability to veto any moves towards constitutional change. The result, she contends, was that 'the popular Malay nationalism which survived independence was a colonial form, encouraged to look to archaisms like the rulers for validation and satisfaction'.

*

That this important study was not published in Donna's lifetime was largely because of the strength of her own self-criticism together with the fact that, after achieving her doctorate, her major focus became less on pursuing her own historical research than on encouraging and assisting Southeast Asians to write their own history. Nevertheless, she did demonstrate the high quality of her own scholarship when, with her husband, Patricio (Jojo) Abinales, she coauthored an award-winning book entitled *State and Society in the Philippines*,[2] a work that provided 'a sustained analysis of state formation over the course of a millennium' and soon became essential reading for students of the Philippines.

At the same time as she was completing her dissertation at Cornell in the mid-1990s, Donna served as assistant editor and then acting editor of Cornell's Southeast Asia Program's publications, where she displayed the meticulous and imaginative writing and editorial skills that characterised her later work. After completing her doctorate she taught at Wright State University in Dayton, Ohio, then accompanied her husband to Japan, where she was appointed a visiting scholar at the Center for Southeast Asian Studies at Kyoto University. It was there in 2002 that she established almost single-handedly the multilingual *Kyoto Review of Southeast Asia*, a remarkable online journal that is one of a kind and of which she was founding editor. Publication of *Kyoto Review* sprang from Donna's strong belief that Asian scholars should be able to disseminate and read scholarly

[2] Patricio N. Abinales and Donna J. Amoroso, *State and Society in the Philippines*, Lanham MD: Rowman & Littlefield, 2005.

writings in their own languages, in order to allow the region's intellectual currents to circulate freely without being confined to the medium of English.

She still, however, recognised that facility in the English language was important for Japanese scholars wishing to reach an international audience. In 2004, when she was appointed an associate professor at the National Graduate Institute for Policy Studies (GRIPS) in Tokyo, she established the Academic Writing Center, which aimed at helping Japanese and non-Japanese students communicate their ideas with greater precision and effectiveness in English.

After bravely combating cancer for several years, Donna, with her husband and beloved young daughter Angela, returned to the United States in the autumn of 2010 to spend a year in Washington DC, where Jojo had been appointed a visiting scholar at the Woodrow Wilson International Center for Scholars. Relaxed and delighted to be back, Donna visited Ithaca again in November of that year, together with Jojo and Angela. Her unexpected death two months later came as she and her family were happily planning another move, to pursue new work and a new life in Hawaii. As a reflection of the breadth and meticulousness of her scholarship, the present work stands as a memorial to Donna, providing some indication of her scholarly achievement and promise, and adding to the deep sense of loss felt by all who knew and loved her.

Ithaca
31 August 2013

Foreword II

Francis Loh Kok Wah

Malaysia is transiting from an era of 'old politics', inscribed above all by ethnic politics, to one of 'new politics', generally characterised by increasing interethnic cooperation in the pursuit of democratic politics. The publication of *Traditionalism and the Ascendancy of the Malay Ruling Class in Colonial Malaya* by the late Donna Amoroso is most opportune, because its focus is on two earlier periods of political transition: first, the transition from Malay rule to British indirect rule during the colonial period; and second, the emergence and eventual triumph of the United Malays National Organisation (UMNO) led by aristocrats over both the Malay rulers and radical Malay nationalists. The insights of the earlier transitions contained in the book resonate with current concerns about the transition from the old politics to new politics.

Although the Barisan Nasional coalition led by UMNO was returned to power again in the general election held on 5 May 2013, the opposition Pakatan Rakyat coalition actually polled almost 51 per cent of the popular vote. Looking back, the results of the previous general election held in 2008 similarly indicated a very close contest between the incumbent Barisan Nasional and the then newly-formed Pakatan Rakyat. For the first time since 1969 the ruling coalition was denied a two-thirds majority of parliamentary seats in both 2008 and 2013. Because a two-thirds majority in parliament is required for amending the 1957 Federal Constitution, this has been the benchmark by which the ruling coalition judges its own performance. Perhaps even more significant was the fact that Pakatan Rakyat assumed control of five state governments, including the three most developed states – Selangor, Penang and (for a while) Perak. In local parlance, a political 'tsunami' occurred in 2008.

The Pakatan Rakyat-led state governments in Penang and Selangor then introduced so-called competency, accountability and transparency policies. Henceforth, all government contracts in those states required an open tender, unlike previously when a 'negotiated tender' was the norm for winning government contracts. Freedom of information legislation was also passed in the two state assemblies to offset the tight control of official information and data under the Official Secrets Act. There was also a new momentum for bringing back local government elections, as well as decentralising social services, funding and decision-making to the local level. These initiatives leading towards the goal of good governance, and the clear trend towards a two-coalition system, constitute what is meant by the new politics. Finally, it seemed, Malaysia was becoming a more 'normal' democracy.

At the same time, alternative political discourses and practices reemerged, not least because of the consequences of economic growth and transformation, societal restructuring and the impact of new information and communication technologies. As a result, alternative oppositional voices came to be more keenly articulated in the federal parliament and state assemblies, as well as in the public domain, due in great part to the spread of the new mass media and the emergence of cause-oriented non-governmental organisations. These developments have been supported by a new middle class, generally young and better educated, representing all ethnic groups. So the new politics further implies that ethnic groups are not as unified as particularist political entities as before. The results of the two general elections clearly indicate that the Malays, like the Chinese and Indians, are also divided into several competing political groupings.

As already noted, Donna's *Traditionalism* is a historical investigation of two earlier periods of political transition. The first involved a shift from traditional Malay political leadership to indirect or protectorate rule under the British colonial administration. How did British rule impact on Malay society? How was the Malay ruling class transformed? Donna highlights the consolidation of the rulers over the aristocrats, a process that involved the centralisation and standardisation of the Malay states as well as the bureaucratisation of the aristocrats, all steered by the British. However, in order to establish the preeminence of the rulers over the aristocrats and the modernising Malay states 'traditionalism' was resorted to. Thus, in spite of all the transformations implied by indirect British rule, traditional norms and rituals continued to be conducted, even elaborated upon, largely to convey the impression, especially to ordinary Malays, that the rulers were still in charge.

The second political transition, the main focus of the book, featured the emergence and triumph of UMNO in the aftermath of the Second World War, especially from 1945 to 1948. During this transition, there occurred a three-way struggle among various Malay groups. The rulers, who with British support had established themselves at the top of the hierarchy during the colonial period, suffered a loss of prestige and status during the harsh years of the Japanese occupation, and compromised themselves by collaborating with the Japanese. When the British returned with their Malayan Union proposal after the war, the rulers were forced to endorse the British proposal that would have resulted in the effective demise of the Malay states and the granting of citizenship to non-Malays on liberal terms. Under these circumstances, the aristocrats sponsored the formation of UMNO and seized the leadership of the Malay community from the rulers. But they also turned the rulers into 'icons' in the process. More than that, Donna also discusses how the UMNO aristocrats learnt the language of nationalism and the practice of mass politics from a third group, the radical Malay nationalists. Mastering these skills, the UMNO aristocrats then defined and defended a narrow and conservative notion of ethnic nationalism that called for a rallying around the ruling class to protect Malay interests. Consequently the radicals, too, were sidelined, not only because of repression by the British but also because the aristocrats successfully established hegemony over the majority of Malays.

In these two previous transitions, and in the present one from old politics to new politics, a fragmentation of political leadership occurs, and the question of identity becomes a contested site. For the contest for popular support involves not only material but also ideational appeals. In this regard, it is commonplace to state that the three most important symbols that define Malay identity are the rulers, the Malay language and Islam.[1] Accordingly, although Malaysia is a multiethnic and multireligious society, the modern nation state acknowledges the Malay rulers as the heads of state, Malay as the national and sole official language, and Islam as the official

---

[1] See, for instance, Muhamad Ikmal Said, 'Malay nationalism and national identity', in Muhamad Ikmal Said and Zahid Emby, eds, *Malaysia: Critical Perspectives: Essays in Honour of Syed Husin Ali*, Petaling Jaya: Persatuan Sains Sosial Malaysia, 1996, pp. 34–73.

religion in the 1957 Federal Constitution. Article 153 of the constitution also 'safeguards' the 'special position' of the Malays (and other indigenous peoples), in providing for quotas to be reserved for them in the public service, in issuing business and trading licences and permits, in awarding scholarships and places in universities and colleges, and so on. Taken together, these provisions define the concept of *ketuanan Melayu* (Malay supremacy) which the conservative UMNO nationalists and proponents of the old politics insist must be the basis of governing Malaysia's plural society.

In the current transition, Malay supremacist groups like Pertubuhan Pribumi Perkasa Malaysia (Perkasa, Malaysian Organisation for the Strengthening of the Sons of the Soil) and Pertubuhan Kebajikan dan Dakwah Islamiah Malaysia (Pekida), and not infrequently UMNO leaders too, closely monitor and quickly condemn, mobilise and even file police reports against those who allegedly question or insult (*menghina*) the rulers, the status of the Malay language, Islam and special rights. During the past decade, leaders of Bersih 2.0, the major umbrella group fighting for clean and fair elections, were hauled up after police reports were filed against them for apparently making remarks deemed derogatory to Islam and/or *ketuanan Melayu*, insulting Malays, and so threatening public order and peace. In the run-up to the 2008 and 2013 general elections, police reports were also filed against ordinary people, especially non-Malays, for uploading or posting 'sensitive' remarks in the internet and social media, deemed to be anti-rulers, anti-Islam, anti-Malay and anti-special rights. A few notable individuals were even charged in court, as in the 2012 case of Mohammad Nizar Jamaluddin, who had previously served as the Pakatan Rakyat *menteri besar* (chief minister) of Perak. In this case, the court found that he had no case to answer. However, in another highly publicised case, the Court of Appeal in October 2013 overturned an earlier High Court judgement that had allowed the *Herald*, a Catholic weekly newspaper published in four languages (including Malay), to use the word 'Allah' in its publications. The justification for the Court of Appeal ruling was that its use by Christians would confuse Muslims, disturb the peace and create unrest. Significantly, the Pakatan Rakyat coalition, which includes both Parti Keadilan Rakyat and Parti Islam Se-Malaysia, headed by Malay political leaders, took the stance that non-Muslims had the right to use the word 'Allah' provided it was used respectfully and not misused. The point here is the political fragmentation of the Malays. For the UMNO-led government, egged on by their Malay supremacist supporters, the word 'Allah' could only be used by Muslims, while for the opposition-led Muslims, Malay–Muslim identity would not necessarily be undermined if Christians and other non-Muslims were allowed to use the same word.

The debate over Malay identity is central to Donna's argument too. She does not focus on Islam, and even less the Islamic resurgence that so many researchers concentrated on over the past three decades.[2] Nor does she discuss the politics of Malay as the national and sole official language, a subject that attracted the attention of many researchers in the 1960s to 1980s. Instead, she investigates the role of the monarchy, a much-neglected topic of research.[3] Although *Traditionalism* focuses on the colonial period and the immediate postwar years, the arguments it makes have important implications for contemporary politics. In particular, its analytical use of the concept of 'traditionalism' sheds light on what we understand to be traditional, and in that regard how other traditional institutions are being used in this current phase of transition from old to new politics too.

*

In the first part of the book, which looks at the transformation of the roles of rulers and aristocrats, Donna uses the correspondence and minutes of the colonial records (in particular the CO273 and CO882 Colonial Office series) and contemporary writings by British authors (for example, R.O. Winstedt,

---

2 See, for example, the essays in Virginia Hooker and Norani Othman, eds, *Malaysia: Islam, Society and Politics*, Singapore: Institute of Southeast Asian Studies, 2003.

3 Only a few studies that link the institution of the monarchy to contemporary party politics come to mind though there does seem to be a new interest in this topic. See Kobkua Suwannathat-Pian, *Palace, Political Party and Power: A Story of the Socio-Political Development of Malay Kingship*, Singapore: National University of Singapore Press, 2011; Anthony Milner, '"Identity monarchy": interrogating heritage for a divided Malaysia', *Southeast Asian Studies*, vol. 1, no. 2, 2012, pp. 191–212; Ahmad Fauzi Abdul Hamid and Muhamad Takiyuddin Ismail, 'The monarchy and party politics in Malaysia in the era of Abdullah Badawi (2003–09): The resurgence of the role of the protector', *Asian Survey*, vol. 52, no. 5, 2012, pp. 924–48; Ahmad Fauzi Abdul Hamid and Muhamad Takiyuddin Ismail, 'The monarchy in Malaysia: struggling for legitimacy', *Kyoto Review of Southeast Asia*, issue 13, 2013, at: http://kyotoreview.org/issue-13/the-monarchy-in-malaysia-struggling-for-legitimacy/; and Syed Husin Ali, *The Malay Rulers: Regression or Reform?* Petaling Jaya: Strategic Information and Research Development Centre, 2013.

R.J. Wilkinson and T.S. Adams) to reconstruct the attitudes, ideas and intentions of British officers and other writers towards the Malay rulers, and of the rulers' attitudes and responses to British policy. Many of the primary sources that Donna consulted have also been researched by others. Whereas they drew on these sources to discuss how the Malay ruling class and Malay politics had changed as a result of the new configuration of power, like the bureaucratisation of the Malay aristocracy after the turn of the century, she uses them in a novel way: to argue that an ideological conversion was underway long before that point. She shows that British power and Malay responses since the mid-nineteenth century had reshaped three important aspects of the conceptual framework in which Malay politics operated: first, the assumptions about the meaning and purpose of government; second, the definition and shape of the political unit referred to as the 'Malay state'; and third, the relation of economic resources to political leadership. Hence the standardisation of the Malay states and the bureaucratisation of the Malay elite are regarded by Donna not as transformations of the first order, but as phenomena resulting from the elite's prior ideological conversion. Unlike others, she stresses that a new idiom of politics underscored that standardisation and bureaucratisation.

Traditionalism is also one of the first works on Malaysian history that offers special attention to political discourses, as opposed to the events and personalities, parties and policies that feature in so much orthodox historiography. Writing her thesis in the mid-1990s, she was particularly influenced by the discursive turn that had developed in the study of the history and social sciences of the Southeast Asian area, including Malaysia.[4]

In the second part of the book, archival sources, UMNO documents, the Colonial Office CO873 series, War Office records, British Military Administration records, political memoirs and contemporary newspaper editorials are consulted to great effect. Significantly, Donna treats the political writings of this period as a public transcript of the ideas and thoughts of the various protagonists – for the debates on the important political issues of the day and not just for historical data about events and activities. Nor does she use her sources merely as a measure and celebration of the emergent nationalist movement but rather as tools for analysing

[4] One of the first books on Malaysia that utilised cultural and discursive lenses was Joel S. Kahn and Francis Loh Kok Wah, eds, *Fragmented Vision: Culture and Politics in Contemporary Malaysia*, Honolulu: University of Hawaii Press, 1992.

changes in Malay political ideas during those heady times from 1945 to 1948. The discourses in the newspapers, periodicals and other occasional publications reflected the attempts of the literate and politically active to shape public opinion and political practice. Much like the internet and social media today, these publications were part of the new idiom of power and power relations in the postwar world. Hence the analysis investigates the medium, discursive style, readership and their effects on political discourse through this public transcript.

Throughout the study, traditionalism is a central theme. Initially, British intentions were to 'civilise' the Malays to enable them to enjoy good government, progress and modernity. However, an important change in British thinking occurred by the middle of the nineteenth century, an observation initially made by the prominent Dutch scholar Hendrik Maier, a position that Donna supports. Apparently, the original Malay system could not provide guarantees for British demands for the protection of property, free labour and security for the movement of capital, the end goals of British colonialism. The Malays, the colonialists surmised, would not be able to progress into modernity as anticipated. The solution, therefore, was to preserve Malay culture in a way that did not obstruct those goals. Indirect rule, she argues, supplied the structure for the project of preservation. Through indirect rule, the British could guide and reshape but also preserve the traditional elites.

As the British worked to restore Malay court culture, and preserve customs and rituals of the past, the meaning of these traditions inevitably changed, because they operated not in the Malay world which had given rise to them but in a new world determined by British economic and political power. Rituals that were once unconscious reflections of the values and practices of a society were now consciously invoked, and they could not but play different roles in the colonial context. Citing Joseph Levenson, who observed the same in his influential study of Confucian China, Donna argues that 'it is this element of conscious innovation which is the difference between tradition and traditionalism'.[5] In essence, traditionalism is the conscious use of traditions by appealing to, selection of, even reconstruction of old idioms and rituals to serve present needs. Invariably traditionalism narrows the vision of tradition. On the one hand, the restoration of Malay

---

5 Joseph R. Levenson, *Confucian China and its Modern Fate: The Problem of Intellectual Continuity*, London: Routledge and Kegan Paul, 1958.

culture was selective. There was a need to forget about piracy, opium-smoking chiefs, and surplus appropriation and exploitation of the peasants by the chiefs. On the other hand, new rituals began to be created, for example council meetings where the Malay rulers sat with British officials, Malay chiefs and Chinese commercial leaders. So the council meeting brought together colonial officialdom, hereditary privilege and foreign capital, but it was adorned with ceremonial features by utilising familiar traditional cultural trappings. So, too, those flag-raising ceremonies on auspicious occasions, and royal visits that the rulers began to adopt, initially riding in carriages with mounted police escorts into neighbouring areas, and later in cars to towns and villages further away. Whichever, the old rituals were being used for new purposes, and the new discourse was being brought into the local idiom.

Borrowing from the insights of Eric Hobsbawm and Terence Ranger in their pathbreaking *The Invention of Tradition*, Donna also argues that the new tradition is always in the service of change.[6] It is invented to make change more palatable for those experiencing it, not to limit change or turn back the clock. She highlights the fact that the so-called traditions associated with the rulers were actually inspired by the British who wanted the rulers not only to play the role of go-betweens, but also to be go-betweens who could continue to inspire loyalty among the Malay *rakyat*. In the Malay case, the novel purpose that the new tradition served was both the legitimisation of British power and the survival of the Malay ruling class. The new rituals of state, the glorification of Malay royalty and the bureaucratisation of Malay aristocrats shielded colonial reality from the peasants who understood themselves to be living in a Malay state still, as defined primarily by the presence of the rulers and the various invented traditions.

The consequence of traditionalism is a reified version of Malay tradition, the manifestation of which, for the uncritical observer, is often misunderstood to be the essential characteristics of Malay culture and identity. In fact, *Traditionalism* opens with a quotation from Mahathir Mohamad, the longest-serving prime minister of Malaysia. In his controversial book *The Malay Dilemma*, Mahathir had observed that Malays were intrinsically obedient to constituted authority.[7] He elaborated that the

---

[6] Eric Hobsbawm and Terence Ranger, eds, *The Invention of Tradition*, Cambridge: Cambridge University Press, 1983.

[7] Mahathir Mohamad, *The Malay Dilemma*, Singapore: Times Books International, 1970.

typical Malay citizen depended on his or her rajas and chiefs, and that the Malay ruling class was central to the preservation of the Malay character of Malaya. In other words, Malay identity relies on the visibility, even the existence of the aristocracy and rulers. This means, incongruously, that the survival of feudal notables is necessary to guarantee Malay social and cultural identity in a modern capitalist society. In her analysis, Donna tries to explain how this judgement that Malays are 'backward', 'traditional' and 'feudal' became so common in writings and observations of the Malays throughout most of the twentieth century. In light of this, she explores how a traditional ruling class under British colonial rule created a 'world after its own image'. For as the economic, demographic and political foundations of colonial rule transformed the Malay peninsula, the British sought to preserve Malay society in its traditional form – rural, politically docile and dependent on traditional aristocrats and royalty – even more so. For Donna, this 'central paradox of British colonial rule' is expressed in terms of how the Malay ruling class resorted to traditionalism and universalised its image and interests onto the entire Malay society in order to survive colonialism.

*

Donna goes on to argue that that image left Malay society ill-equipped to understand itself capable of change during the second period of transition after the Second World War. During the Japanese occupation, the Malay rulers had suffered a loss of status and prestige. Among other factors, they were denied their usual allowances and pensions from the colonial administration while the ceremonies and official visits that they conducted under the sponsorship of the British were shelved. They further lost the respect of the Malay people when they succumbed to British pressure to establish the Malayan Union in 1946. This British initiative was an attempt to reestablish their rule and restore stability over the plural society via the administrative centralisation of the Malay states. Not only would the Malayan Union have eliminated the sovereignty of the Malay states, by offering citizenship rights to Chinese and Indian immigrants on liberal terms, the character of the Malay nation itself would have been radically transformed.

It fell to aristocrats like Onn bin Jaafar to form UMNO, in order to pull together the Malays from the various states to protest against the Malayan Union proposals. In this endeavour, the UMNO aristocrats were challenged by radical Malay nationalists who had emerged as a significant force after the war and posed a threat to the entire ruling class. Influenced by Indonesian nationalists, they were first to introduce the new idiom of mass politics and the new language of nationalism and popular sovereignty to the Malays. The radicals formed the Partai Kebangsaan Melayu Malaya (PKMM, Malay Nationalist Party of Malaya) and the Angkatan Pemuda Insaf (API, Movement of Aware Youth). Through their various publications and mass rallies, they extolled the virtues of freedom and justice, and called for immediate independence. In addition, they attempted to move towards a wider notion of sovereignty – a people's sovereignty – which was not only critical of the privileges of the Malay rulers but also welcoming of non-Malays as part of the nation, and as manifested in the cooperation between Pusat Tenaga Rakyat (PUTERA, Centre of People's Power) and the All-Malaya Council of Joint Action (AMCJA).

How did the UMNO aristocrats respond to this new challenge? Donna suggests that they first resorted to the 'repair work' of traditionalism and then propagated a narrowly defined nationalism anchored in a conservative ideology of *kesetiaan* (loyalty), *derhaka* (treason), *bersatu* (unity) and *kedaulatan* (sovereignty). In essence, it was a political programme that was exclusive to the Malays. In this regard, UMNO condemned the radicals for sidelining the rulers and reaching beyond the Malay community to collaborate with non-Malays, thereby contributing towards Malay disunity. Restoring traditionalism meant rehabilitating the Malay rulers. The rulers, who had earlier lost their credibility, were now projected as icons of the Malay nation. For what would the future be like if Malays were to compete openly against non-Malays, and if there were no more rulers as in the Straits Settlements like Penang and Melaka dominated by the Chinese? Worse, there was also fear of a communist takeover of Malaya in the aftermath of the war. Under a new round of traditionalism, the Malay rulers were touted by UMNO as the 'protectors' of Malay interests and identity, and as the icons of the *bangsa Melayu* (Malay race). In turn, the rulers encouraged people to join UMNO. In fact, the immediate agenda for the aristocrats was not independence from British colonialism, but the strengthening of British protection of Malay special privileges vis-à-vis 'foreign' communities. To protect Malay interests, there ought *not* to be control of an independent state but privileged access to the British colonial state for more administrative positions and educational opportunities. During this period from 1945 to 1948, then, anticolonialism was not intrinsic to UMNO's nationalism.

In his *Bangsa Melayu: Malay Concepts of Democracy and Community*, Ariffin Omar concludes that the struggle for *bangsa Melayu* amounted to one for 'Malay-ism' rather than for nationalism.[8] For although the conservative UMNO aristocrats incorporated the language of nationalism into their discourse alongside the tenets of traditionalistic Malay culture, they avoided articulating that nationalistic discourse in terms of democracy, nationalism and nationality to the awakened masses and the plural society that characterised postwar British Malaya. For Donna, reversing Ariffin's contention, avoiding a definition of the Malay(an) nation was not merely an outcome of the resort to the conservative ideology. It was the very purpose of focusing solely on the demands of the *bangsa Melayu* in the colonial setting. Malays could now take their place in the modern world of nation states without a fundamental change to their society. The appropriation of the language of nationalism for a conservative agenda was responsible for the triumph of the Malay ruling class in this second period of transition. Malay nationalism as sponsored by the UMNO aristocrats was depoliticised, conservative, even feudal, and the Malay world appeared backward, fearful of change and in need of (British) protection. In fact, the images and the identity it sponsored were invented.

*

Donna's use of traditionalism as an analytical tool provides valuable insights for understanding not only the role of the ruling class, the social origins of UMNO, the conservative basis of its ideology, the sidelining of the radicals who pushed for popular sovereignty and a wider notion of citizenship during these two earlier periods of transition. Insofar as UMNO has continued to be the dominant political force in Malaysia for the past 60 years, her study offers valuable insights into understanding UMNO's staying power too. Can UMNO triumph again over the challenges posed by the new transition in early years of the current century? Can UMNO arrest the present political fragmentation of the Malays? How will it modify and utilise traditionalism in this era of globalisation and the reach of the new forms of communication? Or will a new politics triumph over UMNO's old politics and its traditionalism?

To get at a comprehensive answer we have to locate our investigation within the context of yet another political transition that occurred in the aftermath of the 13 May 1969 racial riots. For following that tragic event,

---

[8] Ariffin Omar, *Bangsa Melayu: Malay Concepts of Democracy and Community, 1945–1950*, Kuala Lumpur: Oxford University Press, 1993.

various aspects of Malaysia's political system were restructured and the New Economic Policy (NEP), the affirmative action policy on behalf of the Malays and other indigenous peoples, was launched. Through these initiatives, UMNO apparently succeeded in reestablishing its hegemony over the Malays for several more decades, by reminding them of its role as the new icon and 'protector' of the *bangsa Melayu*. Although the NEP formally came to an end in 1990, pro-Malay policies have persisted until today.[9] On the one hand, non-Malays and many Malays in the opposition believe that meritocracy and an affirmative action policy on behalf of all who are considered poor, regardless of ethnic background, should replace the ethnic policies associated with old politics. On the other hand, there are those Malays who wish for its continuation, perhaps rationalising that they still cannot compete and are still in need of protection, not unlike how the learned Malay judge ruled that Christians cannot be allowed to use the word 'Allah', because Malays could otherwise get confused. Taking after Donna's argument, we would say that these negative notions have been invented by those elites precisely to remain in power.

In the run-up to the 2013 general election, UMNO, under the leadership of Najib Razak, appeared to have campaigned in a contradictory fashion on two fronts. On the one hand, it projected itself as a liberal and moderate force to non-Malays by articulating a multiracial and multireligious slogan '1Malaysia', while at the same time announcing economic reforms that would deregulate and liberalise the economy, threatening to roll back the NEP and transforming Malaysia into a high-income nation. In 2011 Najib's government had also repealed the Internal Security Act and other coercive laws that had allowed for detention without trial which the prime minister had publicly condemned. By contrast, among Malays in the rural areas, the promises made were to uphold *ketuanan Melayu* and to protect Malay political and economic interests. In this regard, the Malay leaders who headed the opposition Pakatan Rakyat parties were, time and again, denigrated for selling out Malay interests and creating disunity among Malays, precisely a refrain from the earlier transition period that Donna investigates.

---

[9] See Edmund Terence Gomez and Johan Saravanamuttu, eds, *The New Economic Policy in Malaysia: Affirmative Action, Ethnic Inequalities and Social Justice*, Petaling Jaya: Strategic Information and Research Development Centre, 2012.

Alas, in the aftermath of the general election, the pretence of moving Malaysia forward along liberal lines has largely been abandoned. Amendments to the Prevention of Crime Act 2013 and several other laws have brought back preventive detention in full force. A new Bumiputera economic empowerment programme has been announced. Meanwhile, there has been little mention of '1Malaysia'. It appears that UMNO, in coming to terms with the governing coalition's losses in the election, has decided to prioritise consolidating its support in the Malay heartland. Reforming UMNO – and its coalition allies – no longer finds any purchase in the government's agenda. This being the case, no doubt UMNO will resort to another round of traditionalism, with the party projecting itself as the ultimate protector of the Malays threatened externally by global forces, and by non-Malays and by sell-out Malay leaders at home. Donna Amoroso's insights will open up important historical antecedents and ways of understanding how traditionalism is in the process of being reinvented once again.

Penang
24 February 2014

Acknowledgements

I would first like to thank those who served on my PhD committee and read drafts of the original dissertation: Benedict Anderson, Sherman Cochran, Charles Hirschman, Isabel Hull, Audrey Kahin, Takashi Shiraishi and David Wyatt. I have learned from all of you and appreciate your patience and guidance over the years. A special thank you goes to William Roff who was my first teacher of things Southeast Asian. And I am especially grateful to the Southeast Asia Program, Cornell University, for making my field research possible.

In Malaysia many people helped me find resources and pointed out avenues of research, especially the librarians and archivists at the Arkib Negara Malaysia, Dewan Bahasa dan Pustaka, University of Malaya Library and Universiti Kebangsaan Malaysia Library. I would especially like to thank Zainal Abidin bin Abdul Wahid, who originally sponsored my research, and Khoo Kay Kim who offered advice to a confused graduate student fresh to the field. Others were generous with their time and insights and simply made me feel welcome doing research in their country: Firdaus Haji Abdullah, Engku Maimunah Md Tahir and Rustam A. Sani. For their excellent companionship during my time in Malaysia, I thank the entire Mandal household, Sarah Maxim, Patricia Pelley and Suriani Suratman. My short research trips to Britain were made abundantly productive by the staff of The National Archives (then the Public Record Office) and the Rhodes House Library. My non-research hours were made enjoyable by the companionship and kindness of Danilyn Rutherford, John Sidel and Florence Tajasque.

Back in the United States, before and after doing research, I benefited from the advice and assistance of the following people: Barbara Watson Andaya, Jomo K.S., Cheah Boon Kheng, George Kahin, Michael Leigh and Oliver Wolters. One always forms a special bond with other dissertation writers and I would like to acknowledge their fellowship during the writing-up period: Thanet Aphornsuwan, David Baldwin, Suzanne Brenner, Jose Cruz, Daniel Dhakidae, Anne Foster, Christoph Giebel, Lotta Hedman, Shawn McHale, Michael Montesano, Jim Oakey, Geoff Robinson, John Sidel and Thaveeporn Vasavakul. For their friendship in Ithaca and elsewhere, for making this stage of my life one I look back on with happiness, I would also like to thank: Andrew Abalahin, Ben Abel, Dominique and Bing-Bing Caouette, Evelyn Ferretti, Penny Dietrich, Jeff Hadler, Carol Hau, Kyaw Yin Hlaing, Jamal Abdullah, Douglas Kammen, Anita Kendrick, Roberta Ludgate, Sumit Mandal, John Najemy, Dolina Millar, James Powers, Teresa Palmer, Hazel Prentice, Saya Shiraishi, Benny Subianto, San San Hnin Tun, Benito Vergara and Amrih Widodo.

Finally, special thanks to Vincent Boudreau and Mary Callahan, who have made my life so much richer; to Coeli Barry, whose friendship has been so crucial in the final stages; to Dominic and Georgette Amoroso, whose home is always a haven of love and encouragement; and to the two Pats – steadfast in different ways, you both never gave up on me.

Donna J. Amoroso

*

From Dissertation to Book: A Second Acknowledgement

After Donna finished her dissertation, I suggested to her that she might start planning the publication of a revised version in a year's time. This was necessary for tenure purposes (she was teaching in Ohio then) but, more importantly, I thought *Traditionalism* could contribute to the ongoing discussions on Malaysian postwar history and politics. She demurred, saying that the study was 'not that good'. She also worried about how a work by a non-Malaysian on a critical phase of Malaysian history would be received by academics and pundits in that country. I persisted and, as has always been the case in our long relationship, she compromised and agreed to think about it.

We shelved the issue until we moved to Kyoto where, now freed from the pressures of the tenure process, she could go back to the dissertation, revise and update it for publication. I once again raised that possibility, and this time got some help from similar encouragements by Jomo K.S. and Sumit Mandal. Donna still dithered for the same reasons, but adding that *Traditionalism* may now be old hat as the reign of Mahathir Mohamad was coming to an end and Malaysians were concerned more about the future than with the past.

Her attention had also shifted elsewhere. She was now working on developing the *Kyoto Review of Southeast Asia*, an online multilingual journal of Kyoto University's Center for Southeast Asian Studies (CSEAS) where she served as editor until her passing in 2011. Donna also became drawn to the Philippines, finding its often vibrant and destabilising politics fascinating, especially when placed alongside that of seemingly sedate, contained and orderly Malaysia. Being married to a Filipino and regularly visiting the in-laws surely added to the curiosity. The result is the book *State and Society in the Philippines* that we co-wrote and which was published by the American publisher Rowman and Littlefield in 2005 (with Anvil Publishing Company producing the Philippine edition).

Since she passed away in January 2011, I have being trying to find ways to preserve the memory of Donna as a scholar. She was already known for the success of *Kyoto Review* which, under her stewardship, survived limited budgets, recalcitrant bureaucrats and occasional haughty authors to become one of the pillars of Kyoto's CSEAS. When she left, *Kyoto Review*'s issues were being translated simultaneously into Bahasa Indonesia, Chinese (Mandarin), English, Filipino, Japanese, Korean and Thai. No journal in Asia and elsewhere, online or printed, has ever achieved this feat.

State and Society in the Philippines has likewise done fairly well; it is being read and used as reference by faculty and students in the Philippines *and* the United States and elsewhere. The book achieved the most important goal we set out when we wrote it: a historical text that undergraduates can read and appreciate. In 2006 it was chosen one of the 'Outstanding Academic Titles in Comparative Politics' by *Choice*, the publication of the American Library Association. In the Philippines it is into its fourth reprint and there is discussion back home on the possibility of a fifth printing.

It was while I was reorganising her stuff that I came across my copy of *Traditionalism*. As I reread the dissertation, memories of our past conversations about it also came back. I thought that publishing it was worth another try again, alas *sans* Donna's input. (A humorous aside: I told myself that I will surely be getting an earful from her about this unilateral decision, but only when I join her in the Great Beyond.)

As I was too biased to evaluate the manuscript, I asked Ben Anderson, who was Donna's adviser and housing improvement buddy while we were in Ithaca, to take a second look at what she wrote. Ben suggested that I also write to Gareth Richards, who now works as an editorial consultant for Strategic Information and Research Development Centre, on the possibility of SIRD publishing the dissertation if it passed Ben's and an anonymous reader's critical eyes. SIRD, the Kuala Lumpur-based publishing group famed for producing some of the best critical and progressive books on Malaysian society and politics to date, was my hands-down choice. I know it would be Donna's too. Gareth replied saying that SIRD was extremely interested in the manuscript.

Ben wrote back this evaluation: 'I have finished reading Donna's thesis with enormous pleasure. Beautifully written, impressively researched, tightly organised, quietly humorous and "nice shooting" in the jungle of Malaysian history and politics'. This note and the positive review of an anonymous reviewer were, I believe, enough to convince SIRD of the manuscript's value. SIRD agreed to publish it. From there, things moved fast. Audrey Kahin, Donna's dear friend, mentor and editorial collaborator at Cornell University's Southeast Asia Program, gladly said yes when I asked her if she could write a foreword that discusses the book's arguments as well as reminisce about Donna. Francis Loh Kok Wah, one of Malaysia's leading political scientists and a fellow Cornell *mafioso*, also accepted my request to write an introduction that puts the book in comparative contexts.

With the publication of *Traditionalism*, Donna's life as a scholar has come full circle. And it would not have been possible without the assistance of colleagues, comrades and friends, old and new. Our daughter Angela wrote this note of thanks to 'everyone for helping publish, (re)write, support my Mom's book'. I wish to add and say that we are extremely grateful to Chong Ton Sin, SIRD's able publisher for supporting the project. Many thanks also to Gareth Richards who, along with Jaime Hang, deftly and with patience guided the editing and production processes, and to Janice Cheong, who crafted the layout and cover design. Finally we wish to express our heartfelt gratitude to Benedict Anderson, Audrey Kahin and Francis Loh for their support and their contributions to this project. Dominic and Georgette Amoroso, Douglas and Michelle Amoroso, and Eleanor Van Cott always held Donna in high regard for her intellect, her broad knowledge and her love of books. We are eternally grateful for their enduring presence in Donna's and our lives.

Patricio N. Abinales

Honolulu, 8 November 2013

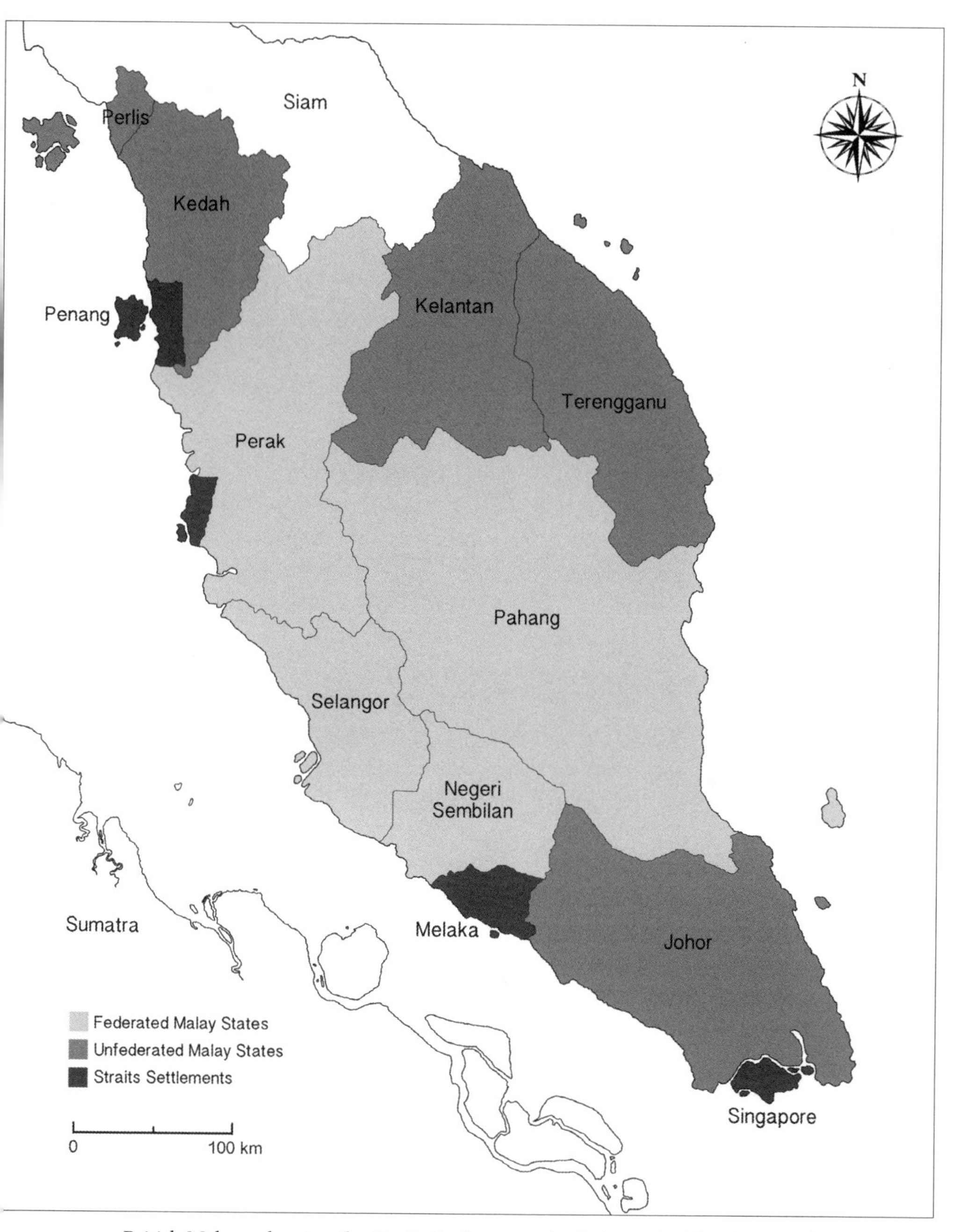

British Malaya, showing the Straits Settlements, the Federated Malay States and the Unfederated Malay States

Chapter One

Introduction

> The Malay is courteous and self-effacing. His world is full of nobility and he is never far from his rajas and chiefs. [T]he vast majority of Malays are feudalist and wish to remain so.... It is the rulers who have in the past furnished, and continue to present the Malay character of Malaya. Remove them, and the last vestige of traditional Malaya would disappear. It is the old values and ways of life which have held the Malays back, cutting them off from the changes continually taking place in the rest of the country and the world.[1]

1969 was a turning point in postcolonial Malaysian history. In the May elections of that year, class and ethnic tensions erupted into riots following the relatively poor showing of the dominant Malay political party, the United Malays National Organisation (UMNO). Constitutional government was suspended while a plan was devised to deal with the social, economic and political divisions within Malaysian society. The following year saw the publication of *The Malay Dilemma*, quoted from above. The author, Mahathir Mohamad, would go on to be the dominant architect of late twentieth-century Malaysia, becoming leader of UMNO and then prime minister of the country from 1981 to 2003. In his book, Mahathir tried to explain the central problem of Malaysian society – the lagging socioeconomic development of the indigenous Malays compared to the immigrant Chinese – and diagnosed a problem within Malay society itself. Mahathir's 'Malay dilemma' was the reluctance of Malays to assert their rights because of the value they attached to politeness and consideration

[1] Mahathir Mohamad, *The Malay Dilemma*, Singapore: Times Books International, 1970, pp. 116, 104, 113.

for the rights of others. At the same time, he argued, due to the economic dominance of the Chinese, Malays felt they were being 'dispossessed in their own land'.[2] It was this unresolvable conflict, according to Mahathir, which erupted, and would erupt again, into violence.

Mahathir placed considerable blame on British colonial policies in diagnosing the origins of this situation, and to remedy it argued that the Malays should be recognised as the 'definitive' citizens of Malaysia in terms of culture, language and education. But his book was more fundamentally concerned with Malay society itself. As suggested by the quotations above, Mahathir held the Malays responsible for their own backwardness through their adherence to 'old values'. Examples of this argument abound in Mahathir's critique. The Malay emphasis on formality and ritual, he argued, was conservative, working against innovation and inventiveness.[3] Fatalism made the pursuit of worldly goods and hard work low priorities.[4] Malay disregard for time was especially symptomatic of backwardness:

> Disregard for time is seen in the careless way in which it is spent. Doing nothing, or sipping coffee, or talking is almost a Malay national habit.... When there is no awareness of time, there can be no planning and work is never reliable.... A community which is not conscious of time must be regarded as a very backward society. What is more, it will remain a backward society. It can never achieve anything on its own and it can never be expected to advance and catch up with superior time-conscious civilisations. There is no doubt that the Malay failure to value time is one of the most important handicaps to their progress.[5]

Further, Mahathir criticised Malays for displaying an 'undeveloped' attitude towards money. They understood and used money as a 'convenience' rather than as capital for investment, making them poor businessmen.[6]

This critique was clearly aimed at bringing Malays into the capitalist economy which was the legacy of colonial rule and large-scale Chinese immigration. Indeed, Mahathir's prescription for Malay progress was that they become urbanised and educated and engage in specialised labour. Yet strangely, Mahathir did not propose sweeping away the remnants of the old order on his march to creating a capitalistic Malay society. Classifying Malays as 'feudalist', he accepted their putative desire to remain so. He thus

---

[2] *Ibid.*, p. 3.
[3] *Ibid.*, p. 157.
[4] *Ibid.*, pp. 158–59.
[5] *Ibid.*, pp. 162–63.
[6] *Ibid.*, pp. 167–69.

placed the retention of an obsolete class structure – commoners paying deference to rajas and chiefs – on the same level as adherence to Islam, as an essential characteristic of Malay culture. To accommodate the ensuing contradiction between feudalism and capitalism, Mahathir argued rather unconvincingly that a feudal society, which he elsewhere condemned as conservative, 'can be a dynamic society if there is dynamism at the top'. He found other virtues as well:

> In itself the feudalist inclination of the Malays is not damaging. It makes for an orderly law-abiding society. People who could follow and observe an unwritten code of behaviour are easily made to observe the written laws of a country. People who accept that a society must have *people of varying degrees of authority and rights* easily make a stable society and nation. A revolution in such a society is unusual unless led from above.[7]

Why did Mahathir exempt the feudal class structure from his condemnation of 'old values' which consigned the Malays to backwardness? The political utility of accepting the continued privilege of an ascriptive ruling class should not be overlooked. At first he may have thought it would make his message seem less radical. (The book was nevertheless banned.) Later, the image of Malays as intrinsically obedient to constituted authority provided an ideological basis for the centralisation of power in executive hands; Mahathir himself would lead a revolution from above. But it is also true that such a characterisation of Malay society was entirely commonplace. Mahathir merely reinforced a truism when he wrote that typical Malay citizens relied on their 'rajas and chiefs' and that the Malay ruling classes 'present the Malay character of Malaya'. Noteworthy here is the sense that Malay identity relies on the visibility, even the existence, of the Malay aristocracy and rulers. The consequences of this commonly held view are suggested by the juxtaposition of the three quotations above. Seeking to discard all other hindrances of traditional culture, Mahathir's acceptance of this essentialist position creates another dilemma. Incongruously, the survival of a feudal class is necessary to guarantee Malay social and cultural identity in a capitalist society.

This understanding of Malay society introduces the fundamental problem explored in this study. Backward, traditional and feudal have been common descriptions of Malay society through much of the twentieth century. In a broad sense, I ask how that judgement became so common. More specifically, I explore how a traditional ruling class, under British

---

7 *Ibid.*, pp. 170–71. Emphasis added.

colonial rule, 'creates a world after its own image'.[8] In trying to survive colonialism, the Malay ruling class successfully universalised its image and interests onto an entire society and left that society ill-equipped, in the early years of independence, to understand itself as capable of change. It was this legacy that Mahathir denounced and this era that, despite his theoretical forbearance towards the feudal remnants, he would do much to end.

Preservation and Change under Colonial Rule

Direct British control over the Malay peninsula was only established in the last quarter of the nineteenth century, but the power of Pax Britannica was felt much earlier. The British acquired the island of Penang in 1786 from the Sultan of Kedah, established a trading entrepôt in Singapore in 1819 and took possession of coastal Melaka from the Dutch by treaty in 1824. These three possessions became crown colonies known as the Straits Settlements. After decades of informal empire – economic and military influence emanating from Singapore – the British signed protectorate treaties with several Malay rulers beginning in 1874. Their territories – Selangor, Negeri Sembilan, Pahang and Perak – were united into the Federated Malay States (FMS) in 1896. Suzerainty over Kedah, Perlis, Kelantan and Terengganu was obtained from the Siamese by treaty in 1909. Over the next decade, administrative control was advanced over these states and Johor, although they all successfully resisted incorporation into the FMS. Collectively, they were known as the Unfederated Malay States.

It was the central paradox of colonial rule in the Malay states that while the economic, demographic and political foundations of the peninsula were transformed, the British sought to preserve Malay society in traditional form – overwhelmingly rural, politically docile and deferential to traditional aristocracies and royalties. This would have been a surprising outcome to any Englishman familiar with the area in the early to mid-nineteenth century. At that time, British opinion was largely hostile to Malay culture and wished to see it recede in favour of something altogether different. British power represented the intrusion of the industrialised world seeking raw materials, areas for investment and free trade. In pursuance of these things, the British demanded within their sphere of influence what they

---

8 Much as Marx described the successful quest of the bourgeoisie, which of course provides the larger context for the particular ideological struggle under consideration here. 'Manifesto of the Communist Party', in Eugene Kamenka, ed., *The Portable Karl Marx*, New York: Viking Penguin, 1983, p. 208.

called good government or civilisation, which was characterised by the rule of law, the creation of wealth through capitalism and free labour. In contrast, Malay culture was condemned as offering mainly piracy, civil war and slavery. The moral condemnation heaped on the Malays is expressed in the following passage by R.O. Winstedt, a British scholar-bureaucrat who was influential in defining Malay culture in the twentieth century for both the British and the Malays:

> As for home policy, both in Malacca and in modern Malay States, there was no expenditure on roads or education or on any of the ends of a modern civilised government. Instead of a regular army there were only a collection of swashbucklers and Indian mercenaries, attached to the court or to the households of the greater chiefs. Justice was not reformative but savage and deterrent. The only civil servants were police and tax collectors. Taxes before the British period were framed to extort revenue to enhance the wealth and importance of ruler and chiefs.[9]

It was argued at the time that the extension of British control over these states would be justified by the imposition of British values and the consequent progress the Malays would make towards civilisation.

Yet by the early 1880s, in the midst of the 'forward movement', a new attitude was ascendant: as an oriental people, the Malays were incapable of achieving the same heights of civilisation as the British and would probably never be able to govern themselves well. The British would therefore provide the legal and economic structure necessary for the territory to progress at a steady pace, regardless of the progress of the Malays themselves. Within this legal structure, backed by military power, those aspects of nineteenth-century Malay society which hindered capitalism were gradually eliminated. The economic structure facilitated a large influx of Chinese labourers who would come to outnumber the Malay population on the west coast.[10] In essence, British control rendered the Malays first harmless, then superfluous to the project of expanding capital. But at the same time, the dynamics of

---

[9] R.O. Winstedt, *The Malays: A Cultural History*, 5th ed., London: Routledge and Kegan Paul, 1961, first pub. 1947, pp. 77–78.

[10] By 1947 Malays and other 'Malaysians' (a category which meant indigenous people of the region, including Indonesians and aborigines) constituted only 43.49 per cent of the population of British Malaya. Chinese made up 44.7 per cent and Indians (including Sri Lankans) 10.25 per cent. Chinese and Indian immigration was connected with the extractive and agricultural industries which grew under colonial rule, mainly tin mining and rubber planting. Although they were considered transients by the British and the Malays, by 1931 one-third of the Chinese and one-quarter of the Indians were locally born.

the changing environment had not left Malay society untouched. Malays had been adjusting for some time to the power of the Straits Settlements by incorporating British ideas – such as progress – into their own political practice, adoptions welcomed by the British even after Malays were no longer considered capable of full civilised status. Less welcome were Malay efforts to benefit from the influx of capital into the tin areas of the west coast. Appearing to result only in more political rivalry and less stability, these developments were interpreted by British observers as the very disintegration of Malay culture. As British control was extended and consolidated in the 1880s and 1890s, and that culture was no longer a hindrance to capital, its demise became a cause for concern. For if the Malays could no longer aspire to be British, and this was what the inability to be civilised really meant, then they must certainly remain Malay. Hence the British became nostalgic about Malay culture and sought to restore and preserve it.

Hendrik Maier, writing about this attitudinal shift and its consequences, describes the 'strange contradiction [that] was created':

> [I]nnovation was to be connected with preservation in such a way that the Malay identity would be safe-guarded in a world that was rapidly changing as a result of economic explorations, the introduction of all sorts of technical achievements. The Malays should not change, but they should.[11]

This contradiction echoes down through the years and forms the basis of the most fundamental Malay dilemma. While Malay culture had grappled with changing conditions in the mid-nineteenth century and had consequently changed itself, in this new conception Malay identity could only be recognised through a culture which was unchanging. R.J. Wilkinson, founder of the colonial Malay educational system, wrote in 1906 in favour of a policy of 'conservation combined with development'.[12] Education was meant to equip the Malays for participation in modern society, but Wilkinson was nevertheless disturbed by the disruption to traditional custom which ensued. He asked in 1925,

> How long are these old Malay ceremonies likely to survive? Not long, perhaps. The Malay is becoming educated; he is commencing to believe in newspapers and books and, above all, he is beginning to have a good

[11] Hendrik M.J. Maier, *In the Center of Authority: The Malay Hikayat Merong Mahawangsa*, Ithaca NY: Cornell University Southeast Asia Program, 1988, p. 51.

[12] Cited in P.L. Burns, 'Introduction', in R.J. Wilkinson, ed., *Papers on Malay Subjects*, Kuala Lumpur: Oxford University Press, 1971, p. 3.

> conceit of himself. Why should he defer to the custodians of these ancient customs, old and ignorant people who cannot read and write? He does not discard – he would not be a Malay if he did – but he improves upon what went before and his improvements are of a most deadly character. There was once a Malay who tried to introduce poetic elements into the official letter-writing of the State Secretariat with which he was connected. The object was laudable enough, but the fond expressions used by Malay lovers seemed singularly out of place in official documents. Anyone who attends a modern Malay ceremony, be it a wedding or an ear-boring or even the installation of a prince, will be struck by the inevitable confusion between the new and the old. Not even Malay conservation will suffice to preserve the old customs of the country from the disintegrating influence of modern improvements.[13]

This impossible ideal – that Malays should preserve their precolonial culture intact while becoming proficient in modern life – permeated British writing on Malaya. One last example throws further light on the postcolonial dilemma. T.S. Adams was a British official known for his pro-Malay sympathies; after the Second World War he became an adviser to the Malay rulers. During the war, Adams wrote a short retrospective on 'the Malay in Malaya' in which he discussed the possibility of unifying the states of the peninsula, a goal long held by London and considered an inevitable stage in the progress of British Malaya. Adams wrote positively of a 'younger educated generation' which 'hopes to keep its culture and tradition and is looking for a way to preserve them', even while adapting to 'a world which thinks in continents and not in villages'. On the future of Malaya, Adams made this curious comment:

> We can at least be sure that if we retain the confidence and loyalty of Malays of all classes, and never weaken their culture and way of life, they themselves will increasingly look for greater unity among themselves, and be ready to associate with them peoples of other nationality, who are willing to share their loyalty and devotion to their land, and their respect for their constituted authorities.[14]

Here we encounter the dilemma in two guises. First was the idea that if Malays were protected from change, they would embrace change. Second, Adams was strangely confident that immigrant communities, who were employed largely in export industries and urban occupations and who

[13] R.J. Wilkinson, *Life and Customs: Part One: The Incidents of Malay Life*, Kuala Lumpur: Federated Malay States Government Press, 1925, pp. 47–48.

[14] Theodore Adams, 'The Malay in Malaya', *Asiatic Review*, vol. 40, no. 141, 1944, pp. 99–100.

had not under British rule been required to assimilate to Malay society, would nonetheless have developed an attachment to the land and a respect for indigenous aristocracies. The unsoundness of this assumption only underlines the increasing marginalisation of Malay culture within British Malaya. Nevertheless, Adams's comment distils the essence of Malay tradition as it was understood on the eve of decolonisation: an agrarian economic base and a feudal class structure.

Traditionalism as a Mechanism of Survival

Why was this particular distillation of Malay culture enshrined as the definitive tradition in a period of rapid change in the Malay world? Several reasons are discernible. During the nineteenth century, British maritime power and the suppression of piracy had forced the Malays to shift from the sea to the land, resulting in a sharp diminution of power and resources. As control of the regional trade passed out of Malay hands, a more cosmopolitan and outward-looking tradition was accordingly less accessible. In the late nineteenth and early twentieth centuries, the influx of immigrant labour to plantations and mines made Malaya a rice-deficient area. In addition to importing rice from other parts of the empire, colonial policy encouraged Malay rice production. The evolving needs of the export-oriented economy thus dovetailed with what was construed as the natural or traditional occupation of the Malays. Finally, the British mechanism for extending control over the Malay states differed sharply from their practice in the Straits Settlements and in Burma. Protectorate treaties, rather than direct rule, necessitated the retention of at least a remnant of a ruling elite.

These factors alone do not explain the elaboration of a particular idea of Malay tradition, but they do provide the preconditions. Indirect rule especially supplied the structure for the project of preservation outlined above. To trace the developments which led to Mahathir's dilemma, we must first clarify what is meant by tradition in the context of changing circumstances and then examine the Malay response to these colonial preconditions.

In a period of change, the way things have lately been (and are no more) is thrown into high relief. Once that way no longer exists, it can be named – tradition – and becomes the beautiful thing that once was, longed for all the more when change is rapid and dislocating. As in the Malay case, there often arise movements to restore, hold fast or return to tradition. Such a thing is not possible in the sense intended, for as Joseph Levenson reminds us in his work on intellectual continuity in China, the conditions surrounding an idea have as much to do with its meaning as the idea itself:

> [A]n idea changes in its persistence as well as in its rejection, changes 'in itself' and not merely in its appeal to the mind.... This apparently paradoxical transformation-with-preservation of a traditional idea arises from a change in its world, a change in the thinker's alternatives.[15]

As the British worked to restore Malay court culture, to preserve customs and rituals of the past, the meaning of these traditions inevitably changed because they operated not in the Malay world which had given rise to them, but in a new world determined by British economic and political power. Rituals which had once been the unconscious reflection of the values and practices of a society were now *consciously* invoked and they could not help but play a different role in the colonial context, no matter what the intentions of those who recalled them. It is this element of conscious invocation which is the difference between tradition and traditionalism. I use the latter term throughout this study to mean the conscious use of tradition – the appeal to, selection of or even reconstruction of old idioms and rituals – to serve present needs. In Levenson's words, 'the conscious will to narrow the vision ... not the blind plodding in the footsteps of the past, is the essence of traditionalism'.[16]

Two aspects of traditionalism are evident in this study of Malay society under colonial rule. The first was the need to be quite selective in restoring Malay culture. As Benedict Anderson writes of nationalist imaginings, so too in traditionalist imaginings, much had to have been 'already forgotten'.[17] In order to remember their traditional culture, Malays were required to have forgotten piracy, to have forgotten opium-smoking rulers, to have forgotten surplus-appropriating chiefs. It was a somewhat expunged tradition, one which, if it did not quite need to foster capitalist relations within Malay society (for that was no longer necessary), still could not be allowed to hinder them in the wider Malayan society. The second

---

15 Joseph R. Levenson, *Confucian China and its Modern Fate: The Problem of Intellectual Continuity*, London: Routledge and Kegan Paul, 1958, p. xiii. David Cannadine makes a similar point when he comments on the anachronism of the British monarchy's horse-drawn coach after the First World War: 'by now, the monarchs' mode of conveyance, already unusual and grand in the preceding period, had become positively fairytale'. David Cannadine, 'The context, performance and meaning of ritual: the British monarchy and the "invention of tradition", c. 1820–1977', in Eric Hobsbawm and Terence Ranger, eds, *The Invention of Tradition*, Cambridge: Cambridge University Press, 1983, p. 142.

16 Levenson, *Confucian China*, p. xviii.

17 Benedict Anderson, *Imagined Communities: Reflections on the Origin and Spread of Nationalism*, rev. ed., London and New York: Verso, 1991, pp. 199–203.

important manifestation of traditionalism was the need to create new ritual where none existed. Late nineteenth- and early twentieth-century Malaya featured innovations in technology and political institutions which had to be incorporated into the tradition being restored and preserved. A Malay ruler, to cite only one example, would find himself attending council meetings with the leading British, Malays and Chinese of his state. To contain this innovation – a meeting of colonial officialdom, hereditary privilege and foreign capital – within the vessel of tradition, it was adorned with new ceremonial utilising familiar cultural material. This process can best be understood using Eric Hobsbawm's idea of 'inventing tradition'.[18] In Hobsbawm's view, the crucial thing is not the familiarity, but the new purpose to which familiarity is put: 'the use of ancient materials to construct invented traditions of a novel type for quite novel purposes'.[19] The new tradition – ritual, custom, ceremonial – is always in the service of change. It is invented to make change more palatable for those experiencing it, not to limit the change or turn back the clock. In the Malay case, the novel purpose which new tradition served was both the legitimation of British power and the survival of the Malay ruling class.

Political changes imposed on the Malay ruling class in the second half of the nineteenth century were sweeping. Malay politics before colonial rule was control of manpower embedded in a spiritual system of leadership. Malay rulers represented 'the organising principle in the Malay world' and their success was measured by graceful demeanour and the spiritual rewards they bestowed, as much as by their military achievements.[20] Successful rulers maintained large retinues of followers and slaves; good relations with more or less autonomous regional chiefs guaranteed stability for peasant cultivators whose response to oppressive leadership would be to flee to the orbit of another chief. In this agrarian setting, rulers did their best to

---

[18] '"Invented tradition" is taken to mean a set of practices, normally governed by overtly or tacitly accepted rules and of a ritual or symbolic nature, which seek to inculcate certain values and norms of behaviour by repetition, which automatically implies continuity with the past. In fact, where possible, they normally attempt to establish continuity with a suitable historic past'. Eric Hobsbawm, 'Introduction: inventing traditions', in *The Invention of Tradition*, p. 1. Clive Kessler uses this approach to analyse colonial and contemporary Malay political culture in 'Archaism and modernity', in Joel S. Kahn and Francis Loh Kok Wah, eds, *Fragmented Vision: Culture and Politics in Contemporary Malaysia*, Honolulu: University of Hawaii Press, 1992, pp. 133–57.

[19] Hobsbawm, 'Introduction: inventing traditions', p. 6.

[20] See A.C. Milner, *Kerajaan: Malay Political Culture on the Eve of Colonial Rule*, Tucson: University of Arizona Press, 1982.

monopolise trade and appropriate economic surplus because the role of wealth was to further political-spiritual power. The British, more and more forcefully as the century wore on, demanded the protection of property, free labour and political security for the movement of capital. These things the Malay system could not provide; they were simply not part of the Malay world on the eve of colonial rule. As the British lost their reluctance to intervene directly on the peninsula, the Malay system was condemned and alternatives for the Malay elite narrowed.

The problem facing Malay leaders then was how to survive the surge of British power that threatened to sweep them away culturally, as well as economically and politically. The idioms of Malay political life – rigid class hierarchy, peasants ruled by ascriptive nobilities, royal ceremonial of indigenous, Hindu and Islamic origins, and rulers who embodied spiritual more than military power – all seemed likely to be lost in the British demand for rationality in administration and the regular collection of taxes. In this context, the shift in British priorities from civilisation to preservation created a second chance for the Malay political idiom and encouraged the mechanism of elite survival to be traditionalism. Very quickly the use of traditional forms created suitable versions of Malay rituals, politics and social relations which were articulated within colonial structures of authority. New rituals of state, the glorification of Malay royalty and the bureaucratisation of Malay aristocrats shielded colonial reality from peasants who understood themselves to be living in Malay states, as defined primarily by the presence of their rulers. The incorporation of British elements and officials into Malay ritual – 'the inevitable confusion between the new and the old' condemned by Wilkinson – usefully subordinated Malay culture to British imperial power. This articulation of tradition also directly served the Malay ruling class in each state, especially the rulers who were complicit in the project, by giving them roles in the colonial state and preserving their privileged position in Malay society. Traditionalism in colonial Malaya should be understood, then, neither as the persistence in old ideas and idioms by an elite resisting change nor as the imposition of a fabricated tradition by a colonial power. Instead, traditionalism in Malay society represented the dynamic interaction of British power and priorities, including the urge to preserve, with the effort of the Malay ruling class to survive in the new order.

The consequences of traditionalism – a reified version of Malay tradition capped by seemingly inherent deference to a hereditary ruling class – were evident to Mahathir in 1969, although he mistook its manifestations for essential characteristics of Malay society. It is the purpose of this study to illuminate that misunderstanding by demonstrating how the Malay ruling class used traditionalism to safeguard its privileged position through two crucial transitions which featured fundamental change in the way political power was exercised. The first, the central issues of which are outlined above, was the transition into colonial rule which I trace by analysing selected Malay–British interactions in the late nineteenth century and by focusing thematically on the transformation of the ruling class after colonial rule was consolidated. The second transition took place after the Second World War and involved not just the Malay ruling class and British colonial officials, but now also 'the people'. The new idiom of power was mass politics and the language it spoke was the language of nationalism. In this transition into the postcolonial era, I focus on the events known as the Malayan Union crisis of 1945 and 1946, in which the restored colonial state tried to impose a unified political structure on the Malay states and which witnessed the first mass mobilisation of peninsular Malays in opposition to that plan under the leadership of Malay aristocrats. The resulting political party, UMNO, went on to claim the mantle of mainstream Malay nationalism and has led every Malaysian government since independence in 1957.

The Ideological Struggle Underlying Nationalism

William Roff's now classic *Origins of Malay Nationalism* was a landmark of the first generation of postcolonial scholarship. Concerned to write from the colonised, rather than coloniser's point of view, and making extensive use of Malay-language sources, Roff's aim was 'to study the effects of British colonial protectorate control and of consequent social, political and economic change'.[21] His groundbreaking study debunked the notion that Malay society before the Second World War had been thoroughly stagnant and that political change had begun only with the anti-Malayan Union campaign.[22] Still, an effective prohibition on political activity, on the traditionalistic grounds that Malays should leave politics to their rulers, had indeed prevented the emergence of what was recognised in other colonial territories as popular nationalism – movements which sought the removal of the colonial power while simultaneously reconceptualising society. British

[21] William R. Roff, *The Origins of Malay Nationalism*, Kuala Lumpur: University of Malaya Press, 1980, first pub. 1967, p. xiv.

[22] For the latter view see, for example, Ishak bin Tadin, 'Dato Onn and Malay nationalism, 1946–51', *Journal of Southeast Asian History*, vol. 1, no. 1, 1960, pp. 56–88.

officials in Malaya, on the lookout for the emergence of nationalism, had hoped it would take the form of a pan-Malay movement which would make easier the administrative unification of the peninsula, if only the loyalty of the Malay ruling class could be retained. We have seen this in the wartime reminiscence of T.S. Adams, who anticipated a pro-colonial nationalism among the educated elite.[23] This unity in ruling class outlook, which was mildly encouraged by the educational grid of British Malaya, was slow to appear, for like political activity, it was caught in the conflicting demands of change versus preservation. Nevertheless, there was Malay attention to the idea of the nation before the war. Roff tells us:

> The concept of a Malay 'nation', though much discussed by the press and the intelligentsia, existed less as an ideal polity than as a defensive community of interest against further subordination to or dependence on 'foreigners', in particular against the domiciled Asian communities now so firmly entrenched in the states and settlements.[24]

The dominant response to this situation – that of the aristocratic bureaucracy and even of the small non-aristocratic intelligentsia – was to call for strengthened British protection of Malay special privilege vis-à-vis the foreign communities in the realms of education and administrative appointment. Significantly, this response did not demand control of the state, only the enhancement of privileged access to it. In fact, the colonial state was relied upon to guarantee the place of the Malays while they modernised and 'caught up with' the other communities. The most vitriolic criticism of the British in the prewar period was reserved for those moments when this guarantee was thought to be in danger.

A study by Ariffin Omar brings the discussion of Malay politics into the postwar period. Ariffin examines the change in status undergone by Malay rulers immediately after the war and argues that the community, *bangsa Melayu*, supplanted the rulers as the focus of Malay identity and loyalty. Ariffin terms this new focus 'Malayism – defined as the belief that the interests of the *bangsa Melayu* must be upheld over all else'.[25] Ariffin does not call this nationalism and it is not hard to see why. Malayism merely advances Malay interests against those of other communities. It is characterised by anti-Chinese chauvinism and the idea of Malay special privilege. Once again,

---

23 'There has been none of those growing pains which have shown themselves in some countries in hostility to the administration'. Adams, 'The Malay in Malaya', p. 99.

24 Roff, *Malay Nationalism*, p. 235.

25 Ariffin Omar, *Bangsa Melayu: Malay Concepts of Democracy and Community, 1945–1950*, Kuala Lumpur: Oxford University Press, 1993, p. 52.

the colonial state may be called upon to play a role in upholding Malay interests; anticolonialism is not intrinsic to Malayism. This phenomenon is clearly a child of the plural society. Can either Ariffin's 'Malayism' or Roff's 'defensive community of interest' be considered an 'origin' of Malay nationalism?

Ethnic identity, such as both of these rest on, may form a primary basis for national identity. At least one scholar has argued that despite geopolitical realities, a pan-Indonesian identification based on cultural, linguistic and religious commonalities was the basis of a Malay 'nation of intent' for much of the twentieth century.[26] But most students of nationalism also point to self-determination or sovereignty as a fundamental aspiration of every nation-in-the-making. Ernest Gellner calls nationalism the principle 'which holds that the political and the national unit should be congruent'.[27] In Anderson's conception, the nation became a visible model 'available for pirating by widely different, and sometimes unexpected hands'. Since that model was pioneered in the American and French Revolutions, crucial components were the sovereignty of the national state and political rights for members of the nation.[28] Popular anticolonial nationalism reflects these twin purposes when it seeks the ouster of the colonial power through mobilisation of national citizens-in-the-making. It is true that the elite leaderships of nationalist movements in turn generate their own 'discourse of order', often to prevent the emergence of socially revolutionary movements,[29] but they must still hold out promise of a better life for citizens in the postcolonial world. This they do by appeal to popular sovereignty: the state, like the nation, will belong to all of us. This dynamic of state and popular sovereignty was not present in the political aspirations of what Roff called the administrators – English-educated bureaucrats largely of aristocratic background. Before the war, this bureaucratic elite tried to protect its privileged access to a state which could not easily be imagined as a national Malay state, ruling as it did over disparate groups of Malays, Chinese, Indians and Europeans. Nor did it see beyond the traditionalistic formulation of its own society in which most Malays were 'peasants', not 'citizens'. Criticism of the colonial state, as Roff tells us, 'took the form of

---

26 Rustam Sani, 'Melayu Raya as a Malay "nation of intent"', in H.M. Dahlan, ed., *The Nascent Malaysian Society: Developments, Trends and Problems*, Bangi: Jabatan Antropologi dan Sociologi, Universiti Kebangsaan Malaysia, 1976, pp. 25–38.

27 Ernest Gellner, *Nations and Nationalism*, Ithaca: Cornell University Press, 1983, p. 1.

28 Anderson, *Imagined Communities*, pp. 7, 67.

29 See Partha Chatterjee, *Nationalist Thought and the Colonial World: A Derivative Discourse*, Minneapolis: University of Minnesota Press, 1986.

special pleas for continued Malay privilege, not of anti-colonial nationalism'. When the war broke out in 1939, conservative Malay associations dominated by these bureaucratic elites declared their loyalty to, and support of, the British empire in its time of need.[30]

It is not surprising, then, that independence, elections, or any other manifestation of state or popular sovereignty were not immediate aims of the aristocrat-led political movement which emerged after the war to oppose the Malayan Union, to form UMNO, and to go on, more than ten years later, to lead the country to independence. How can it be that UMNO, leader of every national government of independent Malaysia, was not a nationalist movement at its inception? I argue in the latter part of this study that these aristocrats-turned-bureaucrats-turned-politicians came late to the nationalist agenda because they had crucial ideological 'repair' work to do after the war. This work involved the restoration and rehabilitation of a tradition which would guarantee ruling class survival in yet another new order. The Japanese wartime occupation of Malaya had shattered the traditionalistic Malay world in many ways, the most important of which were the introduction of mass politics, the decline in the status of the rulers, and the ambiguous standing of Malay bureaucrats whose continuing service to the colonial state (now Japanese) won them the wrath of the Chinese resistance. In the wake of the occupation, colonial restoration could not stop unprecedented violence between the Malays and the Chinese. The seemingly peaceful plural society could not be put back together again. The restored colonial state then made its own assault on its erstwhile allies with the Malayan Union proposals. This new constitutional arrangement would accomplish the long-sought administrative unity of British Malaya at the expense of Malay ruling class privilege. The Malay rulers would lose their sovereign status and become religious figureheads. Access to positions in the state, and all future political rights, would accrue to Chinese and Indian residents – the so-called 'Malayans' – in open competition with the 'backward' Malays. Finally, the war had allowed a small group of radical Malay intellectuals to make the leap into political mass action, resulting in the establishment of the Partai Kebangsaan Melayu Malaya (PKMM, Malay Nationalist Party of Malaya) shortly after the occupation came to an end and well before the aristocrats had conceptualised any response to the new situation. This party fully embraced nationalism, and drew inspiration as well as rhetoric and models from the Indonesian revolution occurring just across the poorly patrolled Straits of Malacca. The PKMM's constant attention to the Indonesian

[30] Roff, *Malay Nationalism*, pp. 240–41.

revolution in its affiliated newspapers also served notice to the ruling class that its days might be numbered.

Forced to defend itself against both colonial state and nationalist rivals, the ruling class waged an ideological battle in the immediate postwar period which would determine the shape of the postcolonial state.[31] Accepting mass politics as the new idiom of power, the aristocrats established a political party (UMNO) and became self-described 'right-wing' politicians. But they also endeavoured to bring traditionalism into the political era. By protesting against the Malayan Union within the framework of colonial discourse – British 'fair play' and the protection of the indigenous culture – conservative politicians successfully established ideological continuity with the prewar colonial past. Then UMNO used the new mass politics to mobilise Malays in support of a traditional Malaya which had emerged during colonial rule. Specifically, the Malays rallied in support of the degraded rulers, whose actions in agreeing to the new constitution could be interpreted as either the result of British intimidation or as selling out their people. UMNO publicly focused on the former, while privately threatening the rulers with the implications of the latter. The restoration of the rulers with the withdrawal of the Malayan Union established for postwar politics the identity of the Malay ruling class with the survival of the Malays.

In order to secure its position, however, UMNO found that tradition was not enough. In yet another spin on the idea of 'conservation combined with development', conservative politicians began to incorporate the language of nationalism into their discourse and simultaneously the tenets of traditionalistic Malay culture into nationalism. The process may be glimpsed in the use of the terms *bangsa* and *kebangsaan* before and after the war. *Bangsa* is an old word meaning descent group, race or nation (in a premodern sense). *Kebangsaan* entered the public discourse in 1940 meaning national. It was one of a number of grammatical innovations which differed somewhat in meaning or connotation from the root from which it derived. Another example was *kerakyatan* (citizenship) from *rakyat* (originally subject), which appeared in 1941.[32] Like *kerakyatan*, *kebangsaan* took an old idea or category and infused it with a contemporary political meaning, in this case the whole package of rights and duties attendant

---

31 In Gramscian terms, the Malay ruling class was engaged in a 'war of position' not only against the colonial state but more fundamentally against the nationalist threat from below.

32 Mohd. Taib Osman, *The Language of the Editorials in Malay Vernacular Newspapers Up to 1941*, Kuala Lumpur: Dewan Bahasa dan Pustaka, 1966, p. 22.

upon modern nationhood. Conservative Malay associations had refused to embrace the word when they met in 1940 for fear of upsetting the traditional order.[33] By 1946, after the establishment of the PKMM, conservatives began using the term as well, although conservative usage disarmed it of much of its potency by simply ignoring its new connotations. According to Ariffin,

> [S]ince the *bangsa Melayu* was the focal point of identity and loyalty, the conservatives did not see the need to define a Malay nation, a definition which would entangle them in such thorny issues as nationality, nationalism, democracy.[34]

I would reverse Ariffin's emphasis here: avoiding a definition of the Malay nation was not merely an outcome but the very purpose of focusing on the demands of the Malay *bangsa* in the colonial setting. Using *kebangsaan* as if it issued unproblematically from *bangsa* served to silence the troublesome questions of nationality, nationalism and democracy in a multi-*bangsa* society. This reading of *kebangsaan* implied that Malays could take their place in the modern world of nation states without fundamental change to their society. Along with the rehabilitation of tradition, this appropriation of the language of nationalism for a conservative agenda was responsible for the triumph of the Malay ruling class in the political transition of the 1940s. The legacy of that triumph can be read in Mahathir's critique of a 'backward' society in 1970, but also in his acceptance that the Malay world is 'full of nobility'.

The Study and the Sources

Chapters two and three deal with the colonial period before the Second World War and the development of traditionalism as an important force in colonial Malay society. Chapter two demonstrates three fundamental ways in which Malay society was changed by the onset of British rule. These changes – in the meaning and purpose of government, the geopolitical definition of the Malay state and the political economy of leadership – represented nothing less than a paradigmatic shift in the fundamental categories and values of Malay politics. This paradigm shift was a necessary precursor to the restoration and preservation of Malay tradition which followed, for it reordered the Malay political world and subordinated it to British political

---

[33] See 'Minit persidangan persatuan-persatuan Melayu semenanjung tanah Melayu yang kedua', in Cheah Boon Kheng, ed., *Tokoh-Tokoh Tempatan dan Dokumen-Dokumen dalam Sejarah Malaysia*, Penang: Universiti Sains Malaysia, 1982.

[34] Ariffin, *Bangsa Melayu*, p. 197.

and economic priorities. This chapter also discusses how the contradiction between preservation and progress began to create a cleavage in the ruling class between royalties and aristocracies, and resulted in the partial bureaucratisation of the latter. Chapter three focuses wholly on the royal embrace of the preservationist project, which is related to the problem of centralisation of power in nineteenth-century Malay politics. Traditionalism proved useful to Malay rulers in their continuing competition with chiefs. The apotheosis of the royalty is demonstrated by innovations in three areas of royal life: personal style, public ceremonial and public visibility. Finally, this chapter argues that the articulation of new royal ritual, ostensibly the strengthening of Malay court culture, just as importantly reaffirmed British paradigms and British superiority over Malay society as a whole.

The sources for the first part of the study are largely British colonial records and dispatches, and secondarily British scholarly accounts of Malay culture and politics. These sources are used to demonstrate the triumph of the new political paradigm, as well as the way traditionalistic constructions of Malay culture were presented as authentic restorations of the Malay past and were subordinated to British imperial power. Just as importantly, Singapore's dispatches to London during the period of the 'forward movement' usually contained voluminous attachments seeking to justify local officials' actions. The attachments often included translations of letters from Malay rulers and chiefs to British officials. In this way, and less directly through reported conversations and transcribed interviews, we can see how Malays themselves sought to manage the transition to British colonial rule. Examination of Anglo–Malay encounters reveals Malay chiefs at times resisting the new paradigm and at other times incorporating British ideas into their own discourse to further their political power in the new order.

Chapter four serves as a chronological bridge to the postwar period. It discusses changes in colonial society which threatened the viability of the traditionalist approach to the Malay role in Malaya. The effect of the Japanese occupation on the ruling class is examined, as is the effort of the colonial state to reestablish its authority after the war. New parameters for acceptable political speech and action that developed in the immediate postwar period provided the conditions for the development of mass politics and the ensuing struggle among rulers, UMNO and the PKMM.

Chapters five to seven discuss the transition from colonialism into the era of decolonisation. I focus on political discourse in the years from 1945 to 1947, a period roughly concurrent with the British Military Administration and the Malayan Union. Soon afterwards, the Chinese-led Communist

Party of Malaya began armed struggle and the colonial government's counterinsurgency measures ended the relatively free political discourse of the immediate postwar years. Chapter five focuses on the threat posed by the Malayan Union to the ruling class and demonstrates how the aristocracy pursued its interests at the expense of both Malay rulers and Malay radicals. UMNO led an unprecedented barrage of press criticism of the rulers in the name of political progress, securing for conservative politicians the status of protectors of the Malays. By updating the tradition of loyalty, UMNO gained control of the meaning of the rulers, and thus of tradition, for the postcolonial future. At the same time, UMNO and its press organs successfully defeated the challenge of the Malay nationalists' drive to depose the rulers altogether, transforming the rulers into symbols of Malay survival. The contradiction between preservation and progress was resolved with the ascendancy of the chiefs within the ruling class.

Chapter six focuses on the contest between UMNO and the PKMM. It argues that UMNO needed more than control over the meaning of the rulers to secure hegemony in the newly politicised postwar atmosphere. In this period, UMNO successfully developed a nationalist credibility through four types of political practice: the intersection of the prescriptive mode of traditional manuscript culture with the new political propaganda, an updating of the Malay hero in the person of Dato Onn bin Jaafar, the attachment of national symbols to party identity, and the appropriation of militaristic youth culture from the radical parties.

Chapter seven indicates the direction UMNO would take nationalism once it had established itself as the mainstream party and the only legitimate voice of the Malays. UMNO redeployed ideas with traditional resonance – unity, loyalty, treason, sovereignty – to construct a particular kind of nationalism which both demobilised its Malay critics and deflected calls for independence, a traditionalist and depoliticised nationalism.

Along with archival sources, party documents and political memoirs, contemporary newspaper editorials provide the main source for the second half of the study. Political discourse in the Malay press has long been used as a source of historical data about Malay political activity, as a measure and celebration of the emergent nationalist movement and, most recently, as a tool for analysing changes in Malay political ideas 'which have long been submerged beneath narrative histories of the 1940s'.[35] In the spirit of this last approach, I have treated political writing of the period 1945 to 1947 as a public transcript of the debate on important political issues of

[35] *Ibid.*, p. vi.

the day. The public discourse found in daily newspapers and weekly and monthly journals reflects the attempt of the literate and politically active to shape public opinion and political practice – the new idiom of power in the postwar world. My examination of this public transcript addresses questions of medium, style and readership and their effect on the new political discourse. As the exchange of ideas found in these publications is part of an ideological battle fought under the conditions of late colonial rule, I also describe the role played by colonial censorship in setting parameters for legitimate political expression.

Many publications of the period under consideration were short-lived and only scattered issues are housed in the Arkib Negara Malaysia (ANM, National Archives of Malaysia). In cases where I have been unable to view the original, I have had to rely on the meticulous monitoring of the press by the colonial government. Newspaper editorials were monitored daily by Malay, Chinese and Indian government employees who prepared English summaries and translations. Extant newspapers were consulted wherever possible and I have relied most heavily on those publications which I consulted directly. The press summaries were very useful, however, in ascertaining the range of Malay opinion being published and the types of arguments put forward. I have indicated in the notes where my reference is to a press summary by including the ANM file number.

Chapter Two

British Power and the Reordering of Malay Politics

British power in the nineteenth and twentieth centuries transformed the demographic, economic, political and cultural landscapes of the Malay peninsula. This chapter analyses one aspect of that transformation: the way the Malay ruling class and Malay politics were changed as a result of the new configuration of power. The most evident and most commented on change in the practice of leadership was the bureaucratisation of the Malay aristocracy which started in earnest in most states after the turn of the century. I argue here that an ideological conversion was under way long before that point, the groundwork being laid in the decades of British paramountcy and in transitions to colonial rule. In the following pages I show how British power and Malay response reshaped three important aspects of the conceptual framework in which Malay politics operated – assumptions about the meaning and purpose of government, the definition and shape of the political unit referred to as the 'Malay state', and the relation of economic resources to political leadership. These fundamental shifts in paradigm set the stage for the survival of the Malay ruling class not only through colonial rule but into the postcolonial period as well.

The following sections examine selected episodes in Anglo-Malay history through which it is possible to see the gradual acceptance by the Malay elite of a British discourse on government and politics. In the first stage, British power is understood as that of an overlord, in indigenous terms, or as the paramount power, as the British termed themselves. Up until direct intervention in the west coast states, British officials advanced the virtues of good government, or civilisation, whenever the economic and military power of Singapore gave them access to a local political incident. At this stage, the successful demonstration of good government by a native state consisted of taking British advice, not inviting in other Europeans, 'opening up' territory to investment and settlement, and keeping the peace. The existence of slavery, 'arbitrary' justice and decentralised rule by powerful district chiefs was still largely accepted.

In the next section, I discuss the advancing of the British discourse through direct intervention in the Malay states. With intervention, the administration of British justice and the centralisation of revenue collection became priorities, thus bringing the colonial power head to head with Malay resistance. The outcome of these struggles brought the affirmation of the new style of government and the reorientation of elite energies to finding political advantage in the new order, which was further entrenched with the establishment of a new political economy.

In the third section, I examine another effect of successful intervention: the standardisation of the political units themselves. This process resulted from the economic imperative to survey and map the land preparatory to capital investment. It was also integral to the triumph of British political definitions over indigenous ideas of sovereignty. In the final section, I discuss the bureaucratisation of the Malay elite, not as a transformation of the first order, but rather as a phenomenon resulting from its prior ideological conversion as well as from a paradox in British attitudes towards the Malays.

Britain as Paramount Power

Throughout the nineteenth century the power of Singapore made the British the paramount power in the Malay peninsula. This meant that, from the 1820s, the independent Malay states 'tended to look on the [British East India] Company as the arbiter of local politics to whom they reported the accession of new Rulers, and appealed for help to settle internal disputes as well as quarrels with their neighbours'.[1] When the Straits Settlements (Singapore, Melaka and Penang) were transferred from company rule, first to the government of India in 1858 and then to crown authority in 1867, government policy still did not allow direct intervention, so Britain remained more of a regional overlord than a colonial power. The period under examination here, the 1870s, was a transitional time in which power was starting to be expressed in more direct ways. But the older form of paramountcy was still very much in evidence as the difficulties of direct intervention elicited caution from London.

As overlord, the British projected their authority, emanating from Queen

---

1 Eunice Thio, *British Policy in the Malay Peninsula, 1880–1910*. Vol. 1. *The Southern and Central States*, Singapore: University of Malaya Press, 1969, p. xvi.

Victoria, in a way that was deemed understandable, yet superior, to Malay authority:

> It has always been the object of this government to impress the Native Rajas and people with the idea that Her Majesty is a Raja very much above all Malay Rajas, therefore it was long ago decided not to style Her Majesty by any of the expressions of respect common amongst Malay Rajas, but that Her Majesty should be known to them as Her Majesty Queen Victoria yang mulia dan yang mulia besar: Her Majesty Queen Victoria, utmost noble and the greatest ... more often without the prefix of Her Majesty, which the natives naturally do not understand. I know of no earthly title greater than this one, and it is the one by which Her Majesty is known and respected all over the Peninsula.

Flowing from the queen, British authority was projected as a powerful personage, a projection which allowed it to operate as an overlord in the Malay world, where power was exercised in a personal way:

> In the same way we call the British Government, British Guberment or Guberment Inggris as something so different from the Malay perintahan ... as to be altogether inadequately described by that word. But the real point ... is that the 'British Government' is here spoken of in its 'personal' character, and in this sense the word perintahan is inadvisable, this word meaning simply the act of governing or the authority of a ruler. The 'British Government' is now as well known and understood in the Settlements and the Peninsula as the old kumpni (Company) of the Indian Government's days.[2]

By playing the role of overlord, the British employed the local idiom of power relations and exercised their paramountcy in symbolic as well as practical ways. Sometimes a practical function incorporated ritual significance, such as the tour of a highly ranked official, which gathered information about land and population while symbolically inscribing the realm. The Malays, being comfortable with this idiom, used it deftly to move at times close to and at other times away from British power. The *bendahara* (chief minister) of Pahang, for example, made a point of receiving Governor William Jervois when he toured the east coast states in 1875, at a time when Pahang was being reimbursed for expenses incurred fighting in Selangor. Despite the ruler's illness, 'the Governor was received most cordially by the Bendahara, who was surrounded by many Chiefs and some three hundred

[2] Frank Swettenham to Governor Jervois, 27 December 1876, CO 273/90.

Malays, sitting in solemn conclave in and about the Balei or Council Hall'.[3] In 1882, however, the expansionist Governor Frederick Weld, draft treaty in hand, had to postpone his proposed visit because as the *bendahara* wrote, 'the entrance reception hall which we are preparing is not yet finished, and so how can we receive our friend?'[4]

Overlords did not always get their way. But the preponderance of British power nevertheless caused the meaning of local idioms gradually to shift according to British usage, introducing new elements and requirements which would eventually transform Malay political life. This can be seen in the way British concerns crept into the discourse of those Malay chiefs who had to deal with them. The central concern was the nature of government, the British promoting the idea that good government was an active institution which had legitimate goals to pursue in society. The British ideology of good government was not compatible with Malay politics, of course. The practice of leadership in Malay society, involving grants of revenue-producing areas, maintenance of armed followers, *kerah* (corvée labour) and debt bondage, clashed with the British agenda of 'opening up the country' to foreign investment and increasing revenue at the disposal of the central authority. The British expressed the difference in moral terms, as between oppression and barbarity on the one hand, and good government and civilisation on the other.

Good government was marked fundamentally by the expansion of capitalist economic relations. The surveying of borders, making of maps, laying of roads and collection of revenue would all eventually be projects of state governments in the Malay peninsula. But these projects depended upon what was understood as the spread of English justice, often referred to simply as civilisation, which consisted of guaranteeing property rights, protecting trade and laying the groundwork for the proletarianisation of the Malay peasantry – ending arbitrary or excessive extraction of goods and labour, and abolishing slavery. This pursuit of justice undercut the traditional Malay political economy.[5] The right of the ruling class simply to appropriate stood in the way of capitalism; the labelling of this right as barbaric and oppressive would signal a paradigmatic shift in social and economic relations.

---

3 *Straits Times*, 31 July 1875, CO 882/3.

4 CO 273/116.

5 See Jomo Kwame Sundaram, *A Question of Class: Capital, the State, and Uneven Development in Malaya*, New York: Monthly Review Press, 1988, ch. 1.

Representing the paramount power, British officials found a variety of opportunities to advance their ideology of civilisation against native practices. The east coast tour of Jervois in 1875 offers a case in point. At this time, the British were beginning to intervene directly on the west coast, but still knew little of the remainder of the peninsula, including those states under Siamese suzerainty. *The Straits Times*, voice of British business interests in Singapore, applauded the governor for establishing relations with these Malay rulers and hoped the rulers would be encouraged to visit Singapore as well:

> So, only, can confidence be established, liberal and enlarged views instilled into the conservative native mind, trade flourish, resources become developed, and the prosperity of the native States as well as of these Settlements be increased and ensured.[6]

Jervois himself was quite direct on these points when he met the *bendahara* of Pahang:

> During the course of this interview I explained to him the advantages which would be derived from a good system of taxation and collection of revenues, and informed him that the British Government was anxious that the resources of his State should be opened up, in order that the natural wealth of the country might be developed, the prosperity of himself and his people increased, and trade improved thereby. I also informed him that I would be ready to assist him with advice, and to instruct him as to the best mode of attaining these ends.[7]

The *bendahara* took advantage of the governor's ignorance of Malay politics in order to fend off this tentative advance; he professed to have no power to accept such an offer and politely promised to consult his chiefs.

The British were far more successful in spreading their ideology where they had more influence, that is, closer to Singapore. The remainder of this section examines two instances in which British authority was exercised in Malay affairs. In both these episodes, concerning the first stage of the Negeri Sembilan consolidation (the Sri Menanti confederation) and Johor's annexation of Muar, direct intervention was prohibited by London, so the paramount power employed the local idiom. Yet in both cases the British successfully began to redefine the meaning of that idiom, and Malay politics began to adjust to the new meaning.

---

[6] *Straits Times*, 31 July 1875. CO 882/3.

[7] CO 882/3.

Negeri Sembilan was an area of Minangkabau settlement in the hinterland of Melaka controlled by territorial chiefs (*undang*) who had, from 1773, agreed unanimously on rulers (*yam tuan besar*) descended from previous rulers originally invited from Minangkabau.[8] In 1869, however, the four *undang* (of Rembau, Sungai Ujung, Johol and Jelebu) could not agree on a successor, one backing Ahmat, a son of the late *yam tuan*, and the others backing Antah, a son of the previous *yam tuan*. Civil war over the issue led to the establishment of a British residency in Sungai Ujung in 1874, during the first wave of intervention, but the subsequent failure of the first Perak residency (discussed below) led the Colonial Office to insist on more indirect means of settling the Negeri Sembilan dispute. The Straits Settlements government eventually solved the problem by backing the more popular Antah, and managing the reconstitution of some of the Negeri Sembilan districts into a confederation which agreed, first, to keep the peace amongst themselves and with the districts which had not joined, and second, to refer all disputes to Maharaja Abu Bakar of Johor. Certain elements in the changing idiom of government and politics can be discerned in this episode.

The most important concerns the advancing of the discourse of good government. Datu Klana of Sungai Ujung accepted a British resident in 1874 for the most conventional of reasons; the British were willing to recognise him as the legitimate ruler over his rival, Datu Bandar. He couched his request in terms of the existing idiom of overlord–vassal relations by requesting protection. Datu Klana wrote to the lieutenant governor of Melaka, relating how he had tried to raise the British flag, 'so as to be under the protection of the Great Governor', but was prevented by Datu Bandar. 'If we raise the flag, perhaps the Datu Bandar will attack our place'. He also requested rice. But then he went on to betray new influences:

> And further we would like very much to have our country populous, and a good straight road for traders to come and go on, so that the country may be populous, and doing good to all men. And further, we would like very much for an officer from the Great Governor, who can give good advice, so that we may do what is right under that protection.[9]

Johor's mediation for the British with the new confederation further advanced the new discourse. Johor was the local exemplar of good government at this time. According to Harry Ord, governor from 1867 to 1873, Abu Bakar was the reason for this:

---

[8] This very abbreviated account is based on Thio, *British Policy*, pp. xxi–xxvi. She gives further references.

[9] CO 882/3.

> In his tastes and habits he is an English gentleman, as a ruler he is anxious to promote in every way the advancement and civilization of his people and is the only Rajah in the whole peninsula or adjoining States, who rules in accordance with the practice of civilized nations.[10]

More concretely, Abu Bakar, following his father Temenggung Ibrahim, fully accepted the British as overlord in the Malay peninsula, embraced the discourse of good government by opening up his territory to foreign investment, took British advice and, by being the first to do these things, achieved a favoured position as mediator in the period before direct intervention.[11]

Abu Bakar's mediation allowed the Singapore government to dictate the terms of the Negeri Sembilan confederation while appearing to conform to the dictates and idiom of local politics. Here is Jervois on his initial meeting with the chiefs and the maharaja:

> Having informed His Highness of my wish to see the Chiefs of the States in question, if they could be induced to come in, he sent some of his officers up the Muar River by Luigga and Sejamet to endeavour to communicate with them, and, with a view of arranging a settlement of affairs. The result of this mission was that these Chiefs, accompanied by some eighty followers, many of high rank, came to Johore.[12]

Following the establishment of the confederation, Abu Bakar would continue to mediate between the chiefs and the British. The Negeri Sembilan chiefs may have thought that his mediation would preserve the local idiom by forming a buffer between themselves and the alien British:

> I ascertained that Tunku Antah was desirous of communicating with this government generally through the Maharajah of Johore; he stated that he did not so well understand the ways of Europeans.[13]

Actually, rather than a buffer, Abu Bakar would act as a conduit for the transmission of the British discourse on good government, a discourse which was ultimately to undermine Malay politics:

> I explained to them that the British Government are desirous to see their states peacefully and properly governed, and pointed out to them that they

10 CO 273/94.

11 See the next chapter for a fuller discussion of these rulers.

12 CO 882/4.

13 *Ibid.*

> should strive to emulate the example of the Maharajah of Johore.[14]

There are two other ways in which the Negeri Sembilan episode suggests the power of the British to change the meaning of the local idiom even while seeming to comply with it. The first is the way British officials inserted themselves into and thus changed the meaning of Malay ceremonial. The resident of Sungai Ujung, Captain P.J. Murray, accompanied Yam Tuan Antah on a kind of vast processional around the districts, picking up important chiefs on the way to an installation-cum-treaty signing in Sri Menanti. The significance of British participation was recognised by Datu Muar, who 'dressed in a complete European costume (white) without a sarong'. Later that day the Malay principals visited the graves of their ancestors and prayed, but the main ceremony occurred the next noon, after more than 500 people had arrived. Murray's account continues:

> At that hour, I took my place in the chair, having the Yam Tuan on the right and Tuanku Ahmat on the left – the remaining Datus, etc. were arranged on benches, right and left, according to rank. The agreement signed by the Chiefs was then read, at the conclusion of which, I shook hands with Tuanku Antah and handed him into the chair, taking my place on his right. The Police (sixty-five) then fired three volleys in the air, after which I read a farewell address, and the ceremony was concluded, with the exception of the shaking of hands with everyone, which occupied a considerable time.[15]

Even if this account is, as one would expect, somewhat myopic, the centrality of the British role is unmistakable. Unlike a conventional overlord, especially a foreign one, the British here insisted on participating in what was, after all, a very local occurrence, and on demonstrating their power unequivocally.

The second innovation in the overlord–vassal relationship was the letter of compliance. Having already signed the treaty, chiefs of the districts were then required to send written assurances to Singapore that they would abide by its terms. Perhaps analogous to paying obeisance, a duty which now could not be avoided, this innovation bears clear signs of the new terms of overlordship. From the *yam tuan*:

> We tender many thanks and compliments to our friend, because at this time with the assistance of our friend we are living in comfort and are now examining all the districts under our jurisdiction and all our subjects and slaves are living happily and quietly. With the assistance of our friend, all

---

[14] *Ibid.*

[15] CO 273/90.

> these countries now are in peace.

From Tunku Ahmed Tunggal:

> As regards the action taken by our friend and Tunku Maharaja of Johor Bahru to appoint Tunku Antah as Sultan, we are much pleased with it and we have presented ourselves before the Petuan Tunku Antah and the twelve Lambaga [chiefs], and we summoned all the people to appear in the Royal presence; they were all agreed.

From Penghulu Muar:

> We will obey all our friend's commands and are all agreed and of one mind.

From Penghulu Eenas to the governor:

> Regarding the Yam Tuan Antah who our friend has ordered to return and rule the countries again, we are very glad of it and thank our friend very much.

And, lest the contents of the letter be mistakenly thought to admit of variance, from Datu Klana:

> We inform our friend that we are very sorry of having omitted to mention in our last letter, that we will keep ourselves and our Country peaceable and in prosperity, and we will not in any way interfere or molest the neighbouring States.[16]

One final point should be made. British officials, when commenting on Negeri Sembilan, were uncomfortable with the very configuration of Malay political authority there. Governor Andrew Clarke, in 1874, said: 'They are small, they are apparently insignificant, and from the very fact of their smallness and insignificance they have been really more difficult to deal with than some of the larger States'.[17] Jervois, after the settlement, was not sure things would go smoothly: 'In these small States, where there are a number of subordinate chiefs, all may not yet be satisfied'.[18] These comments, as well as the confederation itself, demonstrate an impatience with variety and multiplicity in the size and authority structure of Malay political units. They may be seen as the point of departure for the articulation of a new ideal Malay political unit, one in which uniformity of size and clarity of authority structure are prioritised. This point will be returned to below.

---

16 *Ibid.*

17 CO 882/3.

18 CO 273/90.

The second episode in the influence of paramountcy is the Muar succession of 1877. Muar was the only district of the peninsula under the control of Sultan Ali, son of Hussein Shah, who had been named Sultan of Singapore by the British in return for the cession of that island in 1819.[19] Neither Hussein Shah nor his son had exercised effective control over Muar, and when Ali died in 1877 officials in the Straits Settlements did not want the district to pass either to Ali's designated heir, an 11-year-old son by a third wife, or to his eldest son, Alam. They claimed that Alam was not of royal blood, but it appears that his real disqualification was that the British considered him 'a stupid indolent man like his father'.[20] Once again Colonial Office policy forced Singapore to act indirectly, and once again the Maharaja of Johor was the beneficiary. The steps taken to bring about the annexation of Muar to Johor (including the disinheritance of the rightful claimant) furthered the centrality of the British role in local politics, as well as the British discourse on government, and introduced a new element in the political economy of leadership.

Although the assistant undersecretary of state for the colonies, the influential Robert Meade, declared that 'who is to be the ruler of this little state we do not care two pins' and that 'the Straits government should only recognize as Sultan the person who is at once acceptable to the people and who is the rightful claimant according to Malay Custom', he did in fact lay down criteria which the successful candidate had to meet: 'the individual selected should be informed that he will be recognized as long as he behaves himself and governs properly'. What was the state of affairs in Muar that elicited this concern? According to the pro-Johor Colonel Archibald Anson, Muar was characterised by 'the absence of any government' and provided refuge for 'bad characters from our own Settlement of Malacca, as well as from that of Johor'. A reconnoitring trip up the Kessang and Muar Rivers by a British official revealed the telling sign of bad government in the Malay states – underpopulation:

> On the Muar side there is desolation, and I should not be surprised if the estimate of the population of the whole Muar Country which I heard from an independent Native authority was correct: he put it at eight hundred only.

This state of affairs was blamed on the *de facto* ruler in Muar, the *temenggung*, and to prevent his faction from gaining permanent control, the

[19] Thio, *British Policy*, pp. xxvi–xxx.
[20] CO 273/91.

district was placed in the temporary custody of the Maharaja of Johor until the proper election of a new ruler could be held. The *temenggung* and his allies were in favour of Alam, a legitimate choice, but this was interpreted by the British as a way of maintaining the unsatisfactory status quo. The *temenggung* and his men were said to fear the selection of a man of 'energy and ability ... who would reside in the country'. Only a few months later, the maharaja had once again demonstrated good government: he had investors ready to commence tobacco planting and had selected appropriate sites for police stations.[21]

The Straits government used several means to encourage the acceptance of the good government ideology among the Muar elite. They arranged for the younger son of Sultan Ali to be educated in Singapore at the Raffles Institution, where he boarded with other sons of Malay royalty (and deposed royalty). It was particularly important to influence and shape this boy, Mahmud, as he was his father's designated heir, and it was anticipated that he and his younger brothers may be 'fitted for posts of responsibility in the Country on their attaining their full ages ... depend[ing] in a great measure upon the character and talents developed by the young men'.[22] In the shorter term, the government again relied on the maharaja for the muscle the Straits government was prohibited from using:

> The Maharajah of Johore was good enough, at my request, to send one of his small steamers to Muar, and invite the Penghulus, or headmen of the Country, to come to Singapore to see me, and this those that were able have since done.

Here the chiefs 'expressed their strong desire, that the State of Muar should be placed under the charge of the Maharajah of Johore'.[23]

Once again, British officials participated in Malay ceremonial for the purpose of achieving their desired outcome, while appearing to respect local custom. As in Negeri Sembilan, their participation had the unintended consequence of defining Malay custom on British terms. The first intervention was in criticising Ali, posthumously, for naming the 13-year-old

---

[21] *Ibid.*

[22] *Ibid.*; CO 882/3.

[23] CO 273/91. The Colonial Office did not miss the coercion: 'But I observe that they were summoned to Government House at Singapore and it must therefore be borne in mind that it would be in accordance with Malay character in these circumstances if they merely put their signatures to a document which at the moment they thought would be agreeable to and in accordance with the wishes of the Colonial Government by whom they had been summoned to discuss the question'.

Mahmud as his heir on his deathbed:

> The proper course, according to the Malay custom of the country, for Sultan Ali to have adopted in appointing a successor, was to have called a Council of the Chiefs and Penghulus, named 'the Waris' and to have presented to them the person whom he intended should be his heir and declared him to be so. This person would then have been known and acknowledged by them from that time as the 'Tunku Besar' or the great Tunku (Master).

Because the Malay ruler had not appointed a successor in 'proper' fashion (and the British had ruled out the candidate of royal blood on grounds of good government), there was no one to pay for and preside over Sultan Ali's funeral. This became the occasion for the second intervention:

> [Sultan Ali] died in the Settlement of Malacca, and this Government and the Maharajah of Johore advanced money for the expenses of his Funeral, and its accompanying feasts and other ceremonies, thus performing the duty that should have formed part, and a very important part, of the duty of his successor.... At the time of the late Sultan's death, the Colonial Secretary was sent to Malacca, to be present at his funeral, in order to prevent the occasion being made one of riot or disturbance, ... and to see that no one was proclaimed, at the Funeral, as his successor, by any faction, without those persons being present, who had a right to a voice in the matter.[24]

Most significant was the third intervention in Malay custom – managing the election of Ali's successor. The government informed the *temenggung* that it would send an officer to 'witness' the event. The Maharaja of Johor was not to be present, which would give his anticipated election the strong appearance of being 'spontaneous and unrestrained'. It was communicated to the Muar chiefs that the government had no wish to influence the outcome of the election, but that British recognition of the successful candidate 'would naturally depend on his personal merits and the character of his administration'.[25]

The report of the officer who attended the election, A.M. Skinner, reveals not only crass manipulation of the outcome, which is no surprise, but also the adaptation of Malay ceremonial to the new conditions laid down by the overlord. In the first place, there was considerable confusion about the nature of the proceedings and who had a right to participate. There were about 200 people present, including three Germans connected to the new

---

[24] *Ibid.*

[25] *Ibid.*

tobacco plantations[26] and two important officers of the maharaja's. Skinner advised the Johor officers to leave as their presence might be misconstrued. This they did, but they left behind a sealed letter addressed to the governor in the name of the assembled Muar chiefs proclaiming the election of the maharaja. (Skinner called the post-election presentation of this letter, clearly prepared beforehand and by outsiders, 'an unsatisfactory incident'.) The whole procedure seemed to have an ad hoc quality which may be attributed to the government's insistence that its preordained outcome be validated by Malay custom. Skinner had been given a list by the government of village headmen and *penghulus* (subdistrict chiefs) who were entitled by custom to vote and he noted right away that there were too many *penghulus*. It turned out that the additional ones had come from the Johor side of the river, and he inquired of the *temenggung* whether they should participate. The *temenggung* answered 'with a phrase he constantly employed, "*kenapa tidak*" (why not)'. Skinner also noted 'the way the *penghulus* were "nursed", without which they could not I believe have been brought there, or kept together so long'. Although the British officer was clearly confronted with ceremonial manufactured for the occasion ('I could not ascertain that there was any particular or separate custom of Muar'), he did not attribute this to British interference. Instead he concluded merely that what he witnessed was not an election in the British sense, but 'something between the Proclamation and the Coronation of a new Raja'.[27]

There was also evidence that Malays were appropriating the discourse of good government in face of unrelenting British backing for the maharaja. The *temenggung* himself praised Abu Bakar 'for his justice, equity, compassion and liberality towards all his subjects'. Skinner spoke to a *penghulu* who had been particularly close to Ali and had originally opposed the maharaja:

> He told me that he rejoiced now to escape his visit to [the late Sultan's residence in Melaka], for he was always made to work when he went there (under the 'hukum kerah') and never got any pay for his labour. He said a good deal more reflecting on the late Sultan and the Temenggung, his Wakil, the latter he described as a rather selfish and tyrannical old gentlemen, who was on his best behaviour just now, but whose administration had been very unpopular. All this was volunteered as if in self-defence. He also referred to the wretched state of the Country. His

[26] See Thio, *British Policy*, pp. 67–69, for British concerns about German activity in Asia and Africa.

[27] CO 273/91.

> father and grandfather had been Penghulus of Tassek before him and in their days the kampung had numbered one hundred souls; now there were not fifty. He also drew a comparison between the north and south banks of the Muar; and here again in reference to the Maharajah's rule he pointed out that the custom of 'kerah' was not so often enforced on the Johor side, for that in Johor people were paid for their labour and the Raja's rule was less severe (tida begitu kras).

The outcome of the election was a source of great satisfaction to the maharaja's backers in Singapore, who now would not have to contend with the 'feeble and inexperienced' Alam. Abu Bakar, by contrast, had 'both the will and the ability to tranquilize and develop the country'.[28]

The very strength of the claim of the late sultan's family and its patent mistreatment by the government, however, left it with many supporters. In an effort to defuse this threat, the British began to develop another tool which would have long-term impact on Malay politics – the pension. The nephew of Sultan Ali, as representative of the sultan's brother's family, was offered $600 a year, provided he agree to live in Singapore, not return to Muar and remain on 'good behaviour'.[29] Ali proved more difficult to pay off, refusing 'with much abuse' the maharaja's offer of $68 per month. The government eventually determined that his acquiescence was worth much more and offered him $500 per month, plus more for other members of his family 'as long as [he] live quietly and in no way attempt intrigues or disturbances'. The pension was understood to entail the cessation of claims, not only because it was explicitly laid out so, but also because Alam's acceptance of the money would be interpreted by other Malays as 'selling his country', ensuring that 'his friends and supporters would have little left to complain about'.[30] Both the vulnerability of the Malay elite to cash buyouts and their impact on Malay politics are pursued further below.

These episodes of British involvement in Negeri Sembilan and Muar illustrate the adaptation of local politics to the new requirements of the British overlord. First and foremost, the British advanced a discourse of good government. The growing influence of Johor, backed by Singapore, both demonstrated and increased the power of this new discourse. British participation in Malay ceremonial also served to introduce the new discourse into the local idiom, which then compelled Malays themselves to begin to use it. The twofold result of these interventions was that the

---

28 *Ibid.*

29 *Ibid.*

30 *Ibid.* CO 273/95.

meaning attached to Malay political ritual and ceremonial began to change according to British priorities, but the relevance of the forms themselves was extended into the colonial period.

The Wages of Resistance: Payoffs and Payrolls

Transitions to colonial rule brought more heavy-handed imposition of the new discourse and practice of government into Malay political life. It was at this point that room to manoeuvre began seriously to narrow and good government measures to harm the economic, cultural and political interests of Malay elites. Resistance was unsuccessful, but illustrated the way Malays were grappling with the changing idiom of politics, some seeking to master the new discourse and others retreating to the old. The aftermath of resistance occasioned the further incorporation of the Malay ruling class into the British discourse of government. Through the construction of a new political economy of leadership, the British secured not merely grudging accommodation, but active Malay participation in the transformation of their political life. In this section I discuss the experience of Perak, which subsequently served as a warning to other Malays, and make reference to similar processes occurring in Selangor and Pahang.

When J.W.W. Birch arrived in Perak in November 1874 as the first British resident, he 'at once proposed to introduce great changes in the constitution, customs and financial arrangement of the country'.[31] By the following April, he had taken the collection of customs duties out of the hands of two Malay officials 'who kept no accounts, and took what they chose for themselves'.[32] At the time of his murder by the men of Sri Maharaja Lela, Birch was in the process of posting two proclamations in Malay villages in the name of Sultan Abdullah.[33] The first acknowledged the power of the resident and the second served notice on the Malay ruling class that the political economy of the state was (from their point of view) about to be shattered:

> Now it has become necessary to examine into and alter the whole present system of taxation in Perak; for in several places there are taxes which

---

31 Enquiry as to the Complicity of Chiefs in the Perak Outrages. CO 273/86. (Hereafter Enquiry.)

32 Report of the Acting Resident of Perak, 2 April 1875. CO 882/3.

33 For fuller accounts of the first Perak residency see Emily Sadka, *The Protected Malay States, 1874–1895*, Kuala Lumpur: University of Malaya Press, 1968, pp. 77–97, and C. Northcote Parkinson, *British Intervention in Malaya, 1867–1877*, Kuala Lumpur: University of Malaya Press, 1964, pp. 194–233.

> ought to be put a stop to. It is also necessary to raise money to pay fitting allowances to us and to certain Chiefs of Perak, and the expenses of rightly administering the country.[34]

No less related to the economic well-being of the ruling class was Birch's implacable opposition to slavery; he insisted on its speedy abolition and himself sheltered runaway female slaves. For these reasons he engendered widespread opposition. The example of one powerful chief, the *orang kaya menteri*, demonstrates how completely good government was prepared to undercut the Malay ruling class:

> The Menteri was the only chief who made any open objection to signing the Treaty: nor can it be wondered that he should have been dissatisfied with it, seeing that by the conditions of the Treaty, Abdullah, with whom he had never been on good terms, was set up over him as Sultan of Perak, and over Ismail (who had been elected Sultan chiefly through his influence); that he was prohibited from driving the Ghee-Hins out of Perak ... and that he was forced to acknowledge as a debt due by him to the government of the Straits Settlements the charges and expenses to which the colony had already been, or might be put, by their efforts to secure the tranquillity of Perak and the safety of trade. Probably, however, the part of the Treaty which affected him most seriously, and which must have been most galling to his self-pride, was that which declared his future position would be that of Governor of Larut only, on a fixed allowance, and that the revenues of Larut would be merged in those of Perak.[35]

The reaction of the Malay elite to this imposition was varied. The *menteri*'s represented one type of response: eagerness to use the British idiom and discourse to his own advantage, just as the British had used Malay idiom against the Malays in the era of paramountcy. The *menteri* paid a $12,000 retaining fee to a Singapore lawyer in an attempt to get his case taken to Britain and questions asked in parliament. It was from his English lawyers that the *menteri* learned about the different layers of British authority and came to the conclusion (not unreasonable in 1874) that 'the Colonial Office will never interfere in the Malay Peninsula'. On this basis he urged Sultan Abdullah to challenge Birch legally:

> We were all forced to sign the Treaty. It was not with our own consent. Therefore, I think, if we go before the law, the Pangkor Treaty will be void.

[34] CO 882/3.

[35] Enquiry.

Sultan Abdullah, however, did not trust the *menteri* and, under the guidance of closer advisers, pursued other methods of resistance. First, perhaps understanding the central importance of the person and power of the sultan to the success of Birch's government, he tried to disperse his power in several directions and make himself inaccessible to the resident. He issued a *kuasa* (authorisation) to his top chiefs delegating them to represent him in all matters to Birch. 'The kuasa set out that in future whatever they said was what the Sultan said, and what they did was his doing; and that, therefore, he authorized Mr. Birch in future to deal with them, and not with him'. Unfortunately, 'Mr. Birch refused to receive the kuasa'. Second, Abdullah tried to bypass the resident with a personal appeal to the departing Governor Clarke. He sent a deputation to Singapore explaining the troubles he was having with Birch and requesting confirmation of his title so that the new governor might not repudiate it. In attributing power personally to Clarke rather than to the office of governor, Abdullah revealed a less than perfect grasp of the new idiom. He also wrote to a Kim Ching, 'asking him to come to Perak and undertake the collection of the Revenue of Larut under the kuasa which Sultan Abdullah had formerly given him, so that the Sultan might have his assistance to hold his own against Mr. Birch'. These letters failed. Clarke met with the deputation from Perak after Jervois had already taken over as the new governor and lectured them never to send mail over the resident's head again. Kim Ching also refused to help, having 'given up his kuasa long ago to Sir Andrew Clarke'.[36]

Other chiefs were even less comfortable with the new idiom of power relations and thus couched their resistance in wholly indigenous terms. The *shahbandar*, the intermediary between traders and the ruler, who had lost control of the collection of customs duties, confronted Birch with the authority of the sultan, as Birch recorded in his journal:

> [The *shahbandar*] said that he had made his farm at the Qualla by the Sultan's orders, and would not give it up; he also said he would go on collecting on oil, salt, etc., and that we must fight for it if we wanted it. When I met him I told him I would not let him collect any more, and that if he went on breaking the Pangkor Treaty, I would recommend the Governor to send him out of the country. This evidently frightened him. He said that he did not think I could do anything till I got the Sultan's chop.[37]

[36] *Ibid.*

[37] CO 273/86. The chop is a stamp or seal denoting the sultan's authority.

Sri Maharaja Lela, before directing the murder of Birch just one year after his arrival, declared: 'I will not depart in the smallest degree from the old arrangement'.[38] The death of Birch, of course, brought down the might of the British empire on Perak and ensured that the 'old arrangement' was no more. The Perak ruling class had shown a certain willingness to learn the new idiom of power relations, but met disaster by resolving to return to the old.

The most significant consequence of the resident's murder to Perak's future was not, however, the temporary posting of troops from India and Hong Kong, but the participation of Malays in the administration of British justice. Although Sultan Abdullah and the *menteri*, *laxamana* and *shahbandar* were dealt with extrajudicially and exiled from Perak, those of lower social rank were tried in a court of law in the state. Their judges in these summary trials were leading Perak chiefs who had been cleared (some of them just barely) of involvement in the plot. Thus the lowly Siputum, actual wielder of the knife, was sentenced to hang by Raja Dris, a sentence that was carried out in front of the sultan and the leading chiefs.[39] Other Malay judges appointed to investigate the case were Raja Muda Muhammad II and Raja Alang Hussein. Once again the Maharaja of Johor played a mediating role in advancing British discourse, this time the discourse of justice, when he took the surrender of several fugitives in exchange for a guarantee that 'they will have a fair and open trial on the charges made against them before a competent and impartial tribunal with a full opportunity of preparing and making their defence'. After the seven defendants (including Sri Maharaja Lela) had been found guilty and sentenced to death, the British government decided to spare the lives of four. The Malay judge was so informed and was instructed to carry out the sentences against the remaining three as soon as possible.[40] In this matter, the Malay elite had no autonomy but was seen carrying out the judgements.

The visible participation of leading Malays in the administration of British justice suggests a systematic method of consolidating colonial rule and coopting the ruling class. It had been undertaken earlier in the punishment of pirates in Selangor when Governor Clarke 'insisted upon the ruler of the country accepting the responsibility for their act, and punishing them himself'.[41] Frank Swettenham later noted that the local people 'still

---

[38] CO 273/90.

[39] The future Sultan Idris had been made judge in 1875 after successfully giving up opium. CO 882/3.

[40] CO 273/90.

[41] CO 882/3. According to Winstedt, 'It was feared that uncertainty as to the place of

speak with awe of that trial and the executions. What probably had the greatest effect on them was that the pirates were tried and condemned by a court of their own people'.[42] Twenty years later, the recalcitrant Sultan of Pahang received the same treatment when he was forced to punish the rebels of his own state with whom he sympathised.[43]

The use of leading Malays to administer colonial justice took place in the context of a far more fundamental change in the political idiom – the complete restructuring of the political economy of Malay leadership. As noted in the case of Muar, British interference in a Malay political incident usually left one party dispossessed and disgruntled. To preempt the threat of further 'disturbances', the monthly pension was devised to recompense political actors for their enforced retirement from politics. The number of disaffected chiefs, the potential threat, and the opportunity for payoffs were all multiplied when formal colonial rule was extended. In Perak, in 1874, Abdullah's rival for the position of sultan accepted $1,000 per month for stating that 'he resigned all his affairs into the hands of the Governor, and relied entirely on the protection of the British Government'.[44] The compensatory pension, however, was insufficient when good government aimed to dispossess the entire ruling class of its means. In developing a new political economy, the British had to do more than buy acquiescence; they had to replace the old system of economic reward and political power. Highly-placed, well-rewarded Malays dispensing British justice thus represents an early glimpse of what the new political economy would look like.

Along the way, however, the new colonial rulers experienced an early failure that illuminates the development of the new system. In 1876 a plan was proposed, which was eventually abandoned, to present honorary swords

the crime, whether on the high seas or in Selangor waters, might lead to acquittal in a British court, and that punishment in British territory would have little deterrent effect in Selangor.... His Highness readily agreed to the trial of the murdering pirates by a court composed of the Viceroy, Dato' Aru, the Penghulu Dagang and See Ah Keng, the Chinese headman at Langat, with the Colonial Engineer Major McNair and the Viceroy's legal friend, Mr. J.G. Davidson, as commissioners. On 15 February 1874 this court sitting in the stockade at Kuala Jugra condemned seven of the prisoners to be speared and creesed, the eighth being reprieved on account of his youth.... The next morning at eleven o'clock the sentence was carried out with a creese sent overnight by the Sultan'. *A History of Malaya*, Singapore: Malayan Branch of the Royal Asiatic Society, 1935, pp. 240–41.

42 CO 882/3.

43 CO 273/196.

44 CO 273/86.

to five Malay chiefs who had helped the British pursue the Perak fugitives after Birch's death. The specifications of the swords were as follows:

> The swords to be all alike, the blade between twenty-seven inches and thirty inches long, flat, two-edged, light, and sharpened on both edges. A crescent and five-pointed star in the ornamental engraving. The inscriptions on the blade, English on one side, Malay on the other. The handle to be of silver, heavy. The sheath of steel or Mechi's silver steel.

And a sample inscription:

> Presented by Sir William Francis Drummond Jervois, Governor of the Straits Settlements, to Raja Mahmud bin Panglima, Raja of Selangor, in recognition of his spontaneous help, his gallantry and good service to the British Government in Perak in the year 1875.[45]

It was later suggested that the swords should be a gift from the queen herself, but there was disagreement about the best way to represent Victoria's title in Malay. It was consequently decided to inscribe the swords in English only.[46] This was an attempt to use a form familiar to Malays – a gift from one's ruler, heavy with meaning, but not necessarily functional – in order to achieve a new outcome – the acceptance of the British monarch as the Malays' overlord. Yet new meaning also attached to these gifts; they were rewards for past service and were hoped to elicit continued cooperation from the recipients. In other words, the British were endeavouring to transform the gift from ruler to chief from a spiritual reward to a secular contract.

The plan ran into trouble, however, when the activities of the five chiefs were examined more critically and the question arose whether they were deserving of government recognition. Two of the chiefs had engaged in piracy and robbery, both before and after aiding the British in 1875. They were all condemned as 'idle', one in particular as 'an idle, gambling, opium-smoking, free lance, who by his own admission did not murder Sir W. Jervois [during his visit to Perak in September 1874] only because Abdullah did not give the signal'.[47] The new resident of Perak, Hugh Low, felt that 'the Rajas are all, I believe, adventurers who served on the side they hoped would

---

45 CO 882/3.

46 CO 273/90; CO 882/3. Bernard S. Cohn discusses similar debates about the representation of the British monarch to Indian subjects at precisely the same time in 'Representing authority in Victorian India', in Eric Hobsbawm and Terence Ranger, eds, *The Invention of Tradition*, Cambridge: Cambridge University Press, 1983, pp. 184–85, 201–2.

47 This was Bloomfield Douglas, the resident of Selangor, on Syed Mashor. CO 273/91.

pay them best'.[48]

More serious was the suspicion that the intended meaning of the swords would be disregarded. When asked whether there was any danger of the chiefs 'making an improper use of the swords', the residents of both Perak and Selangor answered in the affirmative. Low considered that the chiefs were angry that they had not received 'pecuniary provision' and did not think that swords would satisfy them. Further,

> there is every probability that the swords would be used by Syed Mashor and Raja Indut, and perhaps by the others, as insignia of authority and for imposing upon the people of the Native States. If a reward in money could be substituted, it would, in my opinion, be more appropriate and probably more acceptable.

The resident of Selangor agreed that the swords would be used as 'a means of oppression' and 'a symbol of authority'.[49] Once the contract was feared likely to be misconstrued or unenforceable, the Colonial Office felt it had no choice but to withhold the swords.

The possibility of gifts being wilfully misinterpreted by their recipients exposed the disadvantage of using symbols in making contracts with the Malays. Hard cash proved more successful. Chiefs who had been powerful before the British arrived were incorporated into a civil list which provided a monthly allowance from state revenues. Allowances also had a precedent in Malay political life, being analogous to royal grants of revenue-producing territories. But the royal grant had been a sign of favour from the ruler and thus enhanced the political stature (power) of the recipient; the monthly allowance was contingent upon continued adherence to the principles of good government. In Perak the civil list was reduced considerably as a result of the investigation into Birch's murder; those chiefs who survived the cut were informed that 'they would forfeit all right to their allowances, should they attempt to exact revenue not legitimately due to them'.[50] As Malay chiefs were cut off from more and more income-generating activities, beginning, of course, with piracy, they became vulnerable to the strings attached to the allowances.

Very quickly, the allowance became the cornerstone of a new political economy of Malay leadership. Unlike the pension used earlier to buy a chief out of politics altogether (often with the requirement that he live

---

48 *Ibid.*

49 *Ibid.*

50 CO 882/3.

in Singapore), allowances recognised a recipient's position in society and guaranteed his correct behaviour in political life. Although the punitive aspect did not disappear, the allowance (and its increase) was used as a tool to foster active cooperation with British rule. In Pahang,

> It is based on the average receipts which each chief is calculated to have had for his own use together with some slight addition in order to make these headmen appreciate that the introduction of the Residential system has rather improved than otherwise their pecuniary position, and thus to ensure, if possible, their willing cooperation in the reforms which must be introduced.[51]

Because there were so many chiefs, the civil list had to constitute a considerable portion of state expenditures in the early years of colonial rule, even where the chiefs were not well paid. Perak spent $48,000 on Malay chiefs in 1877 out of a total budget of $272,000; this included over $11,000 granted to the exiled chiefs and their families at home. Selangor spent the same, which constituted 20 per cent of its budget, the same amount as was devoted to public works. Sungai Ujung spent one-sixth of its budget on its chiefs.[52]

The allowances succeeded in creating a new discourse surrounding political behaviour and economic reward. This can be seen in the case of Pahang in the 1890s, when a grant was signed over in the sultan's name to the Straits government to help pay for the cost of putting down a rebellion in that state. No one noticed that some years earlier the sultan had signed over that same grant, amounting to $600 per month, to his eldest son. The aggrieved Tunku Mahmud lost no time pointing out the injustice in that 'he, almost the only Raja of Pahang who was loyal to the Government during the disturbances of 1892, should also be the only one on whom a share of the burden of expenses of the expedition should fall'. Reluctant to dock the sultan's allowance, and equally loathe to increase state expenditure 'because somebody blundered', the Colonial Office delayed a decision on this matter until Frank Swettenham, then resident general of the Federated Malay States, reminded them that 'until we interfered, the Sultan and his family practically constituted the state'. The tunku eventually received $300 per month, but only after he carried out a 'fitting marriage' to the sister of the Sultan of Johor.[53]

---

[51] CO 273/160.

[52] CO 273/90; CO 273/91.

[53] CO 273/228–CO 273/230. The latter requirement probably reflected British efforts to integrate the family of the non-royal Sultan of Johor into the royalty of the peninsula. See the discussion in the next chapter.

The complete success of the new political economy can be seen as early as 1889 in the state of Selangor. The governor's visit that year found Sultan Abdul Samad wearing the badge and star of the Order of St Michael and St George. The sultan declared himself pleased with 'all that was going on in his country [and] perfectly satisfied with the amount of the allowance which he drew and which, with a laughing reference to past times as he was aware I knew, was regularly paid'. The circulation of gifts and economic resources had become thoroughly detached from Malay meaning and control. Their meaning was now commanded by the British and accessed by Malay accommodation of British justice and good government. The new political economy had developed in two stages. In the first, symbolic gifts were liable to be misinterpreted as a mark of favour, as constituting participation in the power of the ruler instead of the agreement to relinquish power. This explained the cancellation of the swords and the consequent preference for cash allowances. With no alternatives in sight, the Malay ruling class endeavoured to get on the civil list and wield a new kind of power, highly circumscribed in comparison with the older power, but offering regular rewards. In the second stage, after colonial rule had been firmly consolidated, symbolic honours could be safely bestowed without fear of misinterpretation. The allowance was recognition of position in Malay society; the Order of St Michael and St George conferred membership in the British empire.

Standardisation of the Malay State: Internal and External

The consolidation of British power in the last quarter of the nineteenth century entrenched the discourse of good government as well as a new political economy in southern Malaya. It also accelerated the standardisation of political units (Malay states) which was shown as an impulse in the case of Negeri Sembilan. The result would be a greater uniformity in the size and structure of Malay states, the clarification of authority as lesser sovereignties disappeared, and a new ordering of relations between states. The process can be seen in brief by surveying the southern peninsula at two points in time: the end of the first quarter of the nineteenth century, after British influence had been clarified through treaties with the Dutch and the Siamese, and again towards the end of the century.

Early in the century, political structures varied and were largely determined by the continuing dissolution of the Johor-Riau polity. The heir to that dynasty by then resided in Dutch-controlled territory and was more and more cut off from the peninsula. The British had recognised a rival claimant to the throne, who became sultan in Singapore, but he had little prestige or power, and two generations later his grandson Alam would be stripped of Muar, the family's last remaining territory on the peninsula. This left *de facto* control in the hands of the *bendahara* in Pahang and the *temenggung* in Johor. Though both Pahang and Johor were seen as discrete political entities, they had neither 'tidy' borders nor ideal political hierarchies and were not understood to be independent states.[54]

In contrast, Perak and Selangor were independent. Perak had an impeccable pedigree, having been founded by a son of the last Malay ruler of Melaka and the Siamese had renounced all claims to the state in the 1826 treaty with Britain.[55] Selangor had been acknowledged as an independent state since 1766, when the Bugis ruler received the Malay mark of royalty from the Sultan of Perak. But civil wars in both states, complicated by the participation of rival Chinese clans and Straits financial interests, fractured the exercise of power. Selangor, for example, was divided by the middle of the century into five autonomous territories; the sultan at Langat controlled one of them.[56] Finally, the interior of Melaka, known as Negeri Sembilan (nine states), consisted of a number of Minangkabau *rantau* (outlying area) districts, some of which were nominally under the suzerainty of Johor, but which were actually quite autonomous.[57]

By the end of the century, all these entities had become proper 'states' with centralised power structures. Most striking was the creation of modern Negeri Sembilan. Relations between these small states were gradually regularised through negotiation and treaties, and they were all finally drawn into one entity between the years 1889 and 1898. Treating this creation as clarification of a messy situation, the scholar-bureaucrat R.O. Winstedt later borrowed a Minangkabau saying to describe the outcome: 'the intricate had been disentangled, the turbid cleared, the rain had ceased and the mist dispersed'.[58] Johor and Pahang were also recognised as independent states by the British overlord and their rulers confirmed in the title of sultan.[59]

---

[54] A.C. Milner, *Kerajaan: Malay Political Culture on the Eve of Colonial Rule*, Tucson: University of Arizona Press, 1982, pp. 29–30.

[55] Barbara Watson Andaya and Leonard Y. Andaya, *A History of Malaysia*, London: Macmillan, 1982, pp. 59–60, 117–18.

[56] *Ibid.*, pp. 96, 147–48.

[57] *Ibid.*, pp. 94–95.

[58] R.O. Winstedt, ed., *Malaya: The Straits Settlements and the Federated and Unfederated Malay States*, London: Constable, 1923, pp. 150–51.

[59] The relation between Malay rulers and the centralisation of state power will be discussed in the next chapter.

As in the areas of government and political economy, British recognition of states involved a restructuring of meaning. In the Malay idiom, politics was about control of manpower rather than land and political entities only acquired meaning through 'the condition of having a ruler'.[60] To the British, states were understood as territorial entities and were defined through the technology of mapping.[61] The new attitude was easily summed up: 'without a complete map the country cannot be opened up'.[62] Malay disregard for precise knowledge of borders was somewhat astonishing to the British and always worthy of note, as in this comment on the governor's 1875 trip to the east coast:

> The boundaries on the western side of the State of Trengganu seem to be little known. The Sultan himself said that there was a great extent of jungle in the interior, but that nobody had ever visited it, nor was it known where the Trengganu boundary ran.... It appears that but little light can be thrown on this subject of boundaries, even by the natives themselves.[63]

Thus not only the 'new' state of Negeri Sembilan but all the states under British dominion found themselves redefined by the new idiom, a process in which the Malay ruling class played an important role.

The clarification of borders through surveying and signed agreements became the principal means of accomplishing the territorialisation of Malay states. One example of this process illustrates how border mapping changed the nature of political authority, while providing opportunities to Malay elites who were astute enough to grasp the new idiom. In 1878 the border between Selangor and Sungai Ujung was 'settled by their respective Chiefs assisted by the advice of the Residents'.[64] Not surprisingly, some areas between the states had been found to be under uncertain authority. As Thongchai Winichakul notes in the case of Siam's tributaries, ambiguous territories under multiple sovereignties were a common manifestation of indigenous political space and sovereignty.[65] This situation was intolerable

---

60 Milner, *Kerajaan*, pp. 8–9.

61 See Thongchai Winichakul, *Siam Mapped: A History of the Geo-Body of a Nation*, Honolulu: University of Hawaii Press, 1994, for the triumph of the new geography in nineteenth-century Siam, as well as Britain's role in that transformation.

62 *Straits Times*, 31 July 1875. CO 882/3.

63 *Ibid.*

64 This account of the border between Selangor and Sungai Ujung is based on documents in CO 273/95 and CO 273/104.

65 Thongchai, *Siam Mapped*. He discusses the transformation of 'overlapping margin' into 'vertical interface' in ch. 5.

to colonial rule. Ambiguous territory became 'territory in dispute [which] was neglected and did not share the advantages reaped by the other Districts of Selangor and Sungai Ujung from the introduction of a better system of government'. Venturing into the murky waters of multiple sovereignty, British officials found the evidence collected to be hopelessly 'contradictory'. Finally, top British officials and the Malay ruler of each state, together with a representative from the Straits government, reached an agreement 'based upon mutual convenience and upon general principles of equity'. Through the exchange of several localities, Sungai Ujung received a coastline, expected to 'prove of much service in developing the country'.

The rearrangement of territory did not please everyone, however, and the subsequent controversy demonstrates one Malay chief's deft leap from the old idiom to the new. Raja Bot objected to the transfer of Lukut from Selangor to Sungai Ujung. He claimed to possess, through his father, a *kuasa* from the Sultan of Selangor to collect the revenues of that district, an authorisation which would be voided by the transfer. The revenues of Lukut had declined to between $200 and $300 per month, and the whole system of autonomous revenue collection was in any case being dismantled, but Raja Bot pressed his claim to better his standing in the new order. He engaged a Singapore lawyer who proceeded to publicise the injustice that had been done to the raja. The British government, which had earlier considered him friendly, tried to approach him with a settlement, but 'acting no doubt under advice, he refused to come to the Secretariat to see Mr. Swettenham, though several times sent for'. Raja Bot's claim to sovereignty over Lukut was disputed by the British, who nonetheless played the raja's game by debating the issue on his terms; they claimed the *kuasa* was of the type which could be revoked at will. The Sultan of Selangor's reaction to Raja Bot's plan to seek legal redress reveals the translation of power from the old idiom to the new from another angle:

> [The Sultan] broke into a fit of laughter and ridiculed the idea of any interference between him and his subject except that of the British Government and the Resident under the existing policy.

The sultan probably understood that the raja's goal was a generous settlement; at that time it was still ludicrous to apply the new idiom to relations between Malays. (On the other hand, perhaps he was worried.) Through tenacity and the expansion of the claim to include the district of Sungai Raya, ruled by his cousin Raja Daud, Raja Bot succeeded in his aims. In exchange for giving up all claims, he received $17,000, 3,000 acres of land, and confirmation of ownership of his family's houses and property.

The clarification of borders and consequent redefinition of political authority proceeded apace. Once again, Johor participated in the new idiom without being under formal colonial rule and, as an independent state, developed a cadre of Malay officials with technical competence to carry out the work. The borders between Johor and Pahang and between Johor and Melaka were surveyed and settled in the 1890s, and much internal surveying was done as well. Like the other Malay states, the old rump of the Johor-Riau empire had become something entirely different by the end of the century. The state official in charge of surveying recognised this when he wrote in 1894, '[t]he truth is that I am older than the present state of Johor'.[66]

The redefinition of political space and authority engendered by mapping intersected with the principles of good government to reorder the internal political landscape of Malay states as well. Selangor and Perak, which felt the most direct intervention, showed these effects quite early. When Birch arrived in Perak in 1874, the sultan had abandoned his usual residence at Batarabit to avoid cholera and was living on boats upriver. Ex-Sultan Ismail's family lived in Kinta but the chief himself stayed in Blanja to be closer to his tin mines. Political authority had no permanent residence, and Birch intended to change that. He looked forward to the time when 'the Sultan is located in his own palace, with the Resident within sight of him, the administration of justice and all business will be centralized there, and the Chiefs brought more together and in a public manner'.[67] Birch did not see these plans brought to fruition, but future residents did. By early 1877 the government had decided to move the residency from Bandar Bahru, which was considered inconvenient, to Kuala Kangsar which had several financial, political and logistical advantages. Its proximity to Larut eliminated the need for a highly-paid assistant resident in that area. It was near the home of Yusuf, the new regent, giving the resident 'facilities for exercising a personal influence over him'. Kuala Kangsar was close as well to Kinta, a mining region and near 'the lately disaffected district of Kota Lama'. Overall, Kuala Kangsar's

> central position renders it the most convenient place for access to other parts of Perak. Again, there is a telegraph wire between Kuala Kangsar and the Port of Larut, which is only seven hours distant from Penang, and ... there is a telegraphic communication between Penang and Singapore.[68]

---

66 Mohamed Salleh bin Perang, whose autobiographical writings are translated and interpreted in Amin Sweeney, *Reputations Live On: An Early Malay Autobiography*, Berkeley: University of California Press, 1980, p. 80. See also pp. 58, 66.

67 Report of the acting resident of Perak, 2 April 1875. CO 882/3.

68 CO 273/90.

Kuala Kangsar quickly became established as the royal seat of Perak as Malay politics coalesced around the site of British power. When Swettenham toured the protected states in the following year (as assistant colonial secretary), he found the place reconstructed with new roads, a bridge over the river and a considerable increase in the population, and number of houses. The regent was planning to build himself a new house and Raja Dris, the future Sultan Idris, had built a house near that of the resident.[69]

A similar process was underway in Selangor. In 1874 the sultan pulled down the stockade around his house at Langat, the effective stockade now being occupied by the police, and allowed a road to go past his door. Four years later he had built himself a better house and was building a good road, at his own expense, connecting it to the dock. Ten years later, although the old sultan could not be persuaded to move to the new centre in Kuala Lumpur, the governor's visit found that town booming and connected by rail to the port in Klang.[70]

A final aspect of the redefinition of political space and authority was the growing uniformity of relations between the Malay states under British colonial rule. In order to define and separate the states, more was needed than border demarcation. Ruling class spheres of influence had also to be restricted to within state borders, something particularly evident in the early years when rebels from one state fled into the jungles of another. The goal was a new type of interstate relations conducted through British mediation. Beginning informally, this new norm would eventually be enshrined in treaties and constitutions. Negeri Sembilan provides an example of this process. After intervening in the Negeri Sembilan succession dispute by installing a resident in Sungai Ujung in 1874, the British sought to regulate that area's relations with Selangor. The Viceroy of Selangor, Tunku Dia Udin, was informed that he was to have no communication with the chiefs of Negeri Sembilan without informing the British.[71] At this stage the British were intent on installing the Maharaja of Johor as their agent of supervision over these states. This was reflected in the Sri Menanti confederation agreement of 1876:

> And we agree that in case of any dispute or difficulty arising among our States which we are unable to settle, we will refer for advice to His Highness the Maharajah of Johore.[72]

---

[69] CO 882/4.
[70] CO 882/3; CO 882/4; CO 273/160.
[71] CO 882/3.
[72] The agreement is reprinted in Parkinson, *British Intervention*, p. 326.

In a separate letter to the maharaja, the governor reserved the right of the British to intervene directly. By 1885, however, when the British had become the colonial power rather than overlord of the region, Johor was prohibited by treaty from interfering with the politics of other Malay states.[73]

The culmination of these trends, both the internal and external ordering of the Malay states, is evident in the federation of Selangor, Negeri Sembilan, Perak and Pahang in 1896. The creation of the Federated Malay States served the interests of further standardisation in administration, transportation and economic policy. Still, it was carefully explained to the rulers that, despite the greater authority the British government possessed to pass legislation for all these states, 'no Raja has any voice in the affairs of any State, but his own'.[74] This was meant to reassure the rulers that their individual sovereignties would not be threatened by each other, but they did not fail to notice that state sovereignty itself had been undermined. At the second conference of rulers, a ceremonial gathering in 1903, Sultan Idris appealed to the recently constructed notion of a standardised Malay state to protest against the overcentralisation of the federation:

> These States are now known as the negri negri bersekutu (the united countries), but the matter of union (persekutuan) I do not quite clearly understand; but you are all aware that the States have become friendly, amicably assisting one another; if, however, the four States were amalgamated into one, would it be right to say that one State assisted the other, because assistance implies something more than one, for if there is only one, which is the helper and which is the helped? A Malay proverb says that there cannot be two masters to one vessel; neither can there be four Rulers over one country.[75]

Despite this critical note, both the first and second conferences of rulers displayed the success of the new standardisation. Having thoroughly disentangled the respective Malay ruling classes from each others' political affairs, Swettenham trumpeted the first meeting of the four sultans in 1897 as 'an event absolutely unprecedented in Malay history'.[76] And so it was,

---

[73] Nevertheless, Abu Bakar played out the final act of his instrumentalist role by helping to bring Pahang into the British fold in 1887.

[74] Report of the Durbar (Federal Council) at Kuala Kangsar, 13–17 July 1897. CO 273/229. (Hereafter Durbar.)

[75] Minutes of the Conference of Chiefs of the Federated Malay States held at Kuala Lumpur, 20–23 July 1903. Printed in the Supplement to the Selangor Government Gazette, 2 October 1903. CO 469/13. (Hereafter Conference of Chiefs.)

[76] Durbar. These meetings are discussed in more detail in the next chapter.

for these four rulers were assembled on British terms, as representatives of a new kind of polity. The ensemble was political insofar as it ratified the new federal structure, but individual relations between the respective rulers were drained of political content. At the second conference held in Kuala Lumpur, one highlight for the visiting rulers was a tour of the Sultan of Selangor's new *istana* (royal residence) in Klang. Once engaged in alliances and rivalries in a system of regional politics, Malay rulers now emerged from their individual states to compare notes on each other's houses. A British participant in 1903 noted how 'the Sultans and Datohs from different States mixed with each other freely and unreservedly', and concluded that such a thing 'would have been impossible before the era of Federation'.[77]

Six years after this conference, British colonial power expanded once again with the transfer from Siam of Kedah, Perlis, Terengganu and Kelantan. The rulers of these states were asked to accept a British officer and to course all their official communications with the other Malay states through him.[78] Warily, the Sultan of Terengganu questioned the clause of the British treaty 'requiring him to refrain from taking part in the administration of any Malay States other than his own'. The British agent reassured him that 'the clause was not intended to limit in any way His Highness's private intercourse with the Rulers of adjacent States, to several of whom he is connected by ties of blood or marriage'.[79] Though the formal mechanism for political interaction was left in place, the marriage alliance was now a purely personal interaction. By this time, the die was cast.

The Bureaucratisation of Malay Chiefs

The creation of the FMS in 1896 was a landmark in the consolidation of British colonial rule. As the northern states and Johor were then incorporated into the residential system, it became clear that the achievement of federation had also been something of an apogee. These latest additions to the colonial fold successfully resisted being merged into the FMS, and colonial policy in the decades before the Second World War was preoccupied with the problems of centralisation and decentralisation. But such limitations should not distract from the conceptual revolution which was ongoing. British ideological premises – good government and

[77] Conference of Chiefs.

[78] Report of Governor Anderson's interview with the Sultan of Trengganu, 27 May 1909. CO 273/350.

[79] CO 273/351.

the delimitation of the Malay state – were triumphing and being reinforced in each new addition to empire through the new political economy. In this triumph of the British idiom, it only remained to define the role of the Malay ruling classes in the working of good government. This task, however, signalled the beginning of a new stage for the Malay elite: the emergence of a fundamental difference in meaning and role between Malay rulers (rajas or sultans) and the non-royal aristocracies (chiefs). The final section of this chapter traces the origins of this divergence and the eventual transformation of Malay chiefs into a bureaucratic elite.[80]

Throughout the century, the British advanced the ideology of good government in the Malay states, first as a discourse and then in actual practice. Ironically, just as the new idiom succeeded in displacing or redefining Malay political idiom, the British seemed to lose interest in the project of conversion. Instead of indoctrinating the largely quiescent Malay ruling class further in good government, the British declined to incorporate more than a small portion of it into the administration of the states until quite a late date. What accounts for this? Hendrik Maier has identified a mid-century shift in British attitudes towards Malay culture that helps explain it. Early British observers – Maier's merchant-scientists – approached the Malay world through the eyes of the Scottish Enlightenment. These men measured the Malays according to a scale of civilisation and found them wanting; they were contemptuous of the Malays for this reason but believed that all nations were capable of progress. Just like the British, Malays could advance from simple agriculture to a complex commercial society. A later generation abandoned this belief in man's perfectibility, becoming more tolerant and fond of Malay culture, but believing it inherently and eternally inferior to the British. 'First free trade and equality of all human beings, then order and superiority of the white race'.[81] The new attitude was no doubt encouraged by the very fact of formal colonial rule: scholar-administrators had control of the peninsula and did not have to rely on the spread of liberal ideas through persuasion.

This shift in thinking was exemplified by expansionist colonial officials like Frederick Weld who were finding their way east in the interventionist

[80] I use the terms chiefs, aristocracy and bureaucratic elite synonymously to identify the non-royal elements of the Malay ruling class under colonial rule. I am not concerned in this discussion with Malay aristocrats who did not successfully make the transition.

[81] Hendrik M.J. Maier, *In the Center of Authority: The Malay Hikayat Merong Mahawangsa*, Ithaca NY: Cornell University Southeast Asia Program, 1988, pp. 31, 33–44.

1870s and 1880s. It was manifest in a new articulation of the purpose of the British presence. To Weld, Malays were incapable of good government, the mark of civilisation:

> Nothing we have done has taught them to govern themselves; we are merely teaching them to cooperate with us in governing under our guidance.... Moreover, I doubt if Asiatics will ever learn to govern themselves, it is contrary to the genius of their race, of their history, of their religious system, that they should. Their desire is a mild, just and firm despotism; that we can give them.[82]

Even the example of the Maharaja of Johor was now discounted. Abu Bakar was, to Weld, 'an exceptional Malay ruler; he has lived all his life among Europeans; he is intimately bound up with our own government and has been the personal friend of successive Governors'; but 'after all he has not done much for Johor yet, and we do not know what will come after him'.[83] To the new generation, Malays might imitate Europeans, but they could never be authentically civilised.

The ascendancy of this view created a paradox in British dealings with the Malays. It called into question the earlier justification for intervention in the Malay states – the ideology of good government – by denying that the Malays could actually achieve this goal. But at the same time it provided a new purpose for the European presence. As Malays were no longer considered capable of meaningful progress on the scale of civilisation, they became an interesting case of an inferior culture whose identity should be preserved as the world changed around it. To accomplish this, 'Malay society had to be primarily defined in terms of its ancient values'.[84] British rule would bestow the double blessing of preserving an ancient culture while showering its contemporary members with the benefits of peace, justice and economic development.

Unfortunately, the 'ancient values' of Malay society were precisely what the colonial system sought to destroy in its quest to expand British capital. Hence the putative preservation of tradition was actually traditionalism, the conscious selection of appropriate ritual and idiom and the reconstruction of Malay culture along lines that were compatible with colonial rule. An early instance of this was the standardisation of the Malay state to facilitate trade, foreign investment and British control, a transformation which was

---

[82] CO 273/104.

[83] *Ibid.*

[84] Maier, *Center of Authority*, p. 51.

presented as a strengthening of Malay sovereignty and which was accepted as such by Malay rulers. As that example shows, the ideology of preservation never actually erased that of good government. The latter was too much at the heart of the whole British project in Malaya to be effaced, the desire to preserve a political culture condemned as unviable in the modern world. Traditionalism was instead an attempt to put preservation in the service of civilisation, to fashion a Malay culture that did not obstruct good government. Traditionalism could not always resolve the inherent tensions between the two ideologies, but it governed how the British approached the role of the ruling classes in colonial Malaya.

In the 1870s the still-cautious Colonial Office criticised the first generation of residents for taking on too much responsibility for the day-to-day running of government in the Malay states and tried to hold them to the treaty terms of advising. The residents' responses made it clear, however, that the establishment of good government would be a British endeavour. In Selangor, the resident protested that the sultan simply was not interested:

> The pliant, easy-going, trouble-avoiding nature of the Sultan of this State renders him at all times careless in assuming the reins of Government, and he too willingly places his power in the hands of the officer accredited to him.[85]

In Perak, Hugh Low came to a country 'under military occupation, and there was no native Government in it.... [With one exception] there was not a single native authority who had exerted any considerable influence in former times ... we must first create the Government to be advised'.[86] Despite reluctance from above, Malay government was being thoroughly remade.

Still, the imperative to preserve Malay culture, as well as expediency and financial austerity, necessitated a certain continuity in the ruling elite. The ruler himself was a visible manifestation of indigenous culture and hence indispensable. In Perak, the unpopular Raja Muda Yusuf, a man passed over by the Malays for the throne, was made first regent then sultan after all other candidates were eliminated by death or implication in the Birch assassination. Without a Malay monarch, indirect rule could not be presented as a 'peculiar system of Malay administration, tempered by English honesty and justice'. The retention of the Malay ruler, however, did not relieve the resident of any responsibility. Low argued that Raja

---

[85] CO 882/4.

[86] *Ibid.*

Muda Yusuf was 'a man of very good natural abilities, but he has no idea of government, except that the rakyat [subjects] were created to produce revenues for the rajas, and to be at their entire disposal'. Without a firm British hand guiding the ruler, good government would be impossible:

> If the Raja Muda is to be led to believe that he can act in spite of the Resident if he pleases, it will soon be seen that the greatest dissatisfaction will prevail, and we may say goodbye to all hopes of introducing capital and skill, whether European or Chinese, into the country.[87]

Rulers could be moulded, however, as attempted with the education of the sons of ex-Sultan Abdullah in Singapore, where they had 'the benefit of obtaining an insight into civilized manners and customs, and of recognizing the advantages which a country derives from a proper system of government'.[88] Good rulers could be recognised, as when Swettenham praised the Sultan of Kedah in 1889 for learning to speak English.[89] And good rulers could be rewarded, as was the Sultan of Selangor, whose acquiescence was read as loyalty. In fact, the reshaping of the Malay monarchy would represent the culmination of traditionalism and is the subject of the next chapter. The role of the non-royal aristocracy under colonial rule was more ambiguous.

From the beginning, British officials were predisposed to see good, or at least malleable, rulers surrounded by bad chiefs. Birch's first report mentioned the 'chiefs who almost always attend' Sultan Abdullah and 'exercise some influence over him'. His comments were expanded by the governor:

> Abdullah is always influenced by the Chiefs around him, and the four mentioned in this paragraph [the *laxamana*, *shahbandar*, *rajah makota* and *mata mata*] are the most respectable of his advisers. He generally listens to the counsel of a set of scamps, who fight his cocks and smoke opium with him.[90]

Besides influencing the ruler, these chiefs and 'petty Rajas' (the descendants of former rulers) were said to 'swarm about the country and oppress the Rakyat immediately under their control'. Their competition with each other, according to the governor, 'has been one of the great drawbacks to progress,

---

87 *Ibid.*

88 These boys, Raja Chulan and Raja Mansur, were possible successors to Sultan Yusuf. CO 882/3.

89 CO 273/162.

90 CO 882/3.

and will never disappear except under British rule'.[91]

Swettenham made similar comments about the chiefs of Selangor. Sultan Abdul Samad declared that 'with the help of Government he will permit no more of those quarrels amongst his Chiefs which have depopulated Selangor, nor piracies which have intimidated honest men from even approaching its shores and rivers'. Swettenham believed that the sultan was sincere in his friendship to the British government, but that without British backing his good intentions would come to naught, 'surrounded as he has been, and would again be, were he left to himself, by unscrupulous Chiefs, who would not only tacitly oppose him, but by open threats would prevent him from making good his promises'.[92] Twenty-five years later, with the expansion of British Malaya into the northern states, this British attitude was still evident. Governor John Anderson met with the Sultan of Terengganu, a man deeply opposed to the transfer of suzerain rights from Siam to Britain, and reported that 'his present attitude is no doubt the result of the influence exerted over him by his relations and advisers'.[93]

With this outlook, there was some feeling for doing away with the chiefs altogether, especially in the wake of the Perak debacle:

> Assuming ... that we are satisfied that most of the principal Chiefs of the country are disaffected towards us, and dealing treacherously with us, the question then arises whether, in the interests of humanity and civilization, we should not enter into their country and break down their power. In Malacca and Province Wellesley, no Chief possesses any political power; indeed the Chiefs are not to be distinguished from the people, and no one can go through the Malay Peninsula ... without being agreeably surprised at the difference between the condition of the Malays under Native rule and the same class of people under English rule.[94]

But the wholesale dispossession of the chiefs had been ruled out implicitly when they were granted allowances. Then too, the opposite lesson was as easily drawn from Perak: without the chiefs, the government would have no way 'of gauging the strength of native feeling on questions of proposed reform'. The aristocracy would not be ignored. Officials in Malaya were enjoined to 'make the best use of existing materials, and ... to find and train up some Chief or Chiefs of sufficient capacity and enlightenment to appreciate the advantages of a civilized government and to render some

---

[91] *Ibid.*

[92] Report of the Assistant Resident of Selangor, 15 December 1874. CO 882/3.

[93] CO 273/350.

[94] Gov. Jervois to the Colonial Office, 2 December 1876. CO 882/3.

assistance in the government of the country'.[95] This decision resulted in the creation of state councils on which representatives of the aristocracy would sit. As there were always more chiefs than available positions, the British were able to ensure, over time, that prominent chiefs would be amenable to working within the new system.

More important than their contribution to administration, the state councils were meant to reinforce the influence of the principal chiefs among the people. Once the Colonial Office had opted for preservation, it became the task of state governments to bolster traditional elites, rather than 'break down their power'. Low, who developed the state council system as resident of Perak from 1877 to 1889, sought 'to raise the prestige of the Council, and indirectly of its members, by appropriate ceremonial at its meetings'.[96] The rituals included a guard of honour, a band and guns firing a salute at the arrival of the regent to the meeting. Despite the addition of these foreign-inspired innovations, the state council meetings resembled what Eric Hobsbawm calls 'responses to novel situations which take the form of reference to old situations'.[97] The ceremonial nature of council meetings in the soon-to-be Federated Malay States, meetings at which no substantive discussion took place, evoked precolonial royal audiences or *muafakat* (consultation), where all the major chiefs were present and were seen to be in agreement with the ruler.[98] The chiefs' influence on the ruler may have been exercised in private discussion, but the state council meetings, marked by European procedure and the presence of the resident, were more analogous to formal, public audiences in the *balai* (ceremonial hall).[99] Perhaps precisely because the new ritual had this historic resonance,

---

95 Lord Carnarvon, secretary of state for the colonies, 1 June 1876. The letter is reprinted in Parkinson, *British Intervention*, pp. 313–17.

96 J.M. Gullick, *Rulers and Residents: Influence and Power in the Malay States, 1870–1920*, Singapore: Oxford University Press, 1992, pp. 39–42.

97 Eric Hobsbawm, 'Introduction: inventing traditions', in Eric Hobsbawm and Terence Ranger, eds, *The Invention of Tradition*, Cambridge: Cambridge University Press, 1983, p. 2.

98 See Milner, *Kerajaan*, pp. 46, 74.

99 Dissent was not often voiced in public. This was a point of contention in the 1914–15 dispute between the Kedah state council and the colonial government over whether the regent, acting as sultan, would attend state council meetings. Kedah argued that as theirs was a *working* state council, there was the possibility that the regent would be outvoted by the council, and this would harm the dignity of the sultan's position. James de Vere Allen, 'The elephant and the mousedeer – a new version: Anglo-Kedah relations, 1905–1915', *Journal of the Malaysian Branch of the Royal Asiatic Society*, vol. 41, no. 1, 1968, pp. 88–92.

membership in the essentially powerless state councils was valued within the Malay community.

Only the most powerful chiefs in a state became members of the state councils, however, and there were consequently many chiefs left with neither role nor means. Descendants of sultans, even if they held no current office, received small pensions, and those with clear claims to traditional sources of revenue were awarded allowances, but most got little and many got nothing. Suddenly finding themselves on the outside of the new system, and having difficulty adapting to their reduced circumstances, many Malay chiefs became indebted to moneylenders and the colonial government.[100] Still, a new type of government needed to be constructed in the states to ensure law and order and collect revenues. Could work not be found for the Malay aristocracy in this endeavour?

In keeping with the mandate to preserve, a strong argument was made for continuity at the level of local administration. Swettenham's views on this topic were influential. Swettenham argued in favour of retaining the jurisdiction of Malay *penghulus* over subdistricts (*mukim*) with populations ranging from 500 to 2,000. By employing these influential headmen, Swettenham hoped, 'we should, in engaging their services, enlist also their sympathies on the side of a Government which supported them and their traditions'.[101] He also noted how successfully native headmen might obstruct justice were they not included in its administration. But here the contradiction between preservation and good government surfaced. Swettenham wanted at the same time 'to preserve the accepted customs and traditions of the country' and 'to teach [the Malays] the advantages of good government and enlightened policy'. The *penghulus* he wanted to retain had inherited their positions from their fathers, along with substantial property and social standing in their villages of residence; this was the source of the influence Swettenham wanted at the disposal of the government. The qualities he sought in native officers would not likely be found in those same individuals: *penghulus* must be able to read and write, file weekly and monthly reports, serve as magistrates, take the census and collect revenue from the local population without 'squeezing' (appropriating surplus in the

[100] J.M. Gullick, *Malay Society in the Late Nineteenth Century*, Singapore: Oxford University Press, 1989, pp. 75–77.

[101] Citations in this paragraph are from Swettenham's 'Proposals for the government of Perak through its Headmen with a small auxiliary police force' and 'Some arguments in favour of governing Perak through its headmen', both written in 1876 and included in the 1883 report, Local District Administration, commissioned by Weld in 1882. CO 273/120.

time-honoured Malay fashion). Swettenham displayed the contradiction at the heart of his recommendations when he considered the relation of the police to the Malay *penghulu*: 'Place a Police Station in this man's village, and what will happen? Can you place the Police under him? Certainly not. You can't place disciplined men under an undisciplined officer'.

When the situation of local administration was reviewed in the early 1880s, it was clear that little had been done to overcome the inherent contradiction. *Penghulus* did not receive regular salaries in the Malay villages of Penang and were judged to be 'a sad failure', 'an obstruction to justice', 'untrustworthy' and of 'little or no assistance … to the police'.[102] The system of *penghulu* administration had 'fallen into disuse' in Sungai Ujung. In Perak there were not very many *penghulus* and those in office were not considered to be successfully fulfilling their duties, especially in the area of revenue collection. This situation was attributed to the lack of European supervision, which was intended to provide instruction and financial oversight. In Selangor the chiefs were 'a useful link between the Government under the Residential system and the rakyat', but were not trusted with revenue collection. The result of these early failures is well known. The office of *penghulu* was indeed retained and expanded so that the face of colonial rule in the village remained Malay. But the substance of the office was to serve good government. To accomplish this reshaping of local Malay government, control of *penghulu* appointments and their supervision was done by a new layer of state administration: the European district officer. Now both the top stratum of government (the ruler) and the bottom stratum (the *penghulu*) remained Malay. The middle ranges, formerly the province of the powerful district chiefs, were replaced by British officers.

There was some effort to match the numerous chiefs needing support with work needing to be done, and some underemployed chiefs were appointed as *penghulus* in the early years. But most considered that title 'derogatory to one of high rank',[103] and the use of formerly powerful chiefs to assist European district officers met with a predictable lack of success. Most of those who held positions on account of their claim to an allowance held those positions in name only, and were embittered by their inability to maintain followers and command the labour of the people – that is, by the final defeat of the Malay idiom of power. Neither did the colonial state in its early stages require so many personnel as to absorb the ranks of the

[102] Citations in this paragraph are from the reports of the lieutenant governor of Penang and the residents of Sungai Ujung, Perak and Selangor. They are included in Local District Administration. CO 273/120.

[103] Sadka, *Protected Malay States*, p. 276.

abundant Malay aristocracy. In fact, with certain exceptions, the chiefs who experienced the transition to colonial rule in the west coast states were something of a 'lost generation'. It was their sons, some of whom were trained by the British, who would be in a position to rebound after the turn of the century. By this time, of course, colonial rule was firmly consolidated and, in the FMS, highly centralised. The tasks of administration were becoming more complex technically and legally, and in the ranks of administrators Malays were scarcely to be seen.

In 1903 Malay ruling class dissatisfaction with its negligible role in state administration was highlighted at the rulers' conference held in Kuala Lumpur. Meant to 'afford the Rulers and Chiefs of the different States an opportunity of meeting and exchanging views in friendly conversation', the conference had no mandate to change policy. Nevertheless, the agenda was supposed to reflect Malay concerns, so it is noteworthy that the second item for discussion was the further employment of Malays in the government service.[104] Although Swettenham in his opening remarks (as high commissioner for the FMS) regretted that the 'national characteristics' of the Malays made it difficult for them to take advantage of the opportunities afforded them, it is clear that the obstacles were more structural. Only 874 Malays were employed by government departments (not including the police) and an additional 587 as *penghulus* and magistrates in the FMS in 1903. Obstacles to the employment of Malays at the higher levels of the civil service were said to be the severely competitive civil service exam and the need to demonstrate knowledge of the law, in other words, a lack of education.[105] Sultan Idris of Perak pointed out the increasing interest of all Malays in education and asked that suitable government employment be reserved for Malays and not offered to other nationalities.

A certain changing of the guard is reflected in the remarks made at this conference. Swettenham, whose views on the educability of the Malays were quite clear, was nearing retirement. Younger officers, members of a 'pro-Malay campaign', were moved by the argument that indirect rule mandated a greater role for Malays in the government.[106] According to J.P. Rodger, the resident of Selangor:

---

[104] Conference of Chiefs.

[105] Three Malay clerks in Perak the following year petitioned the government to exempt them from passing the senior grade examination on the basis of their poor educational background. The request was denied, but helped convince the government to upgrade Malay education. CO 273/303.

[106] See P.L. Burns, Introduction to the 1971 historical reprint edition of R.J. Wilkinson, *Papers on Malay Subjects*, Kuala Lumpur: Oxford University Press, 1971.

> It must never be forgotten that these are protected Malay States and not British Colonies and that the British Officials are here to advise and assist and not to supersede the rulers in the administration of their own States.[107]

The contrivance of a protectorate never hindered the expansion of British dominance over Malay society. The term did accurately describe, however, an important aspect of the task of preservation. The position of the Malay ruling class was consistently protected, both within Malay society and against the growing interests of Chinese and Indian immigrants. This understanding of the protectorate also shaped the consequent expansion of Malay education and participation in the government. When the English-medium Malay College Kuala Kangsar (MCKK) was founded in 1905, it was treated by Malay royalty and British authorities as a preserve for the sons of royalty and the aristocracy. And when, in the 1920s and 1930s, Chinese and Indian residents of the FMS argued strongly for the opening of the civil services to non-Malays, the British reaffirmed their commitment to protect the special position and privileges of the Malays; in practice, the Malay ruling class.

In 1910 the Malay administrative service was established in the FMS as a junior bureaucratic service.[108] Most of its recruits came from the MCKK and were, therefore, sons of the aristocracy. This new bureaucratic elite was the site where traditional authority met the colonial state, where preservation met progress. Malay officers within the Malay administrative service were always subordinate to Europeans, usually posted to remote, all-Malay, non-productive regions, and slowly promoted. As in colonial Africa, the British established 'neo-traditions of hierarchy and subordination' to which aristocracies had exclusive access.[109] Although relegated to subordinate postures, the Malay bureaucrats enjoyed enormous prestige in Malay society. Their place in the official hierarchy gave the impression of 'immense power', which was enhanced by their adoption of Western styles of leisure activity, dress and transportation. The prestige they enjoyed came more from the officers' association with government than with their birth.[110] To the Malay public with whom they were in close contact, 'Malay Officers personified

---

[107] Conference of Chiefs.

[108] See Khasnor Johan's excellent study, *The Emergence of the Modern Malay Administrative Elite*, Singapore: Oxford University Press, 1984.

[109] See Terence Ranger, 'The invention of tradition in colonial Africa', in Eric Hobsbawm and Terence Ranger, eds, *The Invention of Tradition*, Cambridge: Cambridge University Press, 1983, pp. 220–22.

[110] Khasnor, *Malay Administrative Elite*, p. 176.

achievement' and were 'the embodiment of progress and a testimony to the advantages of an English education and a regular income'.[111] Ideologically, the high status of the Malay administrative service represented the adoption of the good government idiom by Malay society.

While Malay bureaucrats in the FMS enjoyed great prestige but little power, those in the Unfederated Malay States (Kedah, Perlis, Kelantan, Terengganu and Johor) retained more actual responsibility and control. These states had undergone varying degrees of self-imposed bureaucratisation in an effort to stave off European control. When the advance eventually came, the British found, in Kedah for example, a 'fully organised central administration composed of Malays, some of them men of considerable ability and individuality.... it would be highly impolitic and undesirable to displace the Malays'.[112] This state of affairs, as well as anticipated resistance to any loss of Malay control, resulted in the retention of more responsibility in Malay hands in the Unfederated Malay States than in the FMS.

Khasnor Johan argues that there was 'no significant conflict' between the traditional ruling class and the new elite in the FMS. The former provided most of the Malay administrative service recruits and had considerable say in the selection process.[113] In fact, the incorporation of the aristocracies into colonial bureaucracies was a real extension of royal power and would be an important bridge to the continued dominance of ruling class families over political power in the postcolonial period. As a ruling class, the royal families and the bureaucratised aristocracies had shared interests vis-à-vis both the British and the lower classes. In the FMS, for example,

> the Malay Officers ... were alert to the opportunities which arose to use the members of the traditional ruling class as their own mouthpiece. It was not uncommon for a small group of the more senior of the Malay Officers to get together informally before their rulers went into conference with the British and decide what subjects each sultan or ruler would be 'made' to raise with the authorities.... In this way some of the sultans and other aristocrats often became channels for the ideas and aspirations of the Malay Officers.[114]

The pursuit of shared interests can be seen in the Unfederated Malay States as well. In Terengganu the colonial government broke the ruling class hold

---

111 *Ibid.*, pp. 177, 190–92.

112 According to Governor Anderson, who visited the state shortly after its transfer from Siam to Britain. CO 273/351.

113 Khasnor, *Malay Administrative Elite*, pp. 3, 48–49.

114 *Ibid.*, p. 171.

on political and economic power in the wake of the 1928 revolt. Aristocrats and royal family alike were reduced to well-compensated functionaries of the colonial state. Unlike in a federated state, however, the ruling class in Terengganu filled most of the non-technical positions in the administration; it used entrenched positions to protect special privileges and economic interests. The Terengganu civil service was the preserve of the old ruling class and retained the hierarchical tone of social superior and subordinate in its relations with the public.[115]

But the wielding of power through bureaucratic positions could also be at odds with royal power. The relatively high educational status and administrative position of the bureaucrats bred attitudes of pride and achievement that were said to jar the sensibilities of those at the Malay courts, where the bureaucrats, especially the small number of commoners among them, were systematically cut down to size. The strict etiquette and social hierarchy at court took no account of the prestige of modern administration, education and function. Malay officers particularly resented performing obeisance and being required to sit on the floor, Malay-style, while British officers were provided with chairs. Nevertheless, these were the terms on which a portion of the Malay aristocracy was incorporated into the workings of government. They had to be accepted, though they represented a real limit to the achievement of bureaucratic competence.

But for the ideology of preservation, the reconstruction of power along bureaucratic lines might have represented the final conversion of the Malay aristocracy to the British ideology of good government, the conversion of *kerajaan* to *pentadbiran* (administration). Traditionalism demanded instead that Malay identity be tied firmly to the deference and hierarchy of court life, an identification actively endorsed by Malay rulers. In 1903 Sultan Idris opposed sending Malay boys to Britain to study, for education abroad 'tends to denationalize them and lessens their knowledge of their own language, religion and country'.[116] The education Malays received at the MCKK was

---

[115] Shaharil Talib, *After Its Own Image: The Trengganu Experience, 1881–1941*, Singapore: Oxford University Press, 1984, pp. 222–27; and Heather Sutherland, 'The taming of the Trengganu elite', in Ruth McVey, ed., *Southeast Asian Transitions: Approaches through Social History*, New Haven: Yale University Press, 1978, pp. 83–84.

[116] R.J. Wilkinson, 12 December 1903. CO 273/303. The sultan was backed up in this opinion by the first-generation British administrator Hugh Clifford, whose fictional resident of a fictional Pahang says of a prince educated in Britain: 'It is a thousand pities, to my thinking, that he was ever taken out of his proper environment. The Malay guided by white influence is all right; the denationalized Malay is the devil'.

informed by this concern. It was not particularly challenging, focusing more on 'character building' than intellectual development. Throughout the prewar period, MCKK graduates had difficulty passing the senior Cambridge exam, qualifying for entrance to Raffles College in Singapore and studying the law they needed in their Malay administrative service posts.[117] Quite simply, the kind of training needed to participate more successfully in British-style administration would inevitably produce a bureaucratised chiefly class poised to compete with the Malay courts and, eventually, the British themselves. To prevent the fulfilment of this potential, access to transformative education was tightly restricted and the objective of limited achievement was built into the system of English education in Malaya.

The strength of the Malay bureaucracy was also kept in check. The number of recruits to the Malay administrative service was low, the total corps never exceeding 91 before the Second World War. In addition to the Malay administrative service elite, a very small number of Malays held technical posts, while a much larger group filled clerical positions at the bottom rungs of the administrative ladder. By 1931 English-educated Malay government servants totalled less than 15,000.[118] British ambivalence towards the chiefs and the fears of the Malay courts resulted in the creation of an aristocracy which perfectly reflected the contradictions between the competing ideologies of good government and preservation.

*

This chapter has described the ideological transformation undergone by the Malay ruling class under first British paramountcy and then colonial rule. It has argued that even before the British extended formal colonial rule over the Malay states, a British discourse of good government and civilisation had become pervasive in Malay politics. Transitions to colonial rule provided further opportunity to entrench the British discourse, as Malay political institutions were reshaped through a newly imposed political economy. The new relationship of economic to political power in Malay society was at once the result of expediency by the British and an attempt to survive as a ruling class by Malay rulers and chiefs. At the same time, the very definition of

---

Saleh: A Prince of Malaya, Singapore: Oxford University Press, 1989, p. 167.

117 See Khasnor, *Malay Administrative Elite*, especially chs. 5–7.

118 *Ibid.*, p. 65; William R. Roff, *The Origins of Malay Nationalism*, Kuala Lumpur: University of Malaya Press, 1980, pp. 120–21. This number does not represent the entire bureaucratic elite, as Unfederated Malay States' administration was conducted in Malay.

the Malay polity was adjusted to accord with the needs of colonial control and capital penetration. The result was a series of territorially defined states with distinct ruling classes who professed the desire for progress, good government, education and bureaucratic positions. Ideological premises, which two generations earlier were seen as alien and English, were universalised, and by the early 1900s seen as modern and good.

Yet the survival of the Malay ruling class was not without contradiction. Once in direct control of Malaya, the British no longer needed, or believed in, the ability of Malays to become civilised. Although good government would still be brought to the Malay states, the indigenous elite itself was no longer essential to the process. Instead, it became representative of an ancient culture that had to be preserved while the world changed around it. The Malay ruling class responded to the contradiction between civilisation and preservation in ways that caused a rift to develop within it. On the one hand, it consistently lobbied the British for the right to govern, leading to the bureaucratisation of the aristocracies. Although the achievement of the new bureaucratic elite was sharply limited, it was clearly imbued with the modern, good government ethos. On the other hand, the rulers took to heart the British project of preservation through traditionalism. This redefinition of Malay court culture in the service of colonial rule will be the subject of the next chapter.

Chapter Three

Rituals of State and the New Malay Rulers

In the previous chapter, I discussed the gradual acceptance by the Malay ruling class of the ideological premises of British colonial rule: good government and economic development within territorially defined, politically distinct and bureaucratically administered Malay states. I also examined the contradiction caused by the British abandoning their belief in the ability of Malays to become truly civilised. The ensuing tension between civilisation and preservation was partially resolved through the mechanism of traditionalism, an effort to construct a modern version of an ancient Malay culture that would not impede good government. The Malay elite responded to the imperatives of both civilisation and preservation. With little British encouragement, the courts sponsored the limited bureaucratisation of the aristocracy in pursuit of good government. At the same time, the rulers developed their own position along traditionalist lines with much stronger British backing. This chapter focuses on the meaning and political purposes of the resulting apotheosis of the Malay sultanate.

J.M. Gullick has provided students of Malay history with a richly detailed narrative, culled from colonial files and memoirs, on the development of the residential system in the late nineteenth and early twentieth centuries.[1] Gullick presents this evidence to show that colonial government was a 'joint effort – a process to which the Malay Ruler, if he chose, could make a substantial contribution'.[2] Here and elsewhere, Gullick offers many examples of the 'partly traditional, partly Islamic and partly colonial' ceremonies that developed in those years.[3] I agree with Gullick that the Malay rulers

[1] J.M. Gullick, *Rulers and Residents: Influence and Power in the Malay States, 1870–1920*, Singapore: Oxford University Press, 1992.

[2] *Ibid.*, p. vi.

[3] J.M. Gullick, *Malay Society in the Late Nineteenth Century*, Singapore: Oxford University Press, 1989, p. 33.

made a substantial contribution, but not so much to administration as to the development of new rituals of state. This chapter benefits from Gullick's work and hopes to build on it by offering a framework for understanding the importance of these new rituals in the years of British influence and rule.

I argue that the centralisation of Malay states, as well innovations in the rulers' public demeanour and ceremonial, were projects embraced by both the rulers and their British protectors, each for their own reasons. The result was a hybrid royalty which articulated a serviceable version of Malay culture within the structures of authority of British colonialism. This new articulation of Malay tradition served to legitimise both the Malay royalty in the Malay context and British overlordship of the Malay world.

It has often been observed that what the Malay ruling class lost in 'real power' to British advisers, it made up in status, wealth and stability. The Malay ruling class lost the right to collect revenues from the *rakyat* (subject class) and the practices of debt bondage and *kerah* (corvée labour); it essentially lost the power to run the affairs of state. In return, the British reaffirmed the fairly rigid class system and regularised the rewards for being in the upper class. The ambivalently regarded chiefs often had to scramble to maintain a place in the smaller British-defined ruling class, but the position, income and prestige of the rulers were guaranteed. At the pinnacle of the system, regular salaries supported the royal retinue, whose increasingly opulent lifestyles came to reflect those of European royalty.[4]

To participants and observers alike, this process was ostensibly the 'strengthening' of elite Malay culture, made possible by the overlordship of a protecting power. This was not, in fact, what was occurring. Underneath the familiar form which Malay leadership retained, the substance and purpose of its existence were being transformed. On the simplest level, glamorised and visible Malay rulers helped disguise the highly interventionist nature of indirect rule, offering proof that British Malaya still consisted of sovereign Malayo-Muslim sultanates. More importantly, new rituals, constructed partly of what Hobsbawm calls 'ancient materials'[5] and partly borrowed from British imperial forms, served to articulate an entirely new structure of authority. The new traditions were thoroughly successful in establishing

---

4 Or of European ideas of Muslim royalty. For the transformation of the Sultan of Selangor's residence from a large Malay house on stilts in 1874 to a Moorish palace in 1899, see William R. Roff, *The Origins of Malay Nationalism*, Kuala Lumpur: University of Malaya Press, 1980, pictures facing p. 146.

5 Eric Hobsbawm, 'Introduction: inventing traditions', in Eric Hobsbawm and Terence Ranger, eds, *The Invention of Tradition*, Cambridge: Cambridge University Press, 1983, p. 6.

'continuity with a suitable historic past',[6] while legitimising British overlordship of the Malay world.

It is important to emphasise that this development of a new-style monarchy was not simply imposed by the British on conquered Malay rajas, though imperial culture and political imperatives had great influence. Rather, the process represented the response of Malay leaders to the changing realities of the Malay world, an accommodation to the cultural and economic power of the overlord in Singapore. The pace of this transformation was set early on by the interest of individual rulers and only later by British control over matters of succession. Rulers of future unfederated states often presented developed versions of the new personal style even before they were under official British control. By and large colonial officials encouraged the development of the new style, which they interpreted as cooperation and as a sign of appreciation for their culture and administration.

The following three sections discuss the project of traditionalism in relation to the centralisation of political power before and during colonial rule; the invention of new royal styles and rituals in the late nineteenth and early twentieth centuries; and the question of initiative – British and Malay – in this invention. The final section examines how the hybrid royalty maintained its meaning in a reified version of traditional Malay society, while lending legitimacy to colonial domination.

Centralising Impulses of Malay Rulers and British Imperialists

By the last quarter of the nineteenth century, Malay politics in the west coast states had been much affected by the changing economic environment in Southeast Asia. This was especially true of those areas where tin was mined. Growing European demand for tin encouraged the immigration of large numbers of Chinese miners, whose labour was financed by European and Chinese capital from the Straits Settlements. In these circumstances, political conflict within the Malay ruling class – a continuing feature of Malay political life – became bound up with competition between Chinese groups and Straits economic interests.[7] Escalating economic conflict and civil wars ultimately lent justification to direct British intervention in those states.

---

6 *Ibid.*, p. 1.

7 Khoo Kay Kim, *The Western Malay States, 1850–1873: The Effect of Commercial Development on Malay Politics*, Kuala Lumpur: Oxford University Press, 1972.

One factor used to justify intervention was what British observers interpreted as the 'decay' of the Malay political system – the dispersal of power from 'central governments' (the rulers) to district chiefs (or aristocrats). Although rulers obtained tax revenues from the tin trade, chiefs could move out of the ruler's reach to gain a far greater share of revenues on the spot from tin, spirits and gambling. These chiefs often had financial stakes in the tin industry as well, backed by Straits merchants who sought their cooperation both to ensure the success of their endeavours and to serve as a check on the Chinese miners.[8] The result in Perak, for example, was that the development of the tin industry 'meant a growing independence among the great Perak chiefs; by the middle of the nineteenth century most of the real power rested in their hands'.[9]

Although the power of the chiefs in this period was marked, it was still within a range of power relations historically observed between rulers and chiefs in the Malay states. Despite the beleaguered court in Perak invoking a *zaman mas* (golden age) when chiefs obeyed the rulers as the normal state of affairs, there was in fact always an 'inner tension within the political system as each individual sultan sought to establish and assert his position vis-à-vis his officials'.[10] Sultans did not rule absolutely; rarely did they act without consulting the powerful chiefs of their state.[11]

Malay history holds examples of both powerful, active rulers and weak, retiring ones, and O.W. Wolters illustrates how Malay society was most successful when it had a ruler 'whose sovereignty benefited his loyal subjects and whose initiative ensured unity of purpose'. Yet he also notes that Malay society was 'riddled with centrifugal tendencies'.[12] A ruler's political power, over and above the meaning he gave to the whole politico-religious system, depended much on his personality, and rulers who successfully arrogated power to themselves stand out as exceptions. In the nineteenth century, with

---

8 J.M. Gullick, *Indigenous Political Systems of Western Malaya*, London: University of London, Athlone Press, 1958, pp. 127–30.

9 Barbara Watson Andaya, 'The nature of the state in eighteenth century Perak', in Anthony Reid and Lance Castles, eds, *Pre-Colonial State Systems in Southeast Asia*, Kuala Lumpur: MBRAS Monograph no. 6, 1975, p. 35.

10 *Ibid.*

11 See, for example, *Ibid.*, p. 30; Gullick, *Indigenous Political Systems*; and Heather Sutherland, 'The taming of the Trengganu elite', in Ruth McVey, ed., *Southeast Asian Transitions: Approaches through Social History*, New Haven: Yale University Press, 1978, pp. 34–35.

12 O.W. Wolters, *The Fall of Srivijaya in Malay History*, Kuala Lumpur: Oxford University Press, 1970, pp. 17–18.

the growing state power of Siam and the Straits Settlements both threatening and providing an example, an increasing number of rulers centralised their own states in order to retain or increase royal power. Baginda Omar of Terengganu (ruled 1839–1876) 'succeeded in overriding the territorial headmen and drawing all revenues directly into his own hands'.[13] Ahmad Tajuddin of Kedah (ruled 1854–1879) built a modernised, yet still personally controlled Malay government out of the ruins of direct rule by Siam.[14] Other examples include Muhammad II (Mulut Merah) of Kelantan (ruled 1836–86) and Temenggung Ibrahim of Johor (ruled 1841–62). Even in Selangor, famous for decentralisation of power, hereditary posts were allowed to fall vacant in an effort to reduce the power of the aristocracy. Differences in the relative power of rulers and chiefs between states and over time, then, argue that the ideal Malay state with an effective ruler at its apex was just that – an ideal. The ideal can be acknowledged to exert a pull on political behaviour without assigning to one or another situation the label of 'true' Malay political culture. A wide range of scenarios, including both highly autonomous chiefs in the west coast states and centralising rulers in the north and east, can still be recognisable as 'Malay politics'.

One mechanism of increasing state power in nineteenth-century Malaya was the creation of effective bureaucracies, but this carried an inherent risk to royal power. Through meritocracy and strict bookkeeping, bureaucratisation could threaten what was increasingly construed as a ruler's arbitrary and excessive power. The challenge to royal power of native meritocracy was avoided for a time by employing foreign talent at the ruler's discretion – Europeans or foreign (i.e. out of state) Malays with experience in the Straits Settlements. Likewise, budgetary control was an area of administration left undeveloped before the British took power. Revenues might have been collected according to increasingly routinised procedures, but their disbursal was still in the form of grants and gifts by rulers, not subject to control by state treasuries. As Gullick notes in the case of Kedah, budgetary control 'would have imposed on the Ruler a degree of self-denial which ran counter to the ethos of the period'.[15] In short, bureaucratisation could easily become a weapon in the hands of 'reformist' chiefs, seeking, in the name of modernisation, to push back the gains many rulers had made.

Once British control had been consolidated in a state, it became clear that effective power would be vested in European-run bureaucracies

---

13 Sutherland, 'Trengganu elite', pp. 37–38.

14 Gullick, *Rulers and Residents*, p. 138.

15 *Ibid.*, p. 139.

and exercised in accordance with the ideology of good government and administrative competence. It was at this point that rulers encouraged the entry of more Malays, and specifically *native* Malays, into their state administrations, as discussed in the previous chapter. Insofar as any members of the Malay ruling class could be inducted into the administrative realm, rulers could extend their influence in the rapidly changing political and economic milieu. This bureaucratic empowerment of the ruling class as a whole, however, was still not without danger to the rulers. The same process that transformed Malay chiefs into bureaucratic, salaried elites threatened to reduce royal families to the level of *primus inter pares*, or worse. Luckily, the prevailing colonial traditionalism gave the rulers an opportunity to elaborate their authority in an entirely different sphere, based not on the idea of administrative competence, but by an appeal to tradition.

In precolonial Malaya, the amount of political and economic power an individual ruler might command was not where the significance of the ruler (*qua* ruler, not paramount chief) was to be found. A.C. Milner's study of precolonial political reality shows the ruler to have been 'the organizing principle in the Malay world', the centre of the Malay political system.[16] This appraisal is confirmed by the longevity of the institution and the desire of a ruler's rivals to occupy, not destroy, the office. According to Milner, 'men considered themselves to be living not in states or under governments, but in a *kerajaan*, in the "condition of having a raja"'.[17] The 'maximization of spiritual rewards', not power or social control, motivated men to action and it was the raja who made these rewards possible:[18]

> Subjects ... received little material benefit from their Rajas: they gained in what appear to be insubstantial ways; they received titles and articles of attire rather than disposable wealth.[19]

The ruler's greatness was measured by his behaviour and propriety, his action in accordance with custom and, above all, his performance of ceremonial functions, whether in everyday life or in wartime:

> The Raja ... is presented [in the *Hikayat Deli*] as being involved not in day-to-day administration but in formal state occasions. Like the ruler portrayed in the *Hikayat Pahang*, he was valued more for his manners

---

16 A.C. Milner, *Kerajaan: Malay Political Culture on the Eve of Colonial Rule*, Tuscon: University of Arizona Press, 1982, p. 94.

17 *Ibid.*, p. 114.

18 *Ibid.*, p. x.

19 *Ibid.*, p. 98.

> than his practical skills.... [W]hen dispatching a force, the Sultan is said to address his men in a graceful (*manis*) voice.[20]

In this political reality, ceremonial – weddings, funerals, rites of passage – was work, not entertainment or mere trappings, and contemporary observers noted that it was the main business of a ruler.[21]

British observers who expected a ruler to monopolise at once military, economic and symbolic power misread the contemporary strength of tin belt aristocrats as a sign of the political system's decay. To those Straits Settlements merchants and officials who favoured intervention in western Malaya, this interpretation justified their preferred course of action. The perceived decay, as well as the overall decline of Malay power in the region vis-à-vis the Europeans, argued the need for European protection. An authoritative British retrospective written on the eve of decolonisation illustrates this interpretation of Malay politics:

> Too often a Malay ruler had little except fear of his divine majesty to enforce his will, and relatives often had little respect for that obsolescent divinity and fought him for the throne. Moreover dense forests cut up the little Malay kingdoms into districts where local chiefs did what was right in their own eyes. These difficulties were surmounted under British protection.[22]

Such protection was meant to halt the decay and preserve the culture by restoring the ruler to his rightful place at the apex of the system, though now political and economic power would rest in (capable) British hands through the system of residential advice within a territorially bounded state.

In the previous chapter, I discussed how the standardisation of state structure was integral to the extension of foreign control. In conjunction with preservation, it also proved useful to ruling families seeking to establish dominance over chiefly competitors. While previously the existence of a ruler had given meaning, though not modern territorial definition, to a state, the territorial clarification of the Malay peninsula produced newly defined states which now required proper rulers. Thus a standardisation of political leadership accompanied that of state structure, as can be seen in the British recognition of the rulers of Johor, Pahang and Kedah as sultans. Until about 1880 the British government in Singapore backed and benefited from the expanding influence of Temenggung Abu Bakar of Johor, as well as

---

[20] *Ibid.*

[21] *Ibid.*, pp. 45, 49.

[22] R.O. Winstedt, *The Malays: A Cultural History*, 5th ed., London: Routledge and Kegan Paul, 1961, first pub. 1947, p. 178.

his elevation to the title of maharaja. As discussed in greater detail below, by the time Abu Bakar aspired to the title of sultan, his usefulness to Singapore was over. Yet because of years of demonstrated commitment to 'enlightened' government, Abu Bakar won from London the right to use the title sultan. In Pahang, Bendahara Ahmad, an autocratic ruler who emerged from civil war in a position of supremacy over the chiefs of his state, declared himself sultan in 1882. He took this step to increase his authority in an ultimately futile effort to fend off British political encroachments which had followed commercial investment. In 1887, with the consolidation of colonial control over his state, the British recognised his title as well. In Kedah, British concern about Siamese intentions was expressed through their attitude towards the Malay ruler:

> [T]here is no disguising the fact that, whereas we regard the Raja of Kedah as the rightful and hereditary Sultan of Kedah, and a decision of the Supreme Court in Penang has recognised him as a sovereign ruler, the Siamese choose to treat him as a Provincial Governor. A pretence might, therefore, at any time be found for getting rid of him if ... Bangkok Siamese wished to handle the revenue of the country.[23]

The case of Negeri Sembilan appears to provide a counter-example, but only at first glance. In 1909 the *yam tuan* appealed to 'old custom' in claiming the right to use the title sultan. The British refused him that right, holding that the two titles were not interchangeable: the position of *yam tuan* had been arranged in the 1898 agreement with the other chiefs of the Negeri Sembilan, while only the British monarch could grant the title of sultan.

> The title of Sultan has a certain meaning to us. It means that the holder of the title is the absolute lawgiver in the place from which he takes the title and the King's permission to use the title in this country is based on that difference.[24]

The *yam tuan* was responding to the standardisation of states and leadership occurring all around him. With the general elevation of Malay rulers to the

---

[23] Report of a Consular Tour in the Malay States and Siamese Provinces, North of Penang, 6 April 1889. CO 273/160.

[24] Notes of a meeting held at Kuala Kangsa on 14 August 1909. Those present were High Commissioner John Anderson, Yang di-Pertuan Besar (Yam Tuan) of Negeri Sembilan (Tungku Mohamed), E.W. Birch (resident of Perak, resident of Negeri Sembilan at the time of the treaty), D.G. Campbell (resident of Negeri Sembilan), R.J. Wilkinson (secretary to the resident of Perak, as translator), the Tungku Besar, the Tungku Laksamana. CO 273/351.

office of sultan, he would have found his own title devalued. The British government, on the other hand, clearly wished to retain the distinctiveness of the Minangkabau-based polity. In practice, the *yam tuan*'s title did not rob him of the benefits of the standardisation process and his status was equivalent to the other rulers. The standardisation of both geography and political authority – the Malay peninsula divided into territorial states headed by sultans – first provided a kind of grammar for the Malays and the British to conduct relations in the era of interstate rivalry in the Malay world. It later provided a way for the Malays to recognise their own culture under colonial rule.

Over this period, then, Malay states became more uniform and centralised in their structure, governance and leadership due variously to the demands of British and Chinese investment (Johor), direct colonial intervention (Selangor, Perak, Negeri Sembilan and Pahang), and the initiative of centralising rulers (in all cases). This centralisation of power occurred throughout the peninsula and was aimed at strengthening royalty vis-à-vis both 'domestic' (chiefly) and 'foreign' (British or Siamese) competition. In this period of rapid change, imperfectly masked by the project of preservation, Malay royalty showed similar initiative in elaborating the style and substance of traditional leadership.

The New Malay Ruler

Confirming a ruler's position while completely undermining his political and economic power was, in British eyes, the making of a 'constitutional monarch', a head of state compatible with good government. To the British, enhancing the ceremonial aspects of a ruler's life while cutting off access to the state treasury, for example, rendered him 'symbolic' – essentially powerless, but still in a better position than as an independent ruler with little control over his district chiefs. The emphasis on a ruler's ceremonial role in the colonial state was consistent with this understanding. To the Malays, however, ceremonial was the most important work a ruler could undertake, even as some became interested in new concerns like education. The evolution of new style and ceremonial under indirect rule therefore had a dual effect – both to perpetuate *kerajaan* through Malay political idiom and to simultaneously legitimise colonial rule.

The emphasis on ceremonial brought changes to the rulers' lives which occurred in three related areas: the development of a new manner of living greatly influenced by European models of royalty; enhanced public ceremonial; and greater public visibility. In process as well as product, the transformation was a joint venture, initiated by the British desire to 'strengthen' the rulers and perpetuated by the rulers themselves, who embraced the opportunity to enhance their own position. The British contributed with the introduction of new ceremonies and functions and also by example, as rulers began to emulate the style of British authority (i.e. governors on tour)[25] and to visit centres of British power.[26] The active participation of the rulers and the enthusiasm of British officials for Malay history ensured that the evolving new traditions retained enough 'ancient material' to look familiar.

The Royal Person

The most basic project in the restoration of the Malay ruler was the enhancement of his personal manner of living. In the mid- to late nineteenth century, the life of a Malay ruler was far from glamorous. In 1846 a European observer described the plain lifestyle of the powerful Baginda Omar of Terengganu; his clothes were good but shabby and worn. The rulers' houses and their furnishings were much like those of their subjects, only bigger. Their food was plain. What distinguished a member of the ruling class was the size of his household and his ability to demand services from the *rakyat*. Rulers often had more than one household; if they had several wives, they needed to support them all in like fashion, which usually meant separate establishments for each with the appropriate number of servants.[27]

The support of a ruler's wives, his dependents and his own household, as well as expenditures on the state, military campaigns and help given to subjects in times of need was accomplished on roughly $100,000 per year. Besides taxes and duties (import duties on opium and spirits; export duties on padi and tin), some rulers had their own estates and businesses. Some

---

[25] The construction of British ceremonial on which the rulers were modelling themselves was occurring at the very same time. See David Cannadine, 'The context, performance and meaning of ritual: the British monarchy and the "invention of tradition", c. 1820–1977', in Eric Hobsbawm and Terence Ranger, eds, *The Invention of Tradition*, Cambridge: Cambridge University Press, 1983, pp. 101–64.

[26] See Charles Burton Buckley, *An Anecdotal History of Old Times in Singapore 1819–1977*, with introduction by C.M. Turnbull, Singapore: Oxford University Press, 1984, originally pub. in 1902, pp. 681, 687. In the two-year period 1860–1861, Buckley mentions visits by the rulers of Pahang, Kedah and Terengganu. The ruler of Johor lived in Singapore at this time.

[27] Gullick, *Malay Society*, pp. 48, 52.

managed to hoard away savings of thousands of dollars against sudden expenses. With the arrival of a British resident, all these sources of revenue were lost, except for privately held businesses. State revenues were now distinguished from the ruler's personal income, which was drawn as an allowance.

It became a commonplace of Anglo–Malay relations that rulers frequently petitioned for their allowances to be increased.[28] The need for more money was understandable because, though traditional claims on their incomes decreased, under British rule there were new activities and lifestyles inspired by trips to Singapore, Penang and occasionally London. For example, most rulers now outfitted their *istana* (royal residence) with European furnishings, usually not for the Malay household itself, but for the public rooms and areas where visiting European dignitaries would be entertained and accommodated. Western modes of transportation considered suitable to the ruler's station in life – steamships, yachts, horse-drawn carriages and later cars – likewise demanded considerable expenditure.

When a new sultan was installed in Selangor in 1903, he professed himself 'anxious to take a more prominent part in affairs than his predecessor did'. This meant that he would be entertaining more, so his allowance was increased the following year to $24,000, plus a privy purse allowance of $6,000 for religious and charitable donations. At the same time, the allowances of the rulers and their heirs in Perak and Negeri Sembilan were reviewed. While ultimately a ruler's allowance depended on his support for the government and the revenues of his state, there was also some concern to bring the allowances of the different ruling establishments in line, so that a *raja muda* (heir apparent) in one state, for example, was not granted more than a sultan in another.[29] By 1909 the Sultan of Selangor was again requesting an increase, now to $30,000. Writing in support of this increase, the resident attested that every penny (and more) went to the maintenance of the ruler's household, the ladies' households, his children's maintenance, palace officials, attendants, servants and watchmen. Although 'nothing in his expenditure savours of extravagance',

> there is no margin to meet the various calls to which it is right that the Sultan should be able to respond, such as contribution in aid of Mosques,

---

[28] At their first interview with returning British officials after the Japanese occupation, even with the threat of collaboration charges hanging over them, several of the rulers were most concerned about the resumption of their allowances, complaining about their treatment in this regard by the Japanese. WO 203/5612 and WO 203/5635A.

[29] Governor Anderson to the Colonial Office, 1 September 1904. CO 273/303.

> Schools, and other local organisations affecting the well being of the Muhammedan community and the betterment of their Institutions, neither has he the means to meet the cost of ceremonial visits and receptions which it may at any time become necessary for him to incur.[30]

The new responsibilities of a Malay ruler, including the English education of his children, were considered of utmost importance. The increase was approved.[31]

The personal attire of Malay rulers also changed to reflect new roles in the states and in the British empire. Emily Innes, wife of a British magistrate in Selangor, described an unreconstructed raja who came to tea in 1876:

> Tunku Panglima Raja wore a black silk handkerchief on his head, stiffened with rice-starch, and twisted into a tremendous erection, something like a bishop's mitre, but with the two ends sticking up like little horns on either side. The rest of his dress consisted of a jacket, buttoned only at the neck, and showing his brown skin from thence to the waist, and a sarong, the twisted part of which was stuck full of krises, that gave him a war-like appearance.[32]

In contrast, the sultan himself

> was usually dressed in nothing but a very scanty little cotton kilt, or a pair of still scantier bathing-drawers and was at first sight hardly distinguishable from an old Malay peasant.... he wore a coloured handkerchief on his head, and on high days and holidays a jacket of sprigged silk with diamonds over his kilt.[33]

Many rulers and chiefs soon adopted the European suit for public occasions. For reasons of modesty, a *sarong* was worn over the trousers to cover the thighs and the new style of dress was completed with a *songkok* (formal rimless hat).[34] Retaining distinctive Malay elements, however, including an

---

30 H. Conway Belfield, resident of Selangor. Request forwarded to the Colonial Office on 1 June 1909. CO 273/350.

31 The Sultan of Selangor's salary has increased to $135,000 by 1946. This was well over half the total ($205,004) spent on the entire traditional establishment of the state, i.e. ruler and chiefs, secretaries and other palace officials, clerks, orderlies, punkah pullers, watchmen, state mosques officials, etc. These were salaries and did not include the upkeep of the various royal residences. Selangor Estimates of Expenditure, 1946: The Ruler and Chiefs. BMA/SCAO 471/45.

32 Emily Innes, *The Chersonese with the Gilding Off*, Kuala Lumpur: Oxford University Press, 1974, originally pub. 1885, pp. 100–1.

33 *Ibid.*, pp. 38–40.

34 Gullick, *Malay Society*, pp. 55–59.

elaborate traditional royal costume, proved important to the British, if not always to the rulers. When Sultan Abdul Hamid of Kedah went to London for the coronation in 1911 with only Western suits, he was informed that he could take part in the official procession only if he wore traditional Malay clothes.[35] In a parade of imperial possessions, a Malay ruler was expected to represent oriental exotica and appear in 'national' costume, not mundane Savile Row. Yet even in Malaya, and especially at such public rituals as described below, traditional Malay attire was an important signifier of a royal culture in which high British officials might participate, sometimes by donning royal costumes themselves.[36]

Like dress, the matter of what the rulers ate and drank was influenced by British norms and the desire to ease relations. Innes described her guest as one of 'the more civilized of the rajas'. He drank Bass pale ale, but only in 'homeopathic doses' of half a glass per day, and he ate with his fingers, explaining that 'he was an old man and could not learn new ways'. The sultan's son-in-law, however, the 'viceroy' of Selangor, took to the new ways with a flourish, drinking brandy and champagne and eating ham.[37] These and other contraventions of Muslim law would eventually become problematic, but for a long time British backing validated such public behaviour.

Malay royalty's enthusiastic adoption of Western styles allows us to see the hybrid nature of the tradition being created. Why in fact would an avowedly traditional Malay ruler want to switch from, say, elephant to steamship? Part of the reason was simply the introduction of new products and technologies; we should not preclude such change from a dynamic tradition. But in these matters of personal comportment – clothing, furnishing, diet and transport – the rulers were presented with new models of authority emanating from Singapore. Private British businessmen and officials like the governor conducted themselves in a style calculated to impress the natives. Malay rulers rose to the challenge and implicitly accepted British notions of what was impressive. At times they outdid

---

35 *Ibid.*, p. 58.

36 See, for example, the picture of George Maxwell (chief secretary, FMS) with the Sultan of Selangor c. 1920s. Maxwell is in royal Malay dress, the richness of which threatens to outshine the outfits of the sultan himself. Gullick, *Rulers and Residents*, photo 24.

37 Innes, *Chersonese*, pp. 100–1, 173. Barbara Watson Andaya and Leonard Y. Andaya, *A History of Malaysia*, London: Macmillan, 1982, p. 151, also refer to the 'civilised' reputation fostered by the viceroy, Tunku Dia Udin, who engaged in 'ostentatious sherry drinking' and kept a pack of dogs.

the Europeans, as in the 1880s, when the governor sometimes borrowed the steamship belonging to Abu Bakar of Johor, for it was much more comfortable than the one owned by the government.[38] This example of successful one-upmanship illustrates how British imperial hierarchies were embraced by Malay rulers who made them their own.

Public Ceremonial

Beyond the rulers' personal lifestyle was the public ceremonial in which they played a central role. At first the British presence seemed merely to sanction that which was traditional, though now it was performed before European witnesses, like this rite in Selangor:

> I was present once on his [Sultan Abdul Samad's] homage-day, when all his subjects, rajas included, came crawling to kiss his hand. None of them dared approach him without grovelling on the ground, their two hands clasped in supplication as before a god; and anyone having to cross the room in his presence, crawled sideways on all-fours like a crab. Datus, rajas, and Tunkus, who were all bold enough when he was not by, subsided on to the floor and spoke in timid whispers, and he gave them his hand to kiss as if it were a great favour.[39]

Public ceremonial was elaborated as the colonial system developed in accordance with the needs of that system. The conference of rulers was a ritual conceived in direct compensation, as it were, for the loss of state power which came with the centralisation of the Federated Malay States (FMS).[40] The first conference of rulers (or durbar, after British Indian usage)

---

[38] Gullick, *Malay Society*, p. 55. When the first governor appointed by the Colonial Office arrived in Singapore in 1867, he found that the paramount power in the Malay world owned only two worn-out steamships. He ordered another one (used) and bought a small one locally. This governor (Harry Ord) sought to infuse his office with a dignity which it had not possessed before. C. Northcote Parkinson, *British Intervention in Malaya, 1867–1877*, Kuala Lumpur: University of Malaya Press, 1964, pp. 10–11, 27. A later governor (William Robinson) complained bitterly when he returned from an unofficial leave and received no gun salute or guard of honour. The Maharaja of Johor had, coincidentally, just been received with full honours. The Colonial Office supported the governor in his quarrel with the officer commanding the troops, noting that 'it is most undesirable that the governor should … be treated lightly in the eyes of the natives'. CO 273/96.

[39] Innes, *Chersonese*, pp. 43–44.

[40] For the more extensive use of durbars and assemblages by the British in India see Bernard S. Cohn, 'Representing authority in Victorian India', in Eric Hobsbawm and Terence Ranger, eds, *The Invention of Tradition*, Cambridge: Cambridge University

in 1897 brought the four rulers of the federated states together for the first time, and the European organisers were apprehensive about protocol. Although rulers travelled abroad and on occasion visited one another, these visits were momentous and expensive occasions, involving retinues numbering in the hundreds, convoys of elephants, flotillas of boats and the building of extensive temporary accommodations. These visits were also apt to highlight competition between rulers, as one sought to outdo the hospitality of another.[41] But there was no broader experience of ordered relations between the rulers, who had genealogies of comparable status.[42] According to Hugh Clifford, then resident of Pahang, 'each State holds that its own ruling House should by right take precedence of all others'.[43] However, the gathering hosted by Sultan Idris of Perak, was a success. Each party was received separately by the sultan, a guard of honour and a 17-gun salute. At the formal meetings, the rulers were arranged so that each sat between his own resident and either the high commissioner or the resident-general. Sultan Idris accommodated each of the rulers and their retinues in his own *istana* and entertained them day and night for almost a week. The leading chiefs of Perak provided transportation to picnics, fish drives and the theatre. The sultan's wife and her attendants embroidered pillows as souvenirs for all the guests. And when the parties left (again accompanied by gun salutes and guards of honour), their departures were staggered so that Sultan Idris could travel down the road a bit with each of his guests. This ruler clearly made an enormous effort, well appreciated by British officials, to inaugurate the new system of interstate relations, a gathering at which the rulers sent a message of loyalty to Queen Victoria.[44]

The second conference was held in Kuala Lumpur in 1903 and did not depend upon the hospitality of one wealthy ruler. Because the Sultan of Selangor did not himself reside in that city, it was necessary to build temporary accommodation for all the rulers, as well as a conference hall for the meeting. This was done in the Lake Gardens:

> For each Sultan a commodious residence was provided in the vicinity of one of the small streams which feed Sydney Lake, within easy reach of the Hall and of each other. These houses contained a roomy hall or balei,

Press, 1983, pp. 165–209.

41 Gullick, *Rulers and Residents*, pp. 231–33.

42 Milner, *Kerajaan*, pp. 1–2.

43 Annual Report, Pahang 1897. CO 437/2.

44 Report of the Durbar (Federal Council) at Kuala Kangsar, 13–17 July 1897. CO 273/229.

> with a private room, sleeping apartments, kitchen, bathroom and other accessories. Surrounding the Sultans' residences were scattered the houses of the Members of their Councils, with the result that there were four picturesque native villages, each flying the distinctive flag of the State to which it was assigned.[45]

No problems of precedence were noted at this conference, while the accommodation itself seemed to confirm the standardisation and equivalency of the states in the FMS.

The second conference of rulers did feature, however, the critical speech by Sultan Idris discussed in the previous chapter. The difficulty in controlling such outspokenness and the danger that the rulers would learn to work in concert probably explain why the conferences did not become a regular feature of federation. Colonial advisers did encourage the elaboration and expansion of other rituals which emphasised the ruler *within* his state and which offered little opportunity for substantive discussion, such as royal weddings and funerals. Important characteristics of such rituals were that they could be tied closely both to tradition and to colonial structures of authority. The celebration of a Malay ruler's birthday, the installation of a sultan or *raja muda*, or the public celebration of Hari Raya served to remind everyone that they lived in a Malayo-Muslim state – all the *penghulus* of the state attended and made formal obeisance, traditional entertainments such as fish drives were mounted, and all eyes were on the spectacle of a glorified Malay monarchy. At the same time, the celebrations themselves were sometimes modelled on those of British royalty, incorporated displays of imperial power, included important roles for colonial officials or were even occasioned by the investiture of a ruler with a British decoration.[46] This juxtaposition of Malay and British rituals served to legitimise colonial rule by creating a colonial Malay tradition. In this new tradition, Malay rituals were located within the ascendant British empire, while the aura of 'timeless tradition' rubbed off on the British imperial project.

An example of colonial ritual which blended old with new elements was the royal installation. The installation of Sultan Idris of Perak in 1889

---

45 Minutes of the Conference of Chiefs of the Federated Malay States held at Kuala Lumpur, 20–23 July 1903. Printed in the Supplement to the Selangor Government Gazette, 2 October 1903. CO 469/13.

46 See Gullick, *Rulers and Residents*, pp. 236–38, for examples of such ceremonies. When the ceremony involved the investiture of the ruler in a British order, care was taken to emphasise the Malayness of the rulers: Sultan Idris of Perak laid the foundation stone of a new mosque when he was awarded the Grand Cross of the Royal Victorian Order.

was marked by an extravagance of ceremony and public celebration. The traditional Malay rites included several days of fasting and prayer; the invocation of divine authority; the propitiation of spirits to ensure long life and prosperity for the new ruler; and a visit by the sultan and his whole family to the tomb of his ancestors. But with the encouragement and assistance of his European advisers, a major ceremony of hybrid Anglo–Malay character was also staged:

> The installation ceremony, attended by the Resident and other European officials as well as a large concourse of Malays, took place at Bukit Chandan, which was the residence of the new ruler. Here he was publicly 'invested with the ancestral sword of state' and took his place on the royal dais (*singgasana*) 'with the regalia displayed on the *peterana* (mat of honour) before him'. He then signed an oath of office, like a colonial governor on taking up his appointment, and this was subsequently published in the official Perak Gazette. A proclamation of accession was read aloud and the appropriate salute of seventeen guns was fired. The new ruler 'descended from the royal seat' and when he was in that less exalted position 'European officers and gentlemen were presented to him'. The Sultan then made a formal speech. In the evening there was a banquet and a fireworks display. The Sultan proposed 'the loyal toast', i.e. the health of Queen Victoria, and the band played 'God Save the Queen'. The Resident made a speech in reply.
>
> After this ceremony there was five days of rejoicing with an 'abundance of sports and races, plays, shooting and rowing matches with feasts for the chiefs and people who are said to have numbered more than 15,000'.[47]

The author of the Straits Settlement dispatch on which the above account was based would have found the inclusion of British officials and rituals in this royal Malay ceremony unremarkable. When the history-minded R.J. Wilkinson referred to this ceremony, however, he spoke only of the Malay aspects, as if 'the inevitable confusion between the new and the old' had not yet occurred.[48] Wilkinson's influential *History of the Peninsular Malays*, originally published in 1908, located the Malay ceremony within the claims of Malay genealogy and history:

> The Sultan of Perak claims to possess the very sword and seal that were inherited by Sang Sapurba from his ancestor Alexander the Great. The Dato' Sri Nara Diraja of Perak is the hereditary custodian of the ancient

[47] Gullick, *Malay Society*, pp. 33–34. His account quotes from the Straits Settlement dispatch of 15 April 1889.

[48] See the discussion of the tension between preservation and change in the Introduction.

> proclamation in a forgotten tongue by which the herald installed Sang Sapurba as ruler of the Palembang world. That form of proclamation is still used (with many old-world ceremonies) at the installation of every Perak Sultan and of all his high officers of state.[49]

Wilkinson continues, emphasising the pre-Islamic origins of the ceremony:

> The coronation formula is in either Sanskrit or Pali; it suffers from having been transcribed into Arabic characters that are ill-adapted for representing Sanskrit sounds. Its text – so far as it can be interpreted – reveals nothing. All that we need infer from the Perak regalia and installation customs is that long before the days when the 'Malay Annals' were compiled (A.D. 1612) – almost certainly as far back as the days of the old kingdom of Malacca – the Malay rulers attached importance to the possession of a seal and sword, both bearing Indian names, and to the use of an Indian installation formula and to a state secret suggesting their Indian descent.[50]

Despite the inauthenticity of the sword, which Wilkinson judged to be a few centuries old, and perhaps because of the very incomprehensibility of the coronation formula, these elements of the ceremony clearly constitute 'ancient material'. But the imported elements are just as striking and important. The oath of office, proclamation of accession, posting in the *Gazette*, 17-gun salute and especially the loyal toast to the foreign overlord, were clearly imported elements which located 'ancient' Malay monarchy firmly within the contemporary greater glory of the British empire. Note that the meshing of the rituals is not seamless; there is a transitional moment when the Malay monarch must 'descend' to the level of the European officials, who are representatives of the overlord, Queen Victoria. In this moment, Malay monarchy is ritually subordinated to British power.

For the Selangor installation of Sultan Sulaiman in 1903, tradition was even more self-consciously invented – no one knew the traditional ritual, the last proper installation having been held in 1826. Additionally, the royal regalia was redesigned; that which survived the calamitous civil wars of the past century was deemed not nearly splendid enough for the new court ceremony. The initiative was taken here by Raja Bot, a relative of the ruler, who travelled to Riau in search of Bugis precedents for the Malay parts of the ceremony. As in Perak, the installation included both Malay and European elements, and it specifically incorporated symbols of

---

[49] R.J. Wilkinson, *A History of the Peninsular Malays with Chapters on Perak and Selangor*, 3rd ed., rev., Singapore: Kelly and Walsh, 1923, pp. 17–18.

[50] *Ibid.*, pp. 19–20.

colonial government, such as the Malay States Guides, the local defence force. Celebrations went on for a month, the guests including members of other royal families of the peninsula.[51] Royal installations had become an important ritual of 'British Malaya', in which the common elements were the presence of British symbols of authority and a concern with restoring (or inventing, if necessary) a lavish Malay past.

The Ruler's Visibility

The defining characteristic of indirect rule is that an indigenous elite is left visible to the conquered people, shielding the reality of foreign domination. Thus it is not surprising that Malay rulers experienced a gradual increase and qualitative change in their public visibility. This was the most tentative and slowly developing change, and its full potential would not be realised until the postwar period. In precolonial and early colonial times, despite the centrality of ceremony to a ruler's life, scattered populations and difficulty of travel meant that the ordinary people rarely laid eyes on their ruler.[52] Even if the ruler held audiences where peasants could bring their grievances, as was the case in Perak,[53] it seems likely that only those in the immediate vicinity could easily attend.

If subjects did not often gather to see their ruler, neither did rulers travel much around their states. When Sultan Abdul Samad went to Kuala Lumpur in 1879, it was said to be the first visit of a ruler to the interior of Selangor in 100 years. According to the ruler of Terengganu in 1875, no one ever visited the interior of his state, though he himself had already been to Singapore. And the Raja of Kelantan, that same year, was said 'never to have gone beyond his own river, nor did he express any inclination to do so'.[54] Thirty-four years later, little had changed. Reporting on his visit to Kelantan in 1909, Governor John Anderson remarked that 'the ignorance of the Rajah and of those about him of the interior of the country was complete'.[55] This reticence to travel on the part of those who were most able has been attributed to the expense of bringing a retinue commensurate with dignity and safety.[56] In the absence of the ruler's personal presence, the state's *penghulus* were considered to be his representatives, having been appointed

51 Gullick, *Malay Society*, pp. 35–36.
52 Gullick, *Indigenous Political Systems*, p. 137.
53 Andaya, 'Eighteenth century Perak', p. 29.
54 *Straits Times*, 31 July 1875. CO 882/3.
55 CO 273/350.
56 Gullick, *Malay Society*, pp. 28, 42n38.

by the ruler and usually carrying a letter of authority from him.[57] District chiefs would also act in a ruler's name, though they were apt to go their own way the further their territory lay from the court. Clearly, the distance of the ruler had repercussions, especially in remote *ulu* (upriver) districts where loyalties might swing from one ruler to another.[58]

Some subjects did see their ruler, however, and those were the people who lived in the town or village where he made his home. Pious rulers of the mid-nineteenth century usually attended Friday prayers at the local mosque.[59] Other rulers appeared even more informally. In the 1870s Sultan Abdul Samad of Selangor took a daily, late afternoon constitutional around his village, visiting shops and discussing the padi crop. He could often be found 'seated astride on a carpenter's bench, or else squatting on the ground … watching a cockfight'.[60]

As with personal habit, changes in public posture and visibility depended on the predilections of the individual ruler. Sultan Idris of Perak, an early admirer as well as critic of Western rule, rode in a carriage with a mounted police escort when making local calls. If he went further away, he was greeted on his return with a 17-gun salute and a welcoming party of European and Malay officials.[61] This ruler travelled more before becoming sultan than afterwards, when he usually limited his journeys to trips along the Perak River. With the other rulers as well, the new habit of travelling around the state started gradually, and not much before 1910, when the improvement of roads permitted it. The linking of towns with the major villages of a state coincided with the arrival of the car in Malaya in 1902. From that time on, rulers of the FMS could easily (and in modern style) do systematic tours of their states.[62]

Actually, most rulers' trips around their states were less 'royal progress' than business trip or even vacation. Rulers sometimes travelled in support of an administrative policy, sometimes to encourage projects in which they took a special interest.[63] Rupert Emerson, the American observer of British and Dutch colonialism in the 1930s, called attention to the following comment in the *Annual Report* for Kelantan for 1913:

---

57 Syed Husin Ali, *Malay Peasant Society and Leadership*, Kuala Lumpur: Oxford University Press, 1975, pp. 124, 128.

58 Andaya, 'Eighteenth century Perak', p. 27.

59 *Ibid.*, p. 26.

60 Innes, *Chersonese*, pp. 38–39.

61 Gullick, *Malay Society*, p. 37.

62 Gullick, *Rulers and Residents*, pp. 238–40.

63 *Ibid.*, p. 240.

> His Highness the Sultan visited the gaol on more than one occasion, opened the new hospital, and having purchased a new motor car, travelled a good deal, with the result of calling attention to several road troubles.[64]

Emerson means to point out the insignificance of the ruler's functions in the modern colonial state. Yet there are two important points that he misses. First, royal legitimacy was lent to such ambivalently received colonial institutions as jails and hospitals, which were 'domesticated' to the sultan's realm by his visit. Conversely, insofar as a hospital was seen as a 'modern' thing, the visit may have served to burnish the ruler's image and have allowed him to take credit for any benefits brought by the colonial institution. Second, the ruler's pleasure jaunts brought him more into the public eye than Malay royalty had ever been; a visibility which was often important to the maintenance of colonial rule.

Royal travel – in the appropriate style – can be explained partly by the rulers' emulation of British practice and the pursuit of new pleasures. But it was sometimes undertaken at British behest to cement a link between ruler and *rakyat*. Before European intervention, Malay politics had offered to the *rakyat* certain representations of the ruler's power – *penghulus* who were appointed by the ruler, district chiefs who could be called to make formal obeisance. Under British colonialism, the middle strata had largely disappeared as independent actors or were clearly under the authority of the British themselves. Without the greater visibility of the rulers, this absence of Malay power holders, especially in the FMS, may have rendered untenable the fiction of indirect rule. A broader comparison can also be made with the newly invented royal tradition of modernising Meiji Japan. There, royal progressions allowed the people to be seen by (and to see) the emperor for the first time, and the people learned how to behave in his sight. Thereafter, photographs of the emperor hanging in public and private places served to reproduce his presence and provide constant surveillance; the people were always in the emperor's sight.[65] In Malaya, the sight of the ruler in the eyes of the *rakyat* could be equally significant when they saw him living and travelling in a style comparable to Europeans. According to John Butcher, the British believed that 'Asians expected their rulers to live in a style befitting their status'.[66] The colonialists took this to heart regarding their own

64 Rupert Emerson, *Malaysia: A Study in Direct and Indirect Rule*, New York: Macmillan, 1937, p. 263n63.

65 Takashi Fujitani, 'Electronic pageantry and Japan's "symbolic emperor"', *Journal of Asian Studies*, vol. 51, no. 4, 1992, pp. 839–40.

66 John Butcher, *The British in Malaya, 1880–1941: The Social History of a European*

standard of living and a status-conscious Malay society would certainly notice that its own ruler looked as well-off as the white overlords. By positioning himself (with British contrivance) high within the colonial hierarchy of style, while remaining recognisably Malay, the ruler maintained the idea for the *rakyat* of living in a sovereign Malay state under foreign protection.

The transformation from old to new traditions was uneven and often slow, but sometimes old ritual gave way swiftly to a new type of public posture clearly in service to the modernising colonial state. There is no more dramatic example of such a transformation than the behaviour of the people and Sultan of Terengganu during and after the uprising of 1928. In April of that year, with tensions rising and peasants refusing to pay their taxes, Sultan Sulaiman agreed to travel upriver and meet with local leaders. The British adviser feared the consequences of allowing the Malay delegation to proceed without British backup, but Sulaiman's *menteri besar* (chief minister) 'held firmly to the view that the meeting – between "the Sultan and his people" – should be conducted without British officials being present'. The sultan was met in an upriver town by two to three thousand of his subjects, who were curious to see him and to present their grievances in a traditional audience.[67] This was an old ritual which took place, if only briefly, out of the control of the colonial state. It soon became clear, however, that the sultan could deliver no relief as he owed his position to the British, who would concede little on the contested issues. The uprising surged again and was put down by colonial troops. In the aftermath of the revolt, the ruler undertook periodic visits outside his capital in an entirely new spirit:

> Sulaiman's efforts to regain popular affection were based less on the actions expected of a traditional Malay ruler than on an English model: the first of Sulaiman's annual tours of the outer districts, in 1929, was patterned after a British royal tour, complete with triumphal arches and speeches.[68]

This is a dramatic example of a transformation which was by no means complete by the end of the prewar era. The public posture of the ruler would experience significant changes during the Japanese occupation and the Malayan Union crisis, as discussed in the following chapters.

Community in Colonial Southeast Asia, Kuala Lumpur: Oxford University Press, 1979, p. 77.

[67] Shaharil Talib, *After Its Own Image: The Trengganu Experience, 1881–1941*, Singapore: Oxford University Press, 1984, pp. 156–57, 163.

[68] Sutherland, 'Trengganu elite', p. 81. See also Emerson, *Malaysia*, pp. 266–67.

Self-invention or British Creature?

No one ruler epitomises the standardisation of state structure and leadership better than Abu Bakar of Johor (ruled 1862–1895), from his elevation to the sultanate of modern Johor to the uniform he wore and his travels to the royal courts of Europe, Asia and the Middle East.[69] In fact, his adoption of European ritual and lifestyle, as well as his usurpation of the throne, was so striking that no one mistook him for a 'restored' Malay ruler. Yet all his innovation was in the service of maintaining his independence as the ruler of a *Malay* state administered by Malays. At the same time, his prosperity was won through the Chinese economy and his power legitimised by the British in Singapore.[70] An examination of Abu Bakar's career reveals a high degree of British complicity in his self-creation.

Abu Bakar's success had its roots in the devastation of the old Johor-Riau empire during the eighteenth century. Years of fighting Bugis domination and Dutch attacks ruined Riau as a trading port and the founding of Singapore in 1819 marked the end of the Malay entrepôt. The Anglo–Dutch Treaty (1824) further cut off the weakened Riau sultanate, not under Dutch jurisdiction, from the peninsula, strengthening the *de facto* independence of the Temenggung of Johor (as well as the Bendahara of Pahang). Although the British had recognised a rival claimant to the Johor throne for the purpose of obtaining Singapore, Sultan Hussein and his line were never serious contenders for either power (vis-à-vis the *temenggung*) or position (lacking the royal regalia from Riau). But the real key to the elevation of the *temenggungs* was Temenggung Ibrahim's 'opening up' the state to economic development, which was of benefit to himself and the British, and his acceptance of British policy imperatives, especially his cooperation in the suppression of piracy.[71]

A Johor official, Mohamed Salleh bin Perang, who shared in the prosperity of this process, tells us Ibrahim's situation in the 1840s:

> Marhum Ibrahim himself was impoverished, and Johor had not yet been opened up. Marhum Ibrahim had to subsist entirely on an allowance from the English Government, and yet his servants were by no means few in number.[72]

---

[69] Detailed accounts of Abu Bakar's travels abroad can be found in Gullick, *Rulers and Residents, passim*.

[70] See the discussion of the transformation of the maritime polity in Carl A. Trocki, *Prince of Pirates: The Temenggongs and the Development of Johor and Singapore, 1784–1885*, Singapore: Singapore University Press, 1979, pp. 207–15.

[71] For Ibrahim's early years and economic success, see *Ibid*., pp. 61–84.

[72] Amin Sweeney, *Reputations Live On: An Early Malay Autobiography*, Berkeley: University of California Press, 1980, p. 74.

At the time of his death in 1862, Ibrahim received the following glowing obituary in the *Singapore Free Press*. It admirably summarises his accomplishments, as well as demonstrating the opinion of the British official and commercial community:

> This native chief, during the course of his long rule, conducted himself with great prudence and secured the friendship and support of the British Government, by whom he was presented with a sword of state for his exertions in putting down the piracy which at one period was so prevalent in the vicinity of Singapore. For many years he devoted himself to the improvement of his territory of Johore, in which he was very successful, the revenues at his death amounting to a very considerable sum, derived principally from the Chinese population that under his encouragement had settled in Johore and engaged in agricultural pursuits. He was succeeded by his eldest son, between whom and the Bandahara of Pahang a treaty was entered into at Singapore in June, with the sanction of the British Government, to regulate the countries of Pahang and Johore, their boundaries, jurisdiction and government, to prevent disputes hereafter and to perpetuate the amity existing between them.[73]

Salleh corroborates the ethos of Ibrahim's administration, in which traditional forms were used for novel purposes:

> Every day ... I heard the beneficial and salutary words of wise men endowed with incisive tongues, speaking in gatherings of rulers and ministers, and I noted their use of parables, their good breeding, cultured manners and refined behavior; for every other day or so, the dignitaries would all meet in conference and consider ways and means to improve the country, to induce more people to seek their livelihood in occupations which would increase the state revenues, and to improve the lot of the people of the country.[74]

Ibrahim's son, Abu Bakar, followed in his father's footsteps. His innovation was to add royal ritual to good government. When, in 1887, he ordered Salleh, then chief of the Land Department, to 'open up Muar', he soon made a ceremonial visit to this recently acquired territory.

> On 5th August, His Highness, together with the Sultanah Fatimah and their daughter, the Tengku Puteri, arrived in Muar on the ship *Pantai*. They were given a ceremonial welcome by the officials in Muar, i.e. Engku Sulaiman and myself, together with the *penghulus* and some modest celebrations were held.

---

73 Buckley, *Anecdotal History*, p. 688.

74 Sweeney, *Reputations Live On*, p. 84.

> On 12th August, His Highness, together with Engku Sulaiman and myself, the Chinese businessmen, officials, and *penghulus* gathered at the stone steps while His Highness himself buried the amulet [to ensure the peace and well-being of the new town] and gave Muar the name *Bandar Maharani*. His Highness thus personally participated in the opening up of Muar.[75]

Abu Bakar was best known for being a Westernised monarch. But he did more than acquire a veneer – affecting a style of dress or learning to appreciate horse racing. He thoroughly assimilated those Western attributes which were of value to him. He had been educated in both English and Malay (at Benjamin Keasberry's school in Singapore), he befriended colonial officials on a personal level, and he embraced Western legal, administrative and business methods, hiring British firms and individuals in Singapore and London to represent his interests.[76] Finally, he shaped his ambitions to accord not only with Malay tradition, but with evolving British colonial tradition. From his first trip to London in 1866 Abu Bakar knew that the highest ranked Indian princes held the title maharaja.[77] So while his elevation to this title in 1868 was approved by the Riau court, as having once been used by the rulers of Melaka,[78] it is also evidence that Abu Bakar quite consciously positioned himself within the British empire, the centre of the world of international royalty. He developed a court ceremonial with both Malay and British colonial elements: 'crimson and green gold umbrellas, Malays with krises, native police, Sikh guards', and a European-style Order of the Crown.[79]

What part did the British, who did not directly control Johor during his reign, play in the elevation of the *temenggung*? The local British government, grappling with London's non-expansionist policy until the 1870s, found in Abu Bakar, as his father before him, a local ally. He was essentially to their taste and also appealed to London, having 'raised himself up to the position

---

75 *Ibid.*, pp. 56–58.

76 *Ibid.*, p. 5; see also Eunice Thio, *British Policy in the Malay Peninsula, 1880–1910*. Vol. 1. *The Southern and Central States*, Singapore: University of Malaya Press, 1969, p. 108, for the composition of the Johore Advisory Council in London. She also informs us that this was a common practice of Indian princes in the 1880s.

77 Sweeney, *Reputations Live On*, p. 5. Abu Bakar discovered that the title '*temenggung*' was hitherto unknown to the protocol experts in London. Gullick, *Rulers and Reisdents*, p. 241.

78 Andaya and Andaya, *History*, p. 153.

79 Gullick, *Rulers and Residents*, p. 245, from a Straits Settlements dispatch describing Governor Weld's visit in 1880; Thio, *British Policy*, p. 108.

of an enlightened ruler of an unenlightened community'.[80] He had prestige and power and, at least initially, he accepted British advice. Internally, he had greater control over his territory than other Malay rulers, having started as a local chief himself.[81] Externally, British governors used him as an agent of sorts, pursuing policies they could not have pursued directly, inadvertently furthering his ambitions. As discussed in the previous chapter, Governor Jervois sponsored Abu Bakar's 'supervision' over the quarrelling chiefs of Negeri Sembilan.

Abu Bakar also received British backing when threatened by supporters of the royal Johor-Riau line. The bombardment of Terengganu in 1862 was undertaken to dislodge the deposed Sultan Mahmud of Lingga from Kuala Terengganu and to back Johor's candidate in Pahang. When the Terengganu-Lingga-backed candidate, Ahmad, won anyway, the *Singapore Free Press* warned: 'if he lends himself to intrigues of the ex-Sultan or anyone else against Johore he will certainly involve himself in much trouble and probably endanger his position as ruler of Pahang'.[82]

From the late 1870s, however, more interventionist voices, including Swettenham's, argued for taking direct control in the Malay states, rather than working through someone like the Maharaja of Johor. Abu Bakar, in any case, was beginning to act more and more independently of British advice and, Singapore complained, to spend more extravagantly on himself than on the development of his state. It was at this time that he began to press his claim to be recognised as sultan and found a friendlier reception in London than at home.[83] Further deterioration of Abu Bakar's relations with Singapore revolved around the slower rate of development in Johor compared with the states now under direct British control, as well as the maharaja's influence in Negeri Sembilan and Pahang, which was thoroughly opposed by Governor Weld. Going on the offensive, Abu Bakar went to London in 1885, where praise for his enlightened administration and 'civilisation' was still ringing in Colonial Office ears. Negotiating a new treaty, Abu Bakar gave foreign relations into the hands of the British (easing fears of French interference), agreed to confine his influence to his own state and accepted a British agent. In exchange, Abu Bakar was recognised as sultan, not of the old Riau-based empire, but of the 'State and Territory of Johor'.[84]

---

80 1878 dispatch to the Colonial Office, quoted in Thio, *British Policy*, p. xxx.

81 Sweeney, *Reputations Live On*, pp. 37–38.

82 Buckley, *Anecdotal History*, p. 694.

83 See Thio, *British Policy*, pp. xxxi–xxxvii, 23–25.

84 See *Ibid.*, pp. 93–107, for the treaty negotiations and the events leading up to them.

Aside from the important role played by Britain, this final transformation of the rump of the old empire into the modern state of Johor ironically reveals the continuing significance of *kerajaan*, the condition of having a raja. For Johor, like Pahang and earlier Perak, it was not a sense of place but the ambition of a raja which led to the existence of a sovereign state where earlier there had been a territory of a larger polity. In the case of Johor, only gradually did the mechanisms of state come to reside within the borders. Nearly all government and judicial work was done in Singapore until 1858. And the new sultan only moved his family to Johor Bahru in 1889.[85]

Towards the end of his life, Abu Bakar tried to prevent further British encroachment by promulgating a written constitution for the state of Johor. The British never recognised it as having any standing which could interfere with the terms of a treaty, a point which would be significant in 1946, for it contained a clause forbidding the ruler to surrender any part of Johor to another power or nation. Yet it is also of interest in the story of Abu Bakar himself. The document was the first of its kind for a Malay state (only Terengganu would follow Johor's example before the Second World War) and very much the product of an invented sultan. The preamble states that the constitution is handed down by the sultan, 'in Our name and on Our behalf, and for and on behalf of Our Heirs and Successors, the Sovereign Rulers or Sultans of Johore'.[86] It states also that it is proper to consult with the ministers, chiefs and elders of the state, and it provides for two councils of chiefs, whose advice the sovereign will find it 'expedient, necessary, and advantageous' to take. While the constitution betrays knowledge of European-style administration (executive vetoes and so forth), it is essentially a modern elucidation of the ideal Malay state. It also legitimises the rule of Abu Bakar himself. By stipulating that each future sovereign be 'of the Royal blood, a descendant of Johore Sovereigns', it asserts Abu Bakar's royal status. The constitution, for all its novelty, should be likened to a court-commissioned *hikayat*, written to justify Abu Bakar's reign, further his dynasty and lay down political norms. Fittingly enough in this case, it was written not by Malay scribes, but by English lawyers.

Abu Bakar, of course, had great need for legitimation. As early as the 1850s, Malay royalty of other states, especially Terengganu, resented both

---

[85] Only capital offences were tried in Johor Bahru; for this there was a jail there. Sweeney, *Reputations Live On*, pp. 82–83. See also Emerson, *Malaysia*, p. 202.

[86] Emerson, *Malaysia*, pp. 203–6.

his territorial ambitions and status pretensions.[87] His further elevation to the title of sultan in 1885 presented the problem of his non-royal birth. Interestingly, it was not the conferring of title by a non-Malay power that offended other rajas. Wilkinson later observed:

> Royalty could be conferred, as the Chinese Emperor conferred it on the Permaisura, or as Sultan Mansur divided up his kingdom between his sons, or as a Sultan creates a 'Junior Sultan' (Sultan Muda or Yamtuan Muda), or as *the British may be said to have created the Sultanates of Johor, Pahang and Kelantan.*

But royal birth was a necessary prerequisite:

> Malay popular feeling is against the powerful *de facto* ruler who assumes that power confers rank. Such a man is a worm who aspires to be a dragon.... The hostility displayed to the Mantri of Larut, to Sultan Ismail of Perak, and for many years to the Maharaja of Johor was due to similar misunderstandings.[88]

Despite Malay scepticism, the British in Singapore accepted a royal genealogy that traced the *temenggung*'s line back to Sultan Abdul Jalil (d. 1721) and which was publicised by Thomas Braddell, one of Abu Bakar's English advisers.[89]

Direct British control over Johor was an inevitability which Abu Bakar was able to defer until after his death. It was his son Ibrahim, reigning until 1959, who experienced that loss of independence. Carl Trocki suggests that Ibrahim's lack of administrative experience upon ascending the throne was calculated by Abu Bakar who, anticipating the impending takeover, foresaw that Johor would need 'not an administrator but a respectable figure-head who could uphold the dignity of the office of Sultan and who knew the kind of people a sovereign ought to know'.[90] That the British were essentially sympathetic to this project can be seen in their treatment of Ibrahim: his perceived stature as 'independent' sovereign was indulged; his demand that the British resident be termed 'general', not 'British' adviser was honoured;

---

87 Trocki, *Prince of Pirates*, p. 120.

88 Wilkinson, *Peninsular Malays*, pp. 62–63. Emphasis added.

89 Buckley, *Anecdotal History*, pp. 45–46. Wilkinson found 'certain doubtful features about this pedigree. It is probable that these families [the Temenggung's and the Bendahara's] are descended from a brother, not a son of Sultan Abdul Jalil, as they would otherwise have borne the royal title of Tengku'. Wilkinson, *Peninsular Malays*, p. 82.

90 Trocki, *Prince of Pirates*, p. 202.

his expensive travel abroad was tolerated; and so forth. After the creative and abetted self-invention of Abu Bakar, his son Ibrahim reverted to type – a 'ceremonial' ruler of British Malaya.

Colonialism and the Reification of Malay Tradition

The colonial invention of Malay royalty was a continuing process. As late as the Second World War, pressure to conform to a certain model of royalty can still be discerned in evaluations of rulers written during the war to facilitate later investigations into Malay collaboration.[91] These short biographical notes reveal how successfully the rulers, as a group, had transformed themselves. Interestingly, the transformation was not entirely contiguous with a ruler's friendliness to the British. Sultan Ibrahim of Johor, for example, was 'said to be anti-British', and 'European officers generally disliked serving in Johore because of his uncertain temper and liability of being persistently vindictive to whom he might happen to take a dislike'. But these attributes were contextualised within the larger, royal qualities he possessed: 'masterful and autocratic, assertive of his own authority'. And he was given the highest compliment of being judged to possess 'considerable practical ability and acumen'. Abdul Aziz of Perak earned an unqualified character endorsement which bears quotation at length:

> Educated in Malaya, speaks English well. At one time served in the FMS government service, was a keen volunteer, first as a private, later as a commissioned officer. Well liked by the European community in his state and enjoys European society. First-class shot and good tennis player. Interested himself greatly in the Boy Scout movement in his state. In 1941, at the start of the campaign, with other Perak chiefs made interest-free loan of $30,500.

The Yam Tuan of Negeri Sembilan was considered 'a good example of the modern generation of educated, progressive and intelligent Malays. He understands his responsibilities and is interested in his people's welfare'. In contrast, Sulaiman of Terengganu (who died during the Japanese occupation), while acknowledged to be 'loyal to his British connection', did not generate much enthusiasm, probably on account of his old-style qualities: 'Quiet and dignified, languid in movement and speech. Never an assertive character'. Ironically, it is this characterisation which accords best with the portrait of Malay kingship described by Milner in *Kerajaan*. And it

[91] WO 203/5612.

is a measure of the success of the colonial invention that his opposite, a man overflowing with 'modern' interests – tennis, education, scouting – could be understood to constitute a traditional leader.

This redefinition of tradition, a joint British–Malay initiative, was a product of the attempted preservation of Malay culture in a changing world. Initially, the analysis of weakness and decay explained the Malay failure to achieve good government and lent justification to the British presence. Later, British concern with Malay culture increased along with the nineteenth century articulation of racial theories. According to Hendrik Maier,

> differences [between 'nations' or 'races'] were no longer formulated in terms of the scale of civilization but in terms of a racial hierarchy in which the white man held a superior and unassailable position, having a knowledge of society and nature that even Malay aristocrats were supposedly never able to grasp.[92]

In this context, British admiration for the aristocratic nature of Malay culture emphasised preservation over progress:

> Improvement now meant primarily the imposition of order and the care of material well-being – these were the keys to the restoration of Malay identity, to the stabilization of Malay culture.[93]

Having access to Chinese and Indian labour for the crucial project of 'opening up' the country, British Malayophiles were free to pursue the freezing of Malay culture in an invented past. The strengthening of the Malay rulers was part of this project, as were the commissioning of royal *hikayat* (histories) and state histories and the authentication of the *Sejarah Melayu* (Malay Annals) as the defining text of Malay political life.[94] Malay culture became a sort of fragile, if admirable, specimen which was to be protected from the harshness of the modern world.

But this was not mere cultural 'butterfly collecting' for the amusement of the foreigners. There was a powerful, if unconscious, connection between British understanding of their own power and the status of the Malay rulers. John Butcher, studying the social history of the British in Malaya, found that

---

92 Hendrik M.J. Maier, *In the Center of Authority: The Malay Hikayat Merong Mahawangsa*, Ithaca NY: Cornell University Southeast Asia Program, 1988, p. 53.

93 *Ibid.*, p. 54.

94 In addition to fact that it was well-known throughout the peninsula, Maier points out that the *Sejarah Melayu*'s simple language and accessible (to a European reader) narrative 'evoked reality in a manner that was fairly familiar to dominant British concepts of historiography'. *Ibid.*, p. 42.

'implicit in British thinking about their rule throughout the Empire was the principle that their power was based on prestige rather than military might.'[95] There is no doubt that the glorified Malay monarchy, restored under the aegis of British protection, added immeasurably to that prestige. And the development of hybrid Anglo–Malay ceremonial held a special appeal for middle-class British officials. Protecting a traditional court culture allowed them to indulge their aristocratic fantasies and enter into Malay royal circles at the highest level.

As the centrepiece of the process of cultural restoration, the new Malay ruler looked so natural and authentic that most observers saw only the obvious – strengthened monarchies. Yet a fundamental change had taken place: the rulers now belonged not only to the Malays, to Malay political culture and to the Malay past. Through their articulation of new structures of authority, they belonged also to the present and future of British colonial rule. Yet their new meaning within the colonial system did not invalidate their older position at the centre of the Malay world. On the contrary, the two meanings became heavily intertwined. The rulers' participation in their own invention helped to institutionalise and legitimise British control, which in turn bolstered their real – not merely symbolic – standing as Malay monarchs.

An important element in maintaining this standing was the idea of loyalty, along with its corollary, the suppression of dissent. Loyalty to one's ruler was said to be a Malay characteristic, an assertion backed up by reference to the origin myth of Malay political culture. The story in the *Sejarah Melayu* tells of a pact made between Sri Tri Buana, the first royal ruler of the Malays, and Demang Lebar Daun, a representative of his subjects. The agreement is this: the raja will always treat his subjects well, will punish them in accordance with Muslim law, and will never defile, shame or ill-treat them. His subjects will always be loyal, even if they are oppressed. Should the ruler break his word, his kingdom will be destroyed by God, but rebellion is not sanctioned.[96] More evidence of this Malay characteristic came from the popular story of Hang Tuah, the Melaka-era hero who remained loyal despite the injustice of his ruler. Frequent repetition has made this a truism of Malay culture, but it should not be accepted uncritically, for two reasons. First, it has been argued that the *Sejarah Melayu* is a ruling class text in which the assertion of Malays'

---

95 Butcher, *The British in Malaya*, p. 77.

96 Chandra Muzaffar, *Protector? An Analysis of the Concept and Practice of Loyalty in Leader-led Relationships within Malay Society*, Penang: Aliran, 1979, pp. 3–4, 6.

absolute loyalty to their rulers is an effort to indoctrinate, rather than a description of an existing situation.[97] Second, the Hang Tuah story should probably be read as prescribing an ideal relationship *within* the ruling class – the proper conduct of a chief to his ruler. A modern exemplar of this type of loyalty was Abu Bakar's land official, Mohamed Salleh bin Perang. Slandered, mistreated and pensioned off by Sultan Ibrahim (who wished to be rid of his father's old retainers), Salleh hinted at his displeasure by proclaiming his loyalty:

> I most solemnly enjoin upon my children and my descendants down through the generations that they should never allow even to cross their minds the idea of wishing ill upon their own raja.... Because down through the generations, our ancestors have all been bound by an oath of loyalty to the ancestors of the Sultan of Johor and have vowed to serve their interests.[98]

Ordinary subjects (*rakyat*), however, make few appearances in texts like the *Sejarah Melayu*. It was thus understandable, no less convenient, that Hang Tuah was usually (mis)read as the exemplary subject and has become an icon of Malay culture.

Nevertheless, deference to authority was an important aspect of court culture and maintaining this deference became part of the colonial preservation of Malay society. Within the ruling class, the concentration of power in royal hands corresponded to a decline in the position of chiefs. An early element in this decline was European intolerance of 'piracy' which, even before direct intervention, eliminated a source of revenue for chiefs amassing a following to challenge a ruler.[99] Once British control had been extended to a state, often by taking sides in a succession dispute, a ruler could demand attendance at rituals of obeisance, which now occurred with more frequency.[100] The British presence also changed the nature of those rituals, as suggested by Innes's remarks on Abdul Samad's 'homage day':

> When it was over the Sultan remarked to us that now, since the white man had come into his country, he was no longer afraid for his life on homage-

[97] Abdul Rahman Hj. Ismail, 'Kewibawaan mutlak raja dan ketaatsetiaan mutlak rakyat kepada raja', *Kajian Malaysia*, vol. 3, no. 1, 1985, pp. 32–57.

[98] Sweeney, *Reputations Live On*, p. 69.

[99] Andaya and Andaya, *History*, p. 131.

[100] According to Wilkinson, 'Historically there is not much authority for the *mengadap* [audience at which the ruler receives the homage of his chiefs] to which so much attention is paid at the present day'. R.J. Wilkinson, 'Sri Menanti' in *Papers on Malay Subjects*, Kuala Lumpur: Oxford University Press, 1971, p. 380, originally published in 1914.

> day; but that formerly, when there were many ambitious rajas who would have liked to become Sultan, he was always expecting that one or other of them would seize the opportunity of stabbing him. He told us that such things formerly often happened when Sultans were receiving homage, as on no other occasion were well-known dangerous characters allowed to come so near the royal person.[101]

Even as Malaya changed around the Malays, loyalty to the ruler and deference to his leadership remained unquestioned tenets of traditional Malay society. Further, loyalty to the ruler was effectively extended to include the colonial overlord. This extension was most plainly manifest when peasant or ruling class revolts were labeled *derhaka* (treason) by rulers forced (or eager) to 'take sides' and who relied ever more heavily on British backing thereafter. Over time, the British insinuated themselves conceptually as well as ritually, as revealed in this reminiscence of 'the Malay':

> Love of his ricefields when the young rice is pale green in water which reflects the sunrise and sunset, until the golden grain is ready for the knife, of his village house, brown thatch among the coconuts, silver at night and murmuring by day, leads up to loyalty to his chief, loyalty to his Sultan, and loyalty to those Englishmen who take the trouble to know him and understand him.[102]

Thus did the British imagine themselves as part of tradition.

*

This chapter has described how the structure of Malay leadership was standardised to accord with an ideal Malay political culture considered by the British to be in decay. The articulation of a court tradition through the creation of new state ritual was the prime accomplishment of colonial traditionalism, which sought a way to preserve Malay culture while radically changing the political and economic milieu in which it lived. The rulers themselves are understood, in this analysis, to have embraced this project wholeheartedly as a way of enhancing their position both within Malay society and in the new imperial context. In return for this collaboration, and ostensibly in order to preserve Malay culture, the colonial state protected Malay rulers as never before from challenges within their own society. The rulers, even if unwittingly, acted as frontmen for that state:

---

[101] Innes, *Chersonese*, pp. 43–44.

[102] Theodore Adams, 'The Malay in Malaya', *Asiatic Review*, vol. 40, no. 141, 1944, p. 98.

their very presence, articulated through new rituals and visibility, attested to a traditional, not colonial, foundation of society, and their monopoly on political activity thwarted the development of Malay critiques of colonialism.

Looking at the Malay ruling class as a whole, we see a crucial difference between the colonial transformations undergone by rulers and chiefs. The hybrid Malay ruler encompassed two superficially similar models, Western constitutional monarch and Malay ceremonial raja. In the British imperial, as well as the Southeast Asian, context, the two fit together neatly, the Malay ruler as vassal to the British overlord. The preservation of the chiefs was more ambiguous. They came to be identified partly with tradition, like the rulers, and partly with good government, as salaried members of the colonial state. Both the Malay College Kuala Kangsar, with its British public school ethos, and the Malay administrative service, in which Malay chiefs read English law, were a way of harnessing tradition in the service of change, a way of creating 'the modern Malay'.

A rift had developed within the Malay ruling class, even while the new bureaucratic elite remained contiguous with and dependent upon traditional Malay rulers and their courts. The interests of the two groups usually coincided because together they could most successfully pursue the small amount of power and considerable amount of prestige available to them in the colonial system. Yet when open competition between ruler and chief, so indicative of precolonial Malay politics, had the opportunity to reemerge, it would become obvious that the colonial experience had left the chiefs with an advantage. In the differentiation of the ruling class, the rulers had become invested in the preservation of tradition and the aristocrats in a good government ethos which was rapidly gaining prestige with the public. As long as colonial rule continued to validate traditionalism, aristocratic ambitions would remain in uneasy abeyance. But should circumstances change, the bureaucratic elite would be able to lay claim to a new kind of leadership in Malaya, one based on the qualifications associated with good government and progress. In the next chapter, I discuss prewar changes within Malay society which strained the credibility of the traditional leadership and the momentous disruption of British colonial rule which brought traditionalism to the point of crisis.

CHAPTER FOUR

Challenges to Traditionalism

Conventional colonial wisdom held that Malays were a tradition-bound people and that nothing much had altered that until the Second World War introduced dramatic changes. According to R.O. Winstedt, 'before the Japanese war the passing of the old order was almost imperceptible'.[1] As I have argued, the old order was not what it appeared to be. Beyond that, however, change was indeed taking place in the 1920s and 1930s, especially in connection with urbanisation and education. To understand the effects of the Japanese occupation and the postwar restoration of colonialism on the ruling class, we must read them against a background of changes taking place in Malay society before the war, even in the heyday of traditionalism.

The following four sections examine these successive challenges to colonial Malay traditionalism. In the first, I discuss how increasing opportunities for education led to a dramatic growth in the size of the Malay reading public. Before the war, this public began to articulate critiques of the condition of Malay society, though these were rarely directed openly at the Malay ruling class or the British. In the second section, I analyse the impact of the war. The interruption of British colonial rule for three and a half years did not destroy traditionalism, but it did seriously destabilise it. By promoting anticolonial rhetoric and political activity, the Japanese allowed suppressed criticism of the ruling class to see the light of day. Just as importantly, the priorities of Japanese administration changed the balance of power within the Malay ruling class in favour of the chiefs, who were placed in more responsible positions, while the rulers lost their sovereign status and ceremonial roles. The third section introduces the conditions of postwar Malaya which provide the setting for the remainder of this study. Economic disruption, political violence and civil disorder all extended the instability of the occupation – and consequent threat to traditionalism – into the colonial restoration. Most importantly, British attitudes towards the Malays

[1] R.O. Winstedt, *The Malays: A Cultural History*, 5th ed., London: Routledge and Kegan Paul, 1961, p. 3.

and Chinese upon reoccupation made it clear that the pro-Malay policies of the prewar years, especially the protection of the ruling elite, were a thing of the past. In the final section, I look specifically at the returning British government's policy towards political and press freedom. Much of my analysis in the following chapters is based on the 'public transcript' of Malay-language newspapers in the years from 1945 to 1947. Here I examine the development of parameters for acceptable political expression in this period.

Change in Prewar Malay Society

The careful preservation of a purportedly traditional ruling class could not deter political, economic and cultural change from occurring in the lower realms of society. During the First World War, while the Malay ruling class made appropriate gestures of loyalty and support for the empire, other Malays speculated about Turkey's entrance into the war and Britain's possible defeat. By the 1920s and 1930s commodity production for the global market had reached down to peasant villages of rubber smallholders, and the consequences of the worldwide depression were felt everywhere. Undoubtedly the greatest changes in Malay society were occurring in the urban crucibles of colonial cities. The narrowing horizons of the *kampung* economy, secular education and ease of transportation brought growing numbers of Malays to the cities.

By 1931 about 11 per cent of the Malay population throughout British Malaya was urban.[2] This low percentage (which had risen from 9 per cent in 1921), as well as the overwhelmingly non-Malay character of the largest cities, can easily obscure the significance to Malay society of even limited urbanisation under colonial conditions. When the aggregate numbers are broken down, it becomes apparent that in the unfederated states of Kelantan and Terengganu, largely Malay cities were developing, and even in Johor and Kedah the proportion of Malays to the total urban population was about 30 per cent.[3] In the cities of the Straits Settlements and Federated Malay States (FMS), where the Malays were only about 12 per cent of the population, they nevertheless underwent an experiential change which would have consequences throughout society.

[2] C.A. Vlieland, *British Malaya: A Report on the 1931 Census and on Certain Problems of Vital Statistics*, London, Waterlow & Sons, 1932, p. 48. Urban areas are defined as towns with a population greater than 1,000, p. 36. See also J.E. Nathan, *The Census of British Malaya 1921*, London: Dunstable & Waterford, 1922, pp. 41–42.

[3] The urban areas of Kelantan were 69.3 per cent Malay, Terengganu 81.5 per cent, Johor 29.3 per cent and Kedah 33.1 per cent. Vlieland, *1931 Census*, p. 48.

Urban Malays may be said to have 'slipped through the cracks' of a system designed to preserve a two-tiered social structure of ruling class and agrarian subject class. In the city, Malays experienced a decidedly non-traditional society characterised by Western lifestyles, new occupations and ethnic heterogeneity. Men found employment in the growing motor industry (mainly as drivers and messengers) and in public service (as clerks, police and labourers). A small professional class, working in education, law and medicine, was also urban based.[4] Wage-earning urban Malays, with salaries and leisure time to spend, participated in a popular culture of commercialised art and entertainment. New forms of theatre, music and dance were joined by film and radio as popular pastimes.[5] Emblematic of the new social, commercial and cultural cosmopolitanism was *bangsawan*, a popular Malay opera incorporating elements of Parsi theatre from India. These foreign elements made *bangsawan* a target of criticism from Malay intellectuals who increasingly articulated Malay identity against a background of growing Chinese strength in Malaya.[6] In the cities, awareness of the economic strength and number of foreign immigrants was inevitable, as Malays interacted with them in public places of entertainment and recreation, like dance halls, cabarets and sports clubs.

It was in the cities, at first, that more Malays became literate in their own language. In early census surveys, in fact, literacy was measured only in urban areas. In 1921 male literacy was found to range from 30 to 50 per cent in most towns. And although literacy rates were higher in the Straits Settlements and the FMS, three in every five Kota Bharu (Kelantan) boys between the ages of five and 15 were attending school.[7] The link between urbanisation, education and new occupations can be seen in the 1926 establishment of a Federal Trade School in Kuala Lumpur, meant to train mechanics, fitters, machine workers and other technicians.[8] Despite an overall reluctance to train or educate Malay commoners beyond the level of basic literacy and elementary agriculture, the director of education, Winstedt, was forced to acknowledge the different experience of urban Malays:

---

4 *Ibid.*, pp. 49, 264–65, 289–90, 313–14.

5 Wan Abdul Kadir, *Budaya Popular dalam Masyarakat Melayu Bandaran*, Kuala Lumpur: Dewan Bahasa dan Pustaka, 1988, pp. 221–23, 227.

6 Tan Sooi Beng, *Bangsawan: A Social and Stylistic History of Popular Malay Opera*, Singapore: Oxford University Press, 1993.

7 Nathan, *British Malaya 1921*, pp. 109–10.

8 Philip Loh Fook-Seng, 'A review of the educational developments in the Federated Malay States to 1939', *Journal of Southeast Asian Studies*, vol. 5, no. 2, 1974, pp. 235–36.

> Although the school is open to pupils of all nationalities, Malays are given first consideration, the original intention being to provide training for, and to open up a career to, those town Malays who up to the present have had nothing more to look forward to than an existence spent as a peon or a messenger.[9]

By 1931, when literacy was measured universally, it was estimated that over half the local-born Malay population in the Straits Settlements and FMS was literate. In addition, nearly 80 per cent of boys in these territories were then being educated, a process that the compiler of the census expected would yield nearly universal male Malay literacy in the next generation.[10] The 1920s and 1930s saw primary education of all kinds spreading beyond urban areas. In addition to government and private secular education, religious schools increased in number with the growing demand for education; their curricula came to resemble those in secular schools with the introduction of modern teaching ideas from the Middle East.[11] The graduates of these schools created the market which made possible a dramatic growth in publishing activity in the 1920s and especially the 1930s. Following the spread of literacy outward from the cities was the influence of newspapers and magazines, driven by advertising and benefiting from improved communications and regional marketing.[12] It was the growth of these publications that fostered the development of a modern Malay public discourse. Like the liberal public sphere which emerged in Europe in the eighteenth century, it was characterised by the participation of the literate population and by 'people's public use of their reason'.[13] This developing public manifested itself in both newspaper discourse and new forms of social organisation, both of which articulated responses to the significant changes occurring in colonial Malay society.

Foremost among the topics discussed was the challenge posed by foreign immigration and the need for Malay society to respond through education

9 Cited in *Ibid.*, p. 236.

10 Female literacy lagged behind considerably, amounting to only 7 per cent of the adult population. But progress was reported in the 20 per cent of girls currently attending school. Vlieland, *1931 Census*, p. 93.

11 Khoo Kay Kim, 'Malay society, 1874–1920s', *Journal of Southeast Asian Studies*, vol. 5, no. 2, 1974, pp. 184–89.

12 Wan Abdul Kadir, *Budaya Popular*, p. 232.

13 Jürgen Habermas, *The Structural Transformation of the Public Sphere: An Inquiry into a Category of Bourgeois Society*, Cambridge: MIT Press, 1989, p. 27. See Anthony Milner, *The Invention of Politics in Colonial Malaya: Contesting Nationalism and the Expansion of the Public Sphere*, Cambridge: Cambridge University Press, 1994, especially ch. 5.

and self-improvement. The earliest critique of Malay 'backwardness' came early in the century from the Islamic reform movement (Kaum Muda), a group that included Malays and immigrant Indonesians, as well as Peranakan Arabs and Indian Muslims who identified with and claimed to speak for the Malays. This reform movement, while imbibing ideas and impulses from abroad, was formulated in Malaya largely in response to the impact of colonialism on Islam. The terms of indirect British control left only residually-defined Malay custom and religion in Malay hands, and British encouragement of a bureaucratised traditionalism had led to 'an authoritarian form of religious administration' in which the royal houses controlled 'extensive machiner[ies] for governing Islam'.[14] Reformists rejected the arbitrary control of the elite and insisted on the use of reason (*akal*) in interpreting Islamic practices (i.e. regarding usury and education for women) in order to improve Muslims' position in the world.[15] Their analysis attacked the traditional practices which were fossilising Malay society and put the reformers in direct conflict with the traditional Malay elite. Adding to this intrinsic conflict, the reformers began to articulate a new idea: that rulers and traditional leaders had responsibilities towards their people in the areas of education, economic development and self-awareness, and that they should be helping Muslims to change in a changing world. In this regard, the reformers found the Malay leadership to be a complete failure and criticised it as well for being 'dissolute and self-indulgent'. In responding to this defiance, the Malay elite was backed by colonial authority. Reformers were barred from speaking in many peninsular mosques, and reformist journals published in Singapore and Penang were denied entry into several states. But although the reformists were blocked from developing mass support amongst the peasantry, the critical public discourse they initiated did not disappear. This rational discourse, concerned with the cultural and social improvement of the community (*umat*), was perpetuated by newspapers and in them by particular modes of analysis. For example, *Al-Imam* (1906–1908), the first organ of the Islamic reform movement in Malaya, differed from earlier Malay newspapers (the first of which appeared in 1876), which had largely translated overseas and local news from the English press. *Al-Imam* concerned itself wholly with problems of the community, initiating critiques of Malay backwardness and disunity – both themes which continue to have

---

[14] William R. Roff, *The Origins of Malay Nationalism*, Kuala Lumpur: University of Malaya Press, 1980, pp. 72–73.

[15] *Ibid.*, p. 78.

relevance to this day.[16] After the demise of *Al-Imam*, other Kaum Muda journals picked up those themes: *Neracha* and *Tunas Melayu* in the 1910s, *Al-Hedayah*, *Al-Ikhwan* and *Idaran Zaman* in the 1920s, and finally *Saudara* in the 1930s.[17] The limitations of the early papers were characteristic of the newly postulated public they spoke to: their circulations were small and the size of their literate public was insufficient to sustain them for long runs. By the 1930s, however, Malay literacy had reached a critical mass capable of supporting a wider public dialogue. Especially notable in this regard was the overnight success of Sahabat Pena (Brotherhood of Pen Friends), which started as a write-in feature on the children's page of the Penang newspaper *Saudara* in 1934.[18] Attracting members and letters from all over the peninsula and even Borneo, Sahabat Pena had, within six months, far outgrown its founders' intentions to become the first national forum for a literate Malay public to air its concerns and exchange ideas.

Meanwhile, another innovation had appeared on the Malay social landscape. The first organisation for the promotion and propagation of Malay language and literature appeared in Johor in 1888.[19] Organisations of this type were formed in reaction to the growing marginalisation of the Malays and their culture in the government and economy of colonial Malaya. They were unofficial, that is, not associated with the colonial state, and because of that had to tread carefully around the political prohibition. Nevertheless, this independence allowed them to play a crucial role in generating the political and cultural ideas and language of twentieth-century Malay society. First, they encouraged the development of a new literature independent from the ruling class, a literature which was influenced more by Middle Eastern and Indonesian innovations than by the mediocre English-language training received by the elite. Second, their membership consisted largely of Malay teachers, people who helped to increase Malay literacy and, in turn, provided a growing audience for the critical discourse developing in the Malay newspapers. Finally, they established the significance of language and literature in developing a Malay national consciousness. By the 1930s newspapers like the Singapore *Warta Malaya* were calling for the standardisation of Malay vocabulary and spelling and for a writers'

---

16 *Ibid.*, p. 57.

17 See William R. Roff, 'Kaum muda–kaum tua: innovation and reaction amongst the Malays, 1900–1941', in K.G. Treggoning, ed., *Papers on Malayan History*, Singapore: Journal of South-East Asian History, 1962, pp. 166n14, 179.

18 Roff, *Malay Nationalism*, pp. 212–22.

19 This paragraph is based on Rustam Sani, 'Badan-badan bahasa dan sastera melayu: satu perspektif sosio-politik', paper given to me by the author.

federation across the peninsula.[20]

In the 1930s several of these trends came together: growing awareness and discontent with the position of Malays in colonial society, rising literacy in Malay (and to some extent in English), new occupations in the urban areas and a boom in newspaper publication. At the same time, Malay associational life increased with the establishment of Malay associations organised along Western lines, with elections, committees, meetings and so forth.[21] Among the ranks of the educated, the colonial rendition of traditional Malay society was becoming increasingly uncompelling. The aristocracy, not as alienated from the mass of society as the rulers, could not fail to notice and some were, in fact, susceptible to the same feelings of disaffection. One notable example is Onn bin Jaafar (the postwar founder of UMNO), who veered from his expected career path in the Johor administrative service to advocate, as a journalist, greater Malay representation in government and education. Another example is the Putera Kelab, a youth organisation founded in Kelantan in 1929 by a small group of Islamic-educated low-ranking government servants who wanted to move beyond literary and cultural uplift activities and who began to criticise the Malay establishment in the pages of their newspaper, *Akhbar Putera*. The Kelantan administration (both Malay officials and the British adviser) soon became openly hostile to the group, forbidding government servants from reading the newspaper, and the enterprise came to an end. Another journal published by the same group a few years later prompted the government to require all editors to swear loyalty to the ruler.[22]

These prewar attempts to reverse the stagnation of Malay society by graduates of all educational streams – Malay and English, secular and religious – attest to the growing strains of colonial traditionalism. Yet two factors limited their effectiveness. First, the way the critiques were formulated demonstrates how successfully 'traditional Malay society' shielded colonial reality. Most prewar discontent was articulated in one of two ways. The first was criticism levelled at Malay society itself (and less commonly at Malay leadership). Thus Malays were urged to overcome their backwardness by attention to language, industriousness, education and cooperation within the community.[23] The second type of campaign

---

[20] Zulkipli bin Mahmud, *Warta Malaya: Penyambung Lidah Bangsa Melayu, 1930–1941*, Bangi: Jabatan Sejarah, Universiti Kebangsaan Malaysia, 1979, p. 99.

[21] Roff, *Malay Nationalism*, p. 182.

[22] Khoo, 'Malay society', pp. 192–94.

[23] It is this strain of self-criticism which continues in Mahathir's *The Malay Dilemma*,

was the constant reminder to the colonial power that its responsibility was to the Malays, not to immigrant Asians who were themselves making new demands. The combining of self-criticism with a continual petition for more English education and more positions in the colonial system essentially conceded that progress would come from the British on British terms. For example, the Singapore newspaper *Warta Malaya*, under the editorship of Onn bin Jaafar, reminded the ruling class of Johor that it was the people's affection for them that was responsible for the peace and security of the state (a foreshadowing of Onn's later success as a populist) and pressed the British, in a tone that was not unfriendly, to fulfil their moral obligation to educate and incorporate more Malays into the administration of the country.[24] The recipients of these positions would inevitably be the well-born, who would perpetuate their privileged access to the colonial state.

Only one nexus of secularly educated young men and politically motivated religious reformers seemed to understand the relationship of colonialism to the Malay ruling class and to be hostile to both.[25] The Kesatuan Melayu Muda (KMM, Young Malays Union) was founded in 1938 as the first Malay organisation to transcend state boundaries. The KMM was explicitly anti-British and anti-ruling class, though it was stymied in expressing its views by the pervasive and ingrained prohibition on political activity upheld jointly by the rulers and the British. Clandestine meetings and veiled fictional satire only gave way to outright criticism in the months before the Japanese invasion and for this the leaders of the organisation were jailed.[26]

Second, I would argue that this increasingly complex and challenging public life limited its effectiveness by refusing to cross the line into the political. Conceiving themselves as literary, welfare or cultural organisations may have served to protect fundamentally political aims, but with the exception of the KMM, none was willing to break the taboo

---

Singapore: Times Books International, 1970 and in his later efforts to construct 'the new Malay'.

[24] Zulkipli, *Warta Malaya*, pp. 76–79.

[25] Firdaus Haji Abdullah mentions the connection between the Kesatuan Melayu Muda and a *madrasah* (modern Islamic school) in northern Perak in *Radical Malay Politics: Its Origins and Early Development*, Petaling Jaya: Pelanduk Publications, 1985, p. 18. More generally, he argues that radicalism (i.e. nationalism) owed its origin as least as much to modernist Islam's combination of religious devotion and worldly concerns as to the more often cited secular preparation received at the Sultan Idris Training College.

[26] Roff, *Malay Nationalism*, pp. 229–35.

against interfering (*campur tangan*) with the rulers' monopoly. This is not merely a semantic distinction. For example, support for the Malay language manifested itself in an enriched literature and vocabulary, but could not hope to make its achievements official through control of the state. Later, when these ideas were expressed in explicitly political ways, they would manifest themselves in calls for Bahasa Melayu to be enshrined constitutionally as the national language. Further, political terms and ideas had been entering the Malay language through newspaper editorials since the time of the First World War, and political movements in other Muslim countries were well known to educated Malays.[27] But to embrace politics would inherently have entailed the destruction of traditional/colonial structures of authority which sheltered the educated Malay elite. Thus educated leaders refused to embrace party politics as a means to their desired ends and so left the mass of rural Malays outside the expanding public discourse, mired in a discourse of blind loyalty to hereditary rulers. This important adherence to a traditionalist conception of Malay public life prevented the development of critiques of colonialism.

The more disaffection grew and change seemed inevitable, the more tenaciously tradition was defended by the British and the Malay ruling class, especially the rulers and more court-oriented members of the aristocracy. The defence was especially efficacious in discouraging political activity, sometimes with the help of the police, but often solely by the power of public disapproval. In many cases, social or literary organisations like the Sahabat Pena were hounded by accusations of secret political activity. Others, like the state-based Malay associations of the late 1930s, which were in fact proto-political organisations dominated by English-educated members of the aristocracy concerned with Malay progress, scrambled to disavow any political intentions. Meanwhile, the British and the more complacent members of the ruling class reassured each other of a certain unchanging quality inherent in 'the Malay'. Writing to inform Europeans about Malay court etiquette, a self-described 'courtier and tutor to the royal family of Kelantan' introduced his brief survey by invoking timeless tradition and displaying stubborn ignorance of his countrymen's demands for change:

---

[27] Mohd. Taib Osman, *The Language of the Editorials in Malay Vernacular Newspapers Up to 1941*, Kuala Lumpur: Dewan Bahasa dan Pustaka, 1966, p. 3. New terms, in both English and Arabic, often found their way into the Malay papers in connection with international events. For example, *siasah* (Ar., politics or policy) appeared in 1925, *hizb* (Ar., political party) in 1932. *Ibid.*, p. 13.

> The rules of this unwritten code preserved from time immemorial, are strictly observed.... It is therefore the duty of Malay parents to teach their children how to behave before elders and superiors so that the humblest Malay may be fit to be a follower or companion of royalty and the aristocracy. Although education of the higher kind is not regarded as of paramount importance, a knowledge of Court language and manners is thought to be a *sine qua non* even by illiterate Malays.[28]

Ten years later, in 1944, a senior British official who had worked closely with the Malay ruling class before the war and who would do so again afterwards, saw Malay society as apolitical and unchanging:

> Those of us who have worked and played with Malays know and think of them as individuals, charming, courteous, friendly, loyal, courageous, democratic, yet welcoming ancient constituted authority imposed on them by custom and religion, democratic, that is, in a different way from British democracy based on the vote.[29]

The colonial power had so convinced itself of the traditional and eternal nature of its protectorate, that it would be thoroughly surprised by the second reordering of Malay politics that began under the Japanese occupation.

War and Occupation

The temporary interruption of British colonial rule during the war (1942–1945) allowed the simmering changes in Malay society to come to a boil, producing a situation with which colonial Malay tradition would eventually have to come to terms. The occupation facilitated the visibility and viability of a political challenge to traditional leadership. It also changed the balance of power between preservation and change within the ruling class itself, giving new government responsibilities to the bureaucratic elite and stripping away the ceremonial trappings of the traditional rulers.

[28] Dato' Muhammad Ghazzali, J.P., D.P.M.K. (Dato' Bentara Luar of Kelantan), 'Court language and etiquette of the Malays', *Journal of the Malay Branch of the Royal Asiatic Society*, vol. 11, pt. 2, 1933, p. 273. I have given the author's name as it appears in the publication. Note the combination of British and Malay status markers.

[29] Theodore Adams, 'The Malay in Malaya', *Asiatic Review*, vol. 40, no. 141, 1944, p. 99. Adams's prewar career in Malaya extended from 1908 to 1936, the last four years of which was spent as resident of Selangor. After the war he became an adviser to the rulers.

Without British backing, the rulers' monopoly over political activity vanished. Malay nationalists, jailed by the British before the war, were freed by the Japanese to organise militia and denounce the British. For a brief period early in the occupation, the KMM was the privileged political organisation of the peninsula, enjoying an access to Japanese officers and growth in membership which extended its influence throughout Malay society.[30] Even after its brief ascendancy had passed, its members staffed Malay-language propaganda organs and joined Japanese-led militias. (The significance of both of these will be discussed in chapter six.)

For the first time, political aspirations could be spoken of openly and without 'making obeisance' to tradition. Two examples will serve to illustrate the change. The KMM leader Ibrahim Yaacob held a meeting soon after the British surrender at which he criticised the fragmentation and state-based orientation of existing Malay organisations and stated as his goal the unity of all Malays without reference to region or state. The group discussed the ideals it should pursue, including unity, humanity, liberty, democracy, fraternity and honesty (rendered in English). When words were sought in Malay to convey these aspirations, the meeting decided on *bersatu* (unity), *setia* (loyalty), *percaya* (belief), *bergerak* (to move) and *mara* (progress).[31] The context in which it appears suggests a new conception of loyalty, one invoking not blind obedience to the traditional ruler, but rather adherence to set of principles. In another example, a magazine under the editorship of Ishak Haji Muhammad was able to say (with Japanese encouragement, of course) that Malays had lived under colonialism, exploited and oppressed by capitalists and European governments.[32] The analysis was not new, but the very words were newly expressed, no longer under the cloak of satiric fiction.

The Japanese occupation also restored fluidity to the balance of power between rulers and chiefs. The bureaucratic elite experienced an enhancement of position and responsibility, because, despite the brief ascendancy of the KMM, the Japanese administration of Malaya depended

---

30 Cheah Boon Kheng, *Red Star Over Malaya: Resistance and Social Conflict During and After the Japanese Occupation of Malaya, 1941–1946*, Singapore: Singapore University Press, 1983, is the best overall account of the occupation. For the KMM and their attempts to move towards independence under the Japanese, see especially pp. 101–23.

31 A. Samad Ahmad, *Sejambak Kenangan: Sebuah Autobiografi*, Kuala Lumpur: Dewan Bahasa dan Pustaka, 1981, pp. 152–53.

32 'Menyusun masyarakat baru', *Semangat Asia*, June 1943. Cited in Abdul Latiff Abu Bakar, *Ishak Haji Muhammad: Penulis dan Ahli Politik Sehingga 1948*, Kuala Lumpur: University of Malaya Press, 1977, p. 95.

heavily on institutional continuity. At the highest levels of government, royalty and the aristocratic elite were fully represented in advisory councils, boards, courtrooms and delegations.[33] Throughout the countryside, rural Malay administrators continued in their jobs, many receiving promotions to replace British officers who had fled.[34] According to Cheah Boon Kheng, Malay administrators gained valuable experience in practical leadership, joining community work projects and doing manual labour after office hours 'instead of keeping their hands clean as in prewar days'. This experience has been interpreted vital in increasing the political self-confidence of the bureaucratic elite, enabling it to act decisively after the occupation.[35] Just as importantly, it served to strengthen the identification of Malay chiefs with good government and progress. As British superiors disappeared and district administration continued, Malay bureaucrats proved that self-government was possible.

At the same time, the Japanese occupation represented a direct blow to the standing and public posture of the rulers. Although no rulers were physically harmed, the policy of the new government effectively dismantled the careful construction of ceremonial rajas who embodied Malay tradition within British imperialism. The sultans were not recognised by the Japanese as sovereign rulers and their stipends were cut by as much as two-thirds,[36] abruptly ending their public life of extravagant, Western-style living. They tried to remain aloof from the occupiers, but were often forced to make speeches which had been composed by the Japanese.[37] They were required to participate in 'grow more food' campaigns by working the soil themselves,[38] the sort of activity that could enhance the stature of a leader who was involved in solving problems (i.e. chiefs), but that would do little for one whose very style of life was meant to symbolise the status of a whole community. Further, the nature of the rulers' connection with European colonialism was made explicit by the Japanese, as illustrated by this propaganda broadcast from late 1942:

---

33 See CO 273/669/50744/7 for examples from Selangor, Kelantan and Johor.

34 Cheah, *Red Star*, pp. 29–32. See also Muda Mohd. Taib A. Rahman, 'Pendudukan Jepun di Terengganu', in Khoo Kay Kim, ed., *Sejarah Masyarakat Melayu Moden*, Kuala Lumpur: Jabatan Sejarah, Universiti Malaya, 1984, p. 164.

35 Cheah, *Red Star*, p. 43.

36 Yoji Akashi, 'Japanese military administration: its formation and evolution in reference to the sultans, the Islamic religion, and the Moslem Malays, 1941–45', *Asian Studies*, vol. 7, no. 1, 1969, pp. 95–96.

37 Intelligence Bulletin no. 33, 13 October 1945. WO 203/2155, WO 203/5635A.

38 Chin Kee Onn, *Malaya Upside Down*, 1946, reprint, Singapore: Federal Publications, 1976, p. 47.

> The British in Malaya treated the Malays very badly, as though they were aliens, while foreigners dispossessed them. They are now rid of the intrigues practised by the British, who bribed the Malay Rajahs to praise the British. The Japanese have eliminated the evils of the old system of conferring distinction on figureheads, and in its place there is nationalism and the Co-prosperity Sphere.[39]

The emergence of critical voices, the increasing responsibility of the chiefs as administrators, and the decline in stature of the rulers were all tremendously destabilising to the power of the elite *qua* traditionalistic ruling class. The first danger emerged from Japanese unwillingness to referee the plural society as the British had. Malay administrators acting as district officers found themselves for the first time in positions of authority over Chinese and Indians, as well as Malays. In these positions they were forced to carry out Japanese orders, like those recruiting labourers for the Burma–Siam 'death' railway, that left them targets of retribution by the Malayan People's Anti-Japanese Army (MPAJA), the largely non-Malay resistance force. Inevitably, they also betrayed their own communities to the demands of the occupying power. Cheah Boon Kheng has argued that the entire local Malay establishment, from district officer to *penghulu* (subdistrict chief) to *ketua kampung* (village head), was implicated in the fulfilment of rice and labour quotas.[40] All Malays in positions of responsibility, whether bureaucrats or the KMM, experienced the hostility of peasant villages in this time of upheaval and violence. Good government is always being measured by its achievements, and by that measurement, the bureaucratic elite failed as often as it succeeded. When, in early 1945, a cycle of ethnic attacks and retaliation began, only religious figures were prepared to offer any practical leadership; the bureaucrats were unable to protect their people, or themselves, from attack.

Another danger involved elite willingness to cooperate with the Japanese occupiers. The issue of Malay collaboration with the Japanese is a complicated one. On one level, the entire Malay community had an easier relationship with the Japanese than did the Chinese, who were punished for their past contributions to the Chinese war effort and their vigorous resistance to the occupation of Malaya. Malays were favoured over Chinese

[39] Extract from Monitoring Report, Penang Radio, 5 November 1942. CO 273/669/50744/7.

[40] Cheah Boon Kheng, 'The social impact of the Japanese occupation of Malaya (1942–1945)', in Alfred W. McCoy, ed., *Southeast Asia Under Japanese Occupation*, New Haven: Yale University Southeast Asia Studies, 1980, pp. 83–84.

and Indians in appointment to administrative positions and in recruitment to the *Koa Kunrenjo* (leadership training schools).[41] As mentioned above, Malay visibility in local government positions invited the accusation of collaboration from the Chinese resistance movement. And finally, it was believed by the exiled British during the war that the fifth column activities of the tiny KMM represented a more widespread 'betrayal' by the entire Malay community. Consequently, upon their return, the British made it known that the activities of all Malays in public life, from sultans to *penghulus*, would be scrutinised on suspicion of collaboration.

Alfred McCoy has suggested that 'wartime allegiance was a matter of little importance to the Southeast Asian wartime leaders'.[42] This was especially true of Malay leaders when accusations of collaboration came primarily from outside the community. According to Cheah Boon Kheng, the numerical preponderance of Malays among the MPAJA's victims, the mutilation of victims' bodies, and Chinese distrust of those Malays who did join the resistance all fostered an interclass alliance of Malays against Chinese.[43] In this context, an MPAJA or even British accusation of collaboration was meaningless, and from the Sultan of Selangor to the nationalist editors of *Seruan Rakyat*, Malays refuted the widespread charges of collaboration.[44]

Within the Malay community, however, the issue acquired some significance as postwar class politics began to take shape. When the British returned, they were intent on restoring Malaya's economic profitability. This made institutional continuity a priority and encouraged them to overlook administrative collaboration once Malay officials had been cleared of acts of betrayal leading to British deaths. Both the British and the Malay community, however, branded the KMM activists collaborators. Clearly, it was not pro-Japanese activities, but anti-British ones that defined collaboration charges after the war. The KMM's motives – using the Japanese occupation to win Malaya's independence from Britain – could not be lauded as long as colonial restoration proceeded. Yet more than 30 years after the departure of the British, the legacy of this definition survived. In

41 *Ibid.*, p. 82.

42 Alfred W. McCoy, 'Introduction', in Alfred W. McCoy, ed., *Southeast Asia Under Japanese Occupation*, New Haven: Yale University Southeast Asia Studies, 1980, p. 5.

43 Cheah, 'Social impact', p. 91.

44 The Sultan of Selangor, in a speech to *penghulus* and village heads, observed that the Japanese had given orders that people had had to obey, for fear of losing their lives or property. BMA/PR 1/7. See also 'Malaya political climate', no. 5, 1–20 December 1945. WO 203/5660.

1989 the daughter of the recently deceased wartime vice president of the KMM, Mustapha Hussain, made public his memoirs 'so that Malaysians and historians alike can judge for themselves whether my father was a hero or a Japanese collaborator'. In the memoirs, Mustapha distances himself from the KMM president, Ibrahim Yaacob, who 'always had a grand design for Malaya – he wanted a republic, but my father felt that the sole aim of KMM was to liberate Malaya from the Japanese and from any form of colonialism and imperialism'. Further, Mustapha's daughter emphasised that her father had not tortured other Malays and had, in fact, saved the lives of many highly placed Malays using special powers conferred on him by the Japanese.[45] Four decades after the war, collaboration had become a question of betraying the Malay elite. The British were not mentioned; neither was the connection between the Japanese military and the end of British colonial rule.

The significance of elite collaboration did not go completely unnoticed, however. British colonialism had prepared Malay rulers and chiefs to perform ceremonial and administrative tasks under the supervision of foreign overlords. The Japanese changed little about day-to-day administration at the local level, providing an important source of continuity which should not be overlooked amidst the violence and dislocation of the war years. Because the Japanese preserved the colonial state, and enhanced Malay positions in it, Malay bureaucrats were not to be found in the resistance. In continuing to serve, they revealed their loyalty to that state – regardless of who was at its head. This easy shift from British to Japanese rule was remarked upon by some, like the Malay who wrote to *The Straits Times* in 1946 in favour of 'cast[ing] overboard the whole cargo of worthless fossils who posed as wise owls but who hooted to the tune of any overlord'.[46]

But this was a superficial collaboration when compared to the deep, or structural, collaboration by which the traditional elite, especially the rulers, flourished under British colonial rule. When the British Military Administration (BMA) arrived in 1945, it interviewed all the rulers to ascertain whether the proper person was on each throne and to evaluate each for collaboration. In these interviews, the rulers related experiences which showed the impossibility of meaningful collaboration between the Japanese regime and traditional Malay rulers whose very identity derived from the British colonial milieu. The experience of the Yam Tuan of Negeri Sembilan is emblematic. The Japanese took away all his cars except one.

45 'A daughter's crusade for an unsung hero', *Sunday Mail* (Kuala Lumpur), 2 April 1989.

46 *Straits Times*, 4 February 1946.

They would not let him live at his *istana* for several months, and then they would not allow him to fly his flag. They forced him to attend functions at the state capital, and in attending those functions he was not allowed to have his royal umbrella-bearer with him. At all the functions he attended, he had been made to sit on the floor with the clerks. The Sultan of Johor was also forthright about his experience and seemed particularly affected by it. The Japanese took away all his European clothes and his *istana* was used as a boarding house. He had been paid nothing at first, then $8,000 per month, and then $20,000, 'which', he said, 'is the same as the British Government paid me'. These exact words were thought by the British interviewer to be 'worthy of special note' because the sultan's monthly allowance was actually paid from Johor state funds. Before the war he would never have said that the British government paid his allowance. The experience of foreign occupation had dampened the independent spirit of Ibrahim of Johor.[47]

Colonial Restoration

British troops returning to Malaya in September 1945 found that although there had not been large-scale destruction, the physical infrastructure of the country was in a serious state of disrepair. Water, electric and gas supply systems, drainage and irrigation canals, sewage systems, roads, bridges and transport would all require extensive renovation before Malaya could be brought back to prewar standards of living.[48] Public health had also suffered with increased incidence of malaria, tuberculosis and venereal disease, the breakdown of urban sanitation leading to typhoid, smallpox and cholera, and the hospitals' lack of all basic supplies to care for patients.[49] There was the great problem of recovering, caring for and repatriating 100,000 Allied prisoners of war and internees. Besides Europeans interned in camps in Malaya, there were some 10,000 Javanese in Malaya and 30,000 Malays, Chinese and Indians found on the Burma–Siam railway. Not forgetting the thousands of Japanese troops requiring repatriation, this amounted to a serious dislocation of population which would take years to correct.[50]

---

47 Intelligence Bulletin no. 33, 13 October 1945. WO 203/2155, WO 203/5635A.

48 F.S.V. Donnison, *British Military Administration in the Far East, 1943–46*, London: Her Majesty's Stationery Office, 1956, pp. 155–56, 161.

49 T.N. Harper, 'The politics of disease and disorder in post-war Malaya', *Journal of Southeast Asian Studies*, vol. 21, no. 1, 1990, p. 98.

50 Vice-Admiral the Earl Mountbatten of Burma, *Post Surrender Tasks: Section E of the Report to the Combined Chiefs of Staff by the Supreme Allied Commander South East Asia, 1943–1945*, London: Her Majesty's Stationery Office, 1969, p. v; Donnison,

But the most immediate threat to both public health and order was the severe rice shortage which was already causing widespread malnutrition.[51] The shortage of rice and other consumer goods in Malayan markets combined with a currency crisis to leave the economy in a serious state. Inflation due to the overproduction of currency and the undersupply of goods had already been a feature of life under the Japanese. As the end of the war neared, British leaflets were dropped announcing that the despised Japanese 'banana' currency would not be recognised upon reoccupation. People responded by buying up everything in sight, trying to use up the soon-to-be-worthless currency. The price of rice more than doubled from July to August 1945. Inflation rose hourly.[52]

Problems of infrastructure and the restoration of institutions like the postal service would largely be on their way to recovery by the end of the military administration in March 1946. Inflation, shortages, low wages and strikes were more intransigent, involving international food allocation and the struggle between local labour and British economic interests. In these areas, neither the BMA nor the civilian government that followed was successful in restoring the conditions of prewar society. These persistent conditions of economic instability and class (as opposed to ethnic) conflict should be understood as underlying postwar Malay politics as much as they did the growth of the Communist Party of Malaya (CPM). Like the prewar development of an urban educated class of Malays and the wartime shifts in ruling class influence, postwar instability weakened the hold of traditionalistic understandings of Malay society and directly threatened those who benefited from them.

Contributing significantly to postwar instability was a high level of crime and political violence. The complete breakdown of order which came with the British withdrawal in 1941–1942 had seen widespread looting and robber gangs preying on the population. Many of those who took advantage of the disorder were army and police officers armed with rifles, shotguns, bayonets, *kris* (daggers) and *parang* (knives).[53] Rural crime and violence – including anti-Japanese resistance – continued throughout the occupation, prompting the Japanese to respond with large-scale mobilisation of young Malay men into organisations given military training and practice.[54] During

British Military Administration, pp. 279–80.

51 Donnison, *British Military Administration*, p. 159.

52 Chin, *Malaya Upside Down*, pp. 38, 43, 181, appendix C.

53 *Ibid.*, pp. 17–24.

54 Cheah, *Red Star*, p. 33. See also ch. 6 below.

the transition back from Japanese to British rule, disorder was even more marked, with violence being committed by bandits, Malay religious cults, Chinese secret societies, communists and Kuomintang guerrillas.

By 1945 violence and militarism were common not only in connection with crime,[55] but had also become part of political life. This was partly due to the vast expansion of the 'political' in the everyday life of Malaya under the Japanese, who had inculcated militaristic mass nationalism against European colonialism in the service of Japanese interests. It was also partly due to the occupation itself – to find violence in a mass political culture under military occupation comes as no surprise. In Malaya, the occupation polarised the population into patterns of resistance or accommodation. This polarisation largely occurred along ethnic lines and, as the end of the occupation neared, erupted into clashes between Malays and Chinese.[56] As noted above, most rural Malays felt they had no stake in the communist-led MPAJA's resistance movement, which was perceived as a purely Chinese force. Malays largely tried to stay neutral or actively betrayed MPAJA camps to the Japanese.[57] Resistance forces began to react to these betrayals with attacks on Malay villages in Johor in April 1945, and Malays responded with increasingly ferocious attacks on Chinese villages. The ethnic violence culminated in horrific incidents of retaliatory mass murder committed by both sides during the interregnum between the Japanese surrender and the British landings in August and September 1945. During this time the MPAJA took over from the retreating Japanese forces in many parts of rural Malaya. In towns and villages under MPAJA control, 'collaborators' of all ethnic groups,

---

55 Violent crime, especially murder, armed robbery and kidnapping, continued to be widespread throughout the BMA period. According to statistics later compiled by the Federation of Malaya government, there were 76 incidents of murder in January 1946 alone. (These statistics do not reveal the actual number of murder victims. One incident may involve multiple deaths, as in cases of ethnic violence.) The monthly average of murder incidents for the rest of 1946 was 31. The total for 1946 was 421. The monthly average dropped in 1947 to 18, totalling 220 incidents in the year, and continued to drop in the first half of 1948 to 11 incidents per month. During the latter half of 1948, coinciding with the CPM uprising, the average shot up again to 59 incidents of murder per month. The total number of incidents involving murder in 1948 was 465. Similar patterns and higher numbers were found for armed robbery. Thus, for only a relatively brief period of time did the residents of Malaya begin to enjoy a more secure environment. Department of Public Relations, Federation of Malaya, 'Political crime in Malaya. Vigilant efforts of police', 4 February 1949. Statistics compiled by the Records Branch of the Criminal Investigation Department, Kuala Lumpur.

56 See Cheah, *Red Star*, chs. 5–8 .

57 *Ibid.*, pp. 45, 68, 70.

but especially Malay and Sikh policemen and Malay public officials, were subject to 'people's trials', which often resulted in torture and death.[58]

Several points warrant attention. First, the Malay–Chinese killings compounded the violence and dislocation prevailing when British troops landed. In Johor, for example, ethnic/political violence produced an additional 14,000 refugees.[59] Although this period represented a peak, such civic disorder had become commonplace over the past three and a half years and would not be quickly or easily reversed. Second, this period saw the identification in Malay minds of 'communist' with 'Chinese' and the rejection of both as intrinsically foreign and harmful to the Malays. Japanese propaganda had encouraged this identification, as had the use of Malay volunteer troops against Chinese guerrillas during the occupation.[60] It was at this time that the communist-led resistance lost nearly all its Malay members.[61]

Finally, in August 1945 Malays not only feared that the Chinese would take over the country, but that they would do so with British approval.[62] The British stay-behind Force 136 had worked mainly with the Chinese resistance. Malay guerrillas, numbering only about 500, were not contacted until late in 1944 because the British suspected Malay collaboration. When Admiral Louis Mountbatten became supreme allied commander, he turned the favour of the British from Kuomintang to the CPM/MPAJA guerrillas, preferring the MPAJA's Malayan outlook to the KMT's Chinese nationalism.[63]

When fighting broke out between Malays and Chinese in April, Force 136 informed Mountbatten's South East Asia Command, and in July leaflets were dropped urging people to stop fighting. The message, in Malay and English, warned that those who had 'attacked and oppressed their neighbours in accordance with the wishes of the Japanese' would be punished when the British returned.[64] This was the first intimation that the British would return without the pro-Malay attitude which had defined prewar colonialism. Other messages, both broadcast and in leaflets, contained thinly veiled political messages about the improved status of non-Malays:

---

58 *Ibid.*, p. 178–79.

59 Mountbatten, *Post Surrender Tasks*, p. 302.

60 Cheah, *Red Star*, pp. 68, 34.

61 Cheah Boon Kheng, 'Some aspects of the interregnum in Malaya', *Journal of Southeast Asian Studies*, vol. 8, no. 1, 1977, p. 70.

62 Cheah, *Red Star*, p. 225.

63 See Cheah, 'Some aspects of the interregnum'.

64 Psychological Warfare leaflet dated 20 July 1945, WO 203/4015, cited in Cheah, *Red Star*, pp. 221–22.

> It will be impossible to restore at once the prosperity that the war has destroyed, but from the moment our first ship arrives in Malaya, we can begin to rebuild together a new and better country, which will be *a real homeland for those who live in it.*[65]

The last phrase of this message would be understood by all in Malaya to signify more rights for domiciled Chinese and Indians and was understood by Malays as further evidence that the British had become 'pro-Chinese'.

British actions when they finally landed did not quieten Malay fears. Essentially powerless to stop the ethnic political violence, the British left it to the Malays to be 'united in their struggle to prevent Chinese political domination of their country'.[66] Malay leaders did little to restrain the violence that represented the protection for which the British could no longer be counted on to provide. It is important to understand the violence in this way, and not as a Japanese-inspired aberration, as the colonial government and the Malay leadership later professed publicly. Without this demonstration of ruthlessness and ferocity – Chinese casualties died by the knife and children were not spared – it is unlikely that public demonstrations later on by the reputedly 'peaceful Malays' would have been taken seriously.

Distrust between the British and Malays coloured the political atmosphere of the initial months of the restoration. Mountbatten himself observed that 'the Malays, as a community, had not in the first instance been completely hostile to the Japanese'.[67] Tales of Malay fifth column activities had been rampant following the British defeat in 1942, though most cases investigated afterwards turned out to be baseless.[68] Nevertheless, Malay morale was low following the punishment of low-level officials by the MPAJA; now British suspicion was focused on the upper levels. The removal of several Japanese-appointed rulers in the early days of the BMA reinforced the policy.[69] In retrospect, the period of suspicion appears quite brief. As noted above, the imperatives of institutional continuity and stability enabled bureaucrats to resume their positions. However, they had to make way for returning British bureaucrats – who now wore uniforms. The BMA,

---

65 Psychological Warfare leaflet (no date). WO 203/4015. Emphasis added.

66 Cheah, *Red Star*, pp. 232–40.

67 Mountbatten, *Post Surrender Tasks*, p. 301.

68 The Ashley Gibson Report, 1945, BMA/PR 1/6, concluded that the vast majority of the population was loyal and that Malay peasants could not have been expected to fight the Japanese once the British had withdrawn.

69 Cheah, *Red Star*, pp. 271–72, 276–77.

as a military administration, ruled directly, another blow to the ruling class, at least conceptually. Senior civil affairs officers[70] took the place of residents in each state and had 'direct and complete responsibility for administrative action in all fields in contra-distinction to the position occupied by British Government officials in the States prior to the Japanese invasion – especially in the Unfederated Malay States'.[71] British officials had, of course, been very powerful before the war. But their 'influence' had always been wielded within the restraint and polite fiction of a protectorate relationship of advice. Now the gloves were off. Rulers no longer received advice; state councils were suspended. The British representative was in uniform and in direct control. This was unprecedented in Anglo–Malay relations and was certainly meant to establish a new norm. In the early period of colonial restoration, these new British attitudes were perceived as serious threats by the Malay elite.[72] In dangerous times, the elite felt it could no longer count on British protection.

Political and Press Freedom under Restored Colonial Rule

The inability of the BMA to fully restore prewar society represented insecurity to some. But it also presented the opportunity of looser control over public speech and action. Making a virtue of necessity, BMA officials heeded world opinion (especially in the United States), social consciousness at home, and the political forces released by the war to encourage a fully

[70] Much of the responsibility for restoring Malaya's administrative machinery fell to the civil affairs service. Major General H.R. Hone was chief civil affairs officer (CCAO) for Malaya. Under Hone, the civil affairs service was broken into two divisions, Singapore and Malaya, both headed by a deputy chief civil affairs officer (DCCAO). The peninsular division was further subdivided into nine regions, each headed by a senior civil affairs officer (SCAO). These nine regions corresponded to state boundaries and the SCAO position was thus analogous to that of the prewar resident. Essentially, the civil affairs service was charged with recreating a civilian administrative structure, but as a military service it was unhindered by prewar constitutional restraints. In instructions given to Mountbatten by the secretary of state for war, the CCAO was clearly charged with a 'dual responsibility' for both the necessities of war and the active resumption of 'good government'. Directive from the Secretary of State for War. Reprinted in Mountbatten, *Post Surrender Tasks*, appendix I.

[71] Extracts from a directive by the supreme allied commander. Reprinted in Mountbatten, *Post Surrender Tasks*, appendix K.

[72] According to the official historian of the British Military Administration, 'the enquiries prescribed for the detection of those who had collaborated with the Japanese, and the resultant delay in making full and immediate use of recovered officials, were felt to spring from a wounding under-estimate of Malay loyalty and ability'. Donnison, *British Military Administration*, p. 156.

developed rhetoric about preparation for self-government.[73] To a colony like Malaya, whose foreign earnings would be essential to Britain's own postwar recovery, the government returned with strategies for updating the colonial social contract, which included a loosening of political control and a new concern with social welfare. T.N. Harper shows how in a 'new conception of empire', postwar policy moved from a rhetoric of protection to one of partnership, inviting local participation in voluntary organisations which were to act as a form of political advancement leading to eventual self-government.[74] It was argued that the major obstacle to self-government in Malaya was the fragmentation of the population into different polities based on ethnicity. Thus, a 'moderate' nationalism, characterised by common loyalty among the population, was to be nurtured, while 'political extremism' was discouraged.

In order to shape postwar social and political development in this way, the colonial power needed to establish legitimacy with the public and assert control over the public discourse. Not yet willing or able to undertake substantial social spending to bolster its position, the government depended on tools ranging from propaganda to censorship and repression. But in a postwar atmosphere of heightened political awareness, in which the government was likely to be reminded of the Atlantic Charter at every turn, heavy-handed repression was unacceptable. Freedom of speech and association were the order of the day. Legislation restricting societies, trade unions and the press was allowed to lapse. A newly established public relations department used propaganda to try to create an informed citizenry with Malaya-centred loyalties and civic consciousness. It was to be an 'experiment in democracy'.[75]

This policy for shaping political development in Malaya was evident from the beginning in the self-proclaimed liberal policy of Mountbatten. In a directive to the BMA, he emphasised the 'understanding and sympathy' with which the people of the country should be approached. Military rule was not to be an affair of 'absolute autocracy':

---

[73] *Ibid.*, pp. 333, 335.

[74] 'Social policy was a means by which the state attempted to equip itself for its new vocation of partnership and was a method by which a rather limited administrative system attempted to transform itself into a polity'. The fatal flaw was the attempt to separate the social from the political, which eventually came into conflict with groups which saw the social *as* political. Harper, 'Politics of disease', p. 113.

[75] *Ibid.*, pp. 100–1.

> On the contrary, it must be the policy of the Military Administration to exercise its powers and discharge its responsibilities, in so far as this may prove possible, with the co-operation and support of the local population.... The more the people themselves can be associated with the mechanism of government, the more successful and effective it will be. It is therefore my direction that a liberal and enlightened policy shall be followed by the Military Administration.[76]

Mountbatten was convinced that this was the only way to restore the public's 'confidence in British good faith, fair dealing and impartial justice'. He went further by explicitly extending this philosophy to political expression:

> The first guiding principle to be observed is that no person shall suffer on account of political opinions honestly held, whether now or in the past – even if these may have been anti-British – but only on account of previous crimes against criminal law or actions repugnant to humanity.[77]

In practice, political liberties were sometimes respected because of policy confusion and often restricted by Mountbatten's own qualifications of the policy. Early in the restoration, local residents tested the strength of the government's control over assembly. In November 1945 the Kuala Lumpur police noted that 'certain sections of the community' were disregarding the prewar enactment which required prior permission from the chief police officer for all processions and assemblies. No previous notice was being given, and there was, therefore, no opportunity to prohibit gatherings in advance. Neither were the police enforcing this enactment, for which violators could incur a fine of $100 or a six-month imprisonment. The police requested a clarification of policy, and later that month the BMA notified the public that the Processions and Assemblies Enactment would be strictly enforced.[78]

In the realm of expression, that which was deemed 'purely political' and was not critical of the BMA was most likely to be left unchallenged. This was the case when authorities allowed Indonesians in Singapore to fly the Indonesian flag, despite escalating hostility between Indonesian and Dutch refugees.[79] But expression or activities which challenged the performance of the BMA or sought fundamental political change were deemed to be an 'abuse' of 'privileges'. This attitude was crystallised with regard to strikes.

---

76 Mountbatten, *Post Surrender Tasks*, pp. 319–20.
77 *Ibid.*, p. 319.
78 BMA/DEPT 17/63.
79 BMA/ADM 8/21.

In a warning banning a general strike planned for 15 February 1946, Mountbatten outlined the government's position:

> Since it was established in Malaya more than five months ago, the British Military Administration has not only allowed but encouraged full freedom of speech and of the Press, in line with the Civil Governments of the United Nations, who fought and won a war to preserve liberties of this kind.
>
> The Administration, however, has no intention of allowing advantage to be taken of this, nor that civil disturbances should be fomented, hatred of the Administration aroused, or the just processes of the law impeded in any way.[80]

Mountbatten made a distinction between economic strikes and those with a political basis. The former were considered 'a normal democratic procedure', but the latter would not be tolerated.[81] The distinction was, of course, meaningless where the largest employer was the government and the chief organiser of labour, the CPM, was the government's only serious political rival. But, as Harper points out, the government's chief economic function before the war had been control of the migrant labour supply; losing control to the CPM represented 'the most serious kind of anarchy'.[82]

The curtailment of liberties was most clear-cut and unapologetic when applied to labour activity, but would eventually have an effect on association generally. In late January 1946 intelligence reports could not even approximate the number of societies functioning in Malaya, so rapid was their proliferation. A conservative estimate ran to several hundred, although many of these were deemed insignificant or merely branches receiving direction from a larger organisation. Nevertheless, the government no longer received notification of the names of principal officials, the number of members, or the location of headquarters. Significantly, this was perceived to be a problem in sorting out the trade unionists from the so-called 'purely political' activists, two categories which were not supposed to mix.[83]

As the BMA period neared its end, so did the experiment in democracy. Although Mountbatten would not revive repressive legislation (like banishment) during his tenure, by early March civil affairs officers began to redraft registration of societies legislation for use by the civil government. Organisations would no longer be 'legal unless declared otherwise', and

[80] Mountbatten, *Post Surrender Tasks*, p. 304.

[81] *Ibid.*, pp. 302–3.

[82] Harper, 'Politics of disease', p. 95.

[83] Fortnightly Report no. 65 (30 January 1946). WO 203/6426. Mountbatten, *Post Surrender Tasks*, pp. 303–4.

where the societies' law was ineffective, it would be backed up by sedition and banishment laws.[84]

A parallel progression from tolerance to repression can be seen in the government's relations with the vernacular press. With the encouragement of the Department of Publicity and Printing, prewar newspapers resumed publication and in an atmosphere of confusion surrounding the applicability of prewar press regulations new ones quickly joined their ranks. (Table 1 showing circulations of selected newspapers indicates the great revival of independent press activity during the BMA period.) In Singapore, the prewar paper *Utusan Melayu* resumed publication on 1 October. In Kuala Lumpur, *Perubahan Baharu* reverted to its prewar name, *Majlis*, and resumed publication on the same date.[85] In Ipoh, Ahmad Boestamam and some associates who had worked for a Japanese-sponsored paper during the occupation appropriated the English-language press (*Perak Shimbun*) to start *Suara Rakyat*, which became an organ of the Partai Kebangsaan Melayu Malaya (PKMM, Malay Nationalist Party of Malaya).[86] The opportunity of gaining control of a fully stocked printing press was only available very early in the reoccupation; soon, new publications would be forced to deal with the government because of a shortage of newsprint.

The government actually favoured the early reestablishment of the local press. An active press had several advantages. First, in the early days of reoccupation, the BMA was itself unable to produce a daily tabloid in the five or six languages necessary to reach all inhabitants of Malaya.[87] Second, monitoring of the local press allowed the department to track public opinion and political developments.[88] Third, an active press allowed the BMA to place announcements in their pages. Besides official announcements, of which the authorship was clear, publicity officials also quietly supplied press releases to editors. In February 1946, 215 items were handed out, of which 130 found their way into print. This was considered a successful way to influence public discourse in the government's favour:

[84] Minutes of SCAOs Conference, 1 March 1946. BMA/SCAO 67/46.

[85] As of 31 October 1945, there were also in publication in Kuala Lumpur two English-language papers (*Malay Mail* and *Malaya Tribune*), two Tamil papers, one Chinese paper and one Punjabi paper.

[86] Ahmad Boestamam, *Carving the Path to the Summit*, trans. William R. Roff, Athens: Ohio University Press, 1979, p. 6.

[87] Memorandum on Planning, February 1945. WO 203/4037.

[88] In January 1946, 49 newspapers and periodicals were being monitored. Report on Department of Publicity and Printing, January 1946. BMA/PR 1/8.

> As necessarily no acknowledgement of the source is made by papers when publishing material issued by this office, it is not generally appreciated how much of the content of the various papers is sponsored by this office.[89]

Table 1
Selected estimates of newspaper circulation during the British Military Administration

October 1945		January 1946	
Singapore		**Singapore**	
Utusan Melayu	2,000	*Utusan Melayu*	6,000
The Straits Times	30,000	*The Straits Times*	25,000
		Nanyang Siang Poh	40,000
Kuala Lumpur		**Kuala Lumpur**	
Majlis	[NA]	*Majlis*	2,000
Malay Mail	3,200	*Seruan Rakyat*	1,000
		Malay Mail	4,400
		Min Sheng Pau	10,000
Penang		**Penang**	
Warta Negara	500–600	*Warta Negara*	2,000
Straits Echo	5,000–6,000	*Straits Echo*	9,500
		Modern Daily News (Chinese)	10,300
Ipoh		**Ipoh**	
[NA]		*Suara Rakyat*	3,000
		Voice of the People	8,000
		Malaya Tribune	5,000

Note: Total estimated daily newspaper circulation in early 1946 was 317,000. October 1945 figures for Singapore can be found in BMA PR 2/19, and for Kuala Lumpur and Penang in BMA PR 1/8. The January 1946 figures are found in BMA PR 2/30.

[89] Report on Department of Publicity and Printing, February 1946. BMA/PR 1/8. It was felt that the British effort in Java in this regard was not as successful and as a result, the papers in Malaya reflected 'a great deal of exaggeration and distortion of news from Java'. The activities of the Netherlands Indies information services and Indonesian publicity organisations were considered responsible and British officials there were urged to give more frequent statements to the press. WO 203/4410.

This practice continued into the Malayan Union period, as recalled by the first director of public relations in his memoir: 'One day in early April [1946] I sent a copy of a four-page Kuala Lumpur paper to [Malayan Union Governor] Gent in which ninety percent of the news had been supplied by "PR".'[90]

Despite this influence, the government was very quickly irked by 'extreme' anti-BMA views appearing in left-wing publications. Why then was there no early censorship of the press? The brief answer is a shortage of resources and an assessment of what could realistically be accomplished. Given the BMA's initial inability to produce a daily newspaper in all the languages Malaya required and its consequent reliance on the local press, this planning memorandum concluded:

> I doubt whether it is a practical proposition for the editors of local newspapers to submit all their copy for censorship prior to publication. This, I believe, is not the policy which is adopted by British authorities in regards to newspaper publications, and in any case, it is doubtful whether we can provide sufficient staff to undertake the complete pre-censorship of all matter. A delay of even 12 hours in censorship would probably cripple any newspapers run on commercial lines.[91]

Another clue can be found in the political situation encountered by the British in reoccupied territories. As the BMA's 'every action [was] suspect and liable [to] misinterpretation',[92] it was hoped that the combination of propaganda and tolerance towards self-expression would convince the public of British goodwill. Clearly, given the events of the last four years and the tenor of opinion at home and in the United States, a greater range of opinion in the colonies, especially nationalism, would have to be tolerated. Further, without freedom of speech, it would be difficult to gauge public opinion, and the whole project of 'partnership' between a maturing public and an enlightened colonial government would be impossible.

But the biggest influence on BMA censorship policy was probably the supreme allied commander himself. Once there were no possible operational repercussions arising from uncensored mails or press, Mountbatten would not condone censorship on political grounds:

> We are fighting for freedom of the press, and although censorship is always necessary in war on the grounds of security, I could never agree to any

---

[90] Mubin Sheppard, *Taman Budiman: Memoirs of an Unorthodox Civil Servant*, Kuala Lumpur: Heinemann, 1979, p. 145.

[91] WO 203/4037.

[92] WO 203/4437.

> political censorship being exercised in my name, unless overridden by His Majesty's Government in a manner which would clear me on this charge.[93]

The result was a qualified freedom of the press – more lenient than before the war in its tolerance of explicitly political opinion. Nevertheless, in accordance with the BMA policy of reviving prewar legislation,[94] the public was given notice that the Printing Presses Ordinances and Enactments of the Unfederated Malay States, Federated Malay States and Straits Settlements would again be enforced. These required printing presses to be licensed and publications to be registered.[95] Notified on 11 November 1945, presses and publishers were given until 15 November to comply.

The reimposition of prewar regulations was perceived by BMA officers and the public alike as requiring publishers to receive 'permission' to produce a newspaper. However, the regulations at best allowed the government to keep track of all existing and new publications and did not in themselves afford BMA officers much actual control over what was published. In the peninsula, the relevant legislation was chapter 89 of FMS Laws 1935; it required the licensing of printing presses and the registration of publications, but did not permit the government to refuse permission to publish. The legislation of the Straits Settlements did contain an additional clause which could have facilitated such control over the press.[96] But both in Singapore and in the peninsula, where prewar legislation could have been strengthened by proclamation, the chief civil affairs officer exercised restraint in accordance with the wishes of the supreme allied commander. This was a matter of some discussion as those further down the chain of command sought clarification of government policy:

---

93 Undated memorandum from supreme commander. WO 203/4437.

94 As a military government, the BMA's authority derived from the chiefs of staff in London and was based on military necessities. However, as in all reoccupied British territories, prewar laws were revived. According to Donnison, this protected the administration from 'the charge of wielding dictatorial powers'. It also saved it 'the formidable task of building up a legal system from nothing and ensured that the law to be administered … should, fundamentally at least, be familiar … to the people living under it'. Donnison, *British Military Administration*, p. 289. In practice, however, chaotic conditions and a severe shortage of personnel made uniform enforcement of laws impossible. Thus, the revival of prewar legislation was conditional on what the CCAO considered 'practicable'.

95 Licences for printing presses would be signed by the DCCAO or the SCAO, registration of newspapers by the registrar of the Supreme Court. BMA/PR 2/1.

96 Memorandum, J.N. McHugh, Asst. Dir., Publicity and Printing, Kuala Lumpur, to HQ, Seremban, 26 January 1946. BMA/PR 2/1.

> There is no confusion between licensing of presses and the registration of papers nor under existing regulations has the Registrar power to refuse to register a newspaper. Whilst it is true that the GOC [general officer commanding, or CCAO] has extraordinary powers as you say, the legal situation at present is that use is not being made of such powers.... [P]rovided the Printing Press is registered and provided the newspaper (which includes most publications vide a definition of 'newspaper'), is registered – this department has no legal right to withhold permission to publish.[97]

Thus the parameters of official policy allowed for no political censorship, despite the legal ability of the government to impose it.

Thereafter, limitations on freedom of the press can be understood as falling informally into two categories. The first applied to publications which were deemed seditious and the second to those which were considered merely objectionable. 'Seditious' publications usually adopted a hostile attitude to the BMA early in the administration and tended to criticise the government in the following terms: the BMA did not consider the welfare of the people, did not abide by the Atlantic Charter, interfered with freedom of speech and assembly, and was determined to bring back conditions of colonial rule.[98] In response to these attacks, the government subjected these papers to harsh official action. In October *The Guardian* of Taiping was 'suspended for publishing seditious articles'.[99] In November the *Min Sheng Pau* offices in Kuala Lumpur were raided, the editor and president being detained, and *Chiu Kua Jit Poh* of Ipoh was suspended.[100] Such actions continued in early 1946, with the development of a protocol for warning and suspending newspapers:

> At the meeting of the Security Committee held yesterday it was decided that the proper way of dealing with Newspapers which publish seditious or nearly seditious matter will be to call for the Proprietor and Editor and warn them that the repetition of any such matter will result in

---

97 Excerpts from letter, J.N. McHugh to Col. J.S. Dumeresque, Publicity and Printing, Singapore, 19 December 1945. BMA/PR 2/1.

98 Cheah, *Red Star*, p. 261.

99 Fortnightly Report no. 4. CO 273/675/50822/56/3.

100 *Ibid.*, Weekly Intelligence Review no. 59. WO 203/2076. It is noted in Weekly Intelligence Review no. 60 that the *Modern Daily News* of Penang, 'which is in no way deterred by the fact that the BMA has taken strong action against newspapers in Kuala Lumpur and Ipoh, continues to publish scurrilous allegations against the BMA'. WO 203/2076.

> the suppression of the paper under Regulation 18 of the Emergency Regulations. Such warning to be confirmed in writing. If after such a warning any further objectionable matter be published, then the Newspaper should be suppressed for such period as may be considered proper in the circumstances by Order of the DCCAO [deputy chief civil affairs officer].[101]

It is not clear what made a publication fall into this category.[102] But certain characteristics of 'seditious' papers can be observed: first, a predominance of attacks on the BMA; second, communist affiliation; and third, Chinese proprietorship. CPM propaganda offered an immediate challenge to the BMA and its effort to influence public discourse. As a result, early BMA political intelligence focused almost exclusively on the Chinese and failed to delve deeply into political developments in the Malay community. This was in spite of an early understanding of the degree to which the whole country had changed in the intervening years:

> Singapore and Malaya have changed, and more than anything have changed psychologically. The people basically are the same, no doubt, but the conditions they have had to endure, the forces to which they have been subjected, have brought a new set of reactions to the forefront.[103]

Further:

> Certain sections of Malays and Chinese have become, as a result of Japanese occupation, increasingly politically conscious and articulate, and now they are permitted to organize themselves and to express their feelings freely, while talk and overstatement, some of a seditious nature, are apt to be indulged in *on the Chinese side*.[104]

This otherwise astute observer, the one who was largely responsible for the government's understanding of political change in Malaya, did not see any outward manifestations of Malay political sentiment:

> The activities of the Chinese in the political field are plain from the number of associations existing and meetings held and the spate of printed matter issuing from their presses, the slogans pasted up on the walls in every town and village. These are things that strike the attention of any observer.[105]

---

[101] Undated minute (probably February 1946). BMA/PR 2/24.

[102] Proving sedition in a court of law seems not to have been a key factor, as papers were apparently suspended without actually being prosecuted. *Ibid.*

[103] WO 203/5660.

[104] Fortnightly Report no. 4. CO 273/675/50822/56/3. Emphasis added.

[105] The author of these passages, Victor Purcell, was the principal adviser on Chinese affairs and received some criticism from Brigadier A.T. Newboult (DCCAO,

It was perhaps this focus on Chinese communist activities that caused even radical Malay newspapers to fall into the second category of publications subject to some form of censorship – those which were found to be politically objectionable, but not seditious. While not meriting suspension, they were still subject to the efforts of local officials to discourage, within policy limits, publications they deemed potentially harmful. For example, Ahmad Boestamam recalled being summoned to BMA offices almost daily to make written, though not published, apologies for *Suara Rakyat* editorials deemed 'harsh and improper'.[106]

Some use was also made of the severe shortage of newsprint to discourage publication of objectionable newspapers. The initial aim of the military administration was to have sufficient newsprint to allow for an increase over prewar circulation, as vigorous press circulation was felt to be important in counteracting Japanese propaganda.[107] But as with other commodities, newsprint was quickly in short supply and high prices continued into 1949.[108] The shortages sometimes proved to be a *de facto* means of controlling the press, because government assistance was necessary for many papers to begin publication.[109]

In October 1945 meetings between government publicity officers and press representatives were held in Singapore to discuss the newsprint situation. The government declared its intention to cooperate with the press in locating and collecting stocks of newsprint and in devising a fair system

---

Malay peninsula) for offering an unbalanced perspective. Purcell admitted that he did not know Malays well, but maintained that there was no indication of articulate political thought or activity beyond 'an amorphous mass of prejudice and suspicion', unworthy of review. See memorandum by A.T. Newboult, 22 January 1946 and Victor Purcell, 'Malaya political climate', no. 7, both in WO 203/5660. Other government officials were more familiar with the Malay community, but like Newboult, who accompanied Sir Harold MacMichael to collect the sultans' signatures on the new treaties, they were mainly concerned with pushing through the Malayan Union proposal. During the BMA, no one besides Purcell was responsible for assessing the overall political atmosphere. His early series of reports, entitled 'Malaya's Political Climate', seem to have been quite influential; his language and analysis are reflected in later local intelligence reports.

106 Ahmad Boestamam, *Carving the Path*, pp. 13–14.

107 Donnison, *British Military Administration*, p. 244.

108 CO 273/675/50822/56/2; MU 6730/47; Malayan Security Service (hereafter, MSS), Political Intelligence Journal (hereafter, PIJ), no. 13, 1947.

109 In late September, for example, the publishers of *Malaya Tribune* notified the government of its intention to resume publication and requested paper, its stocks having been lost to the Japanese. BMA/PR 2/19.

of allocation. Part of the collection process included getting possession of newsprint from those who had 'looted' it or bought it from the Japanese. But fear of losing access to newsprint led the left-wing presses to keep what 'illegally' obtained newsprint they had.[110]

To help regulate the situation, the government agreed to assist in supplying newsprint and imposed a temporary four-page limit on daily papers. '[A]nxious that the circulation of all papers should go up as high as possible' and concerned about new publications laying claim to existing stocks, the Department of Publicity and Printing also proposed a standstill on new publications until the shortage eased.[111] But the latter policy was challenged within the government and rejected on legal and political grounds. It was argued that newsprint was not a requisitioned commodity, so there was no legal basis for denying it to new publications.[112] Further, it was feared that a ban on new publications would be seen as censorship. To the Department of Publicity and Printing, benevolent moulder of public opinion, it was important that 'political considerations [not] influence the decision on the birth of a new organ'.[113]

Although newsprint never became an officially controlled commodity, the Department of Publicity and Printing remained responsible for its control and fair distribution. But despite the four-page limit which applied equally to all newspapers, not all presses enjoyed the same access to newsprint. It was clear that government presses had enough, while the most severe shortages were experienced by the independent vernacular press.[114] Pro-government, English-language papers like the *Malay Mail* were supplied with additional paper when they ran short.[115]

Being a competitor in the propaganda war, the department had difficulty maintaining the neutrality required to distribute resources 'blindly'. The temptation to use newsprint as an informal means of censorship was great,

---

[110] This situation eventually led to Newsprint Order no. 127 of 12 January 1946, which required anyone in control of newsprint to report it to the authorities and forbade removing it without written permission. This order was based on Emergency Regulations of 1939. BMA/PR 2/19.

[111] Minutes of meeting 1 October and 9 October 1945. BMA/PR 2/19. Present at the 9 October meeting were representatives of two Tamil, one Malayalam, four Chinese, two English and one Malay newspaper (*Utusan Melayu*).

[112] Memorandum from Col. Thomson, Publicity and Printing, Singapore, to CCAO, 5 October 1945. BMA/PR 2/19.

[113] Minutes of meeting, 1 October 1945. BMA/PR 2/19.

[114] Letter, 11 December 1945. BMA/PR 2/19.

[115] Letter from *Malay Mail* to BMA/Selangor, 17 December 1945. BMA/PR 2/19.

as can be seen in the experiences of two different publications. In Kelantan, the Majlis Ugama Islam wanted to resume publication of its prewar journal, *Pengasoh* (Guardian), in April 1946. The resident commissioner of Kelantan requested paper supplies from Kuala Lumpur, noting that there were currently no Malay publications in Kelantan. He also described the journal in question: it had enjoyed wide circulation before the war and was concerned only with educational, cultural and religious matters, not politics. The request for paper was approved.[116] Those who proposed a weekly magazine named *Berjuang* (Struggle) had a different experience. In January 1946 Mohamed Mustaza of the PKMM notified the Department of Publicity and Printing, Melaka, of his intention to publish, seeking 'advice and assistance'. As this was one of the cases that prompted officials to seek clarification of policy, it allows us to trace the steps taken to discourage the publication of an anti-British paper.[117]

The senior civil affairs officer, Melaka, Lieutenant Colonel Harold Luckham, informed headquarters in Seremban of Mustaza's request, including the publisher's description of the proposed magazine: a 32-page weekly to be published in *rumi* (romanised Malay), of a semi-political, literary and cultural nature, with a print run of 750. In Luckham's view, the paper would be explicitly political in nature, following the style of the PKMM's Ipoh English bi-monthly, *Voice of the People*, which advocated the union of Malaya with Indonesia. While Seremban sought clarification from Kuala Lumpur, Luckham informed Mustaza, in an interview on 6 February, that his publication was 'unnecessary'. In a letter to Seremban, he explained that the magazine would have no value except as 'propaganda' and that Mustaza had been given the justification of newsprint shortage. Luckham was challenged from both sides for this action. Mohamed Mustaza followed up his interview with a letter arguing that his publication was important 'for our nationalist cause'. He noted that Indians and Chinese were allowed to promote their nationalist causes through print and any discrimination against the Malays was 'wholly unjust and undemocratic'. If his publication was to be barred, he requested the reasons to be given in writing. At headquarters in Seremban, Major J.M. Gullick wrote to the head of the Department of Publicity and Printing asking whether refusal on the grounds of newsprint shortage was not, in fact, contrary to existing policy. Further, he asked, should permission 'be refused to an extreme Malay Nationalist publication as such?' A month after the initial refusal,

[116] Memoranda, April 1946. BMA/PR 2/1.

[117] The following discussion is based on correspondence in BMA/PR 2/1.

the PKMM representative was still pressing for permission to publish, and the policy came down from the chief secretary in Kuala Lumpur on 11 March. The Straits Settlements Ordinance that could be used to prevent publication, Sec. 6A of Cap. 38 as amended by Ord. 38 of 1939, was a war measure not currently in use. Therefore, if both the press and the publication were registered, the PKMM should be allowed to publish. But the letter concluded: 'It should be pointed out again that newsprint is in very short supply and there is no guarantee as to when a supply will be available'.

By this time, military administration and the censorship restraint of Mountbatten were drawing to a close. Mountbatten's policies had provided a window of press freedom in keeping with the new liberal, 'public relations' philosophy of colonial government, but this approach had failed to persuade Chinese communists and Malay nationalists to welcome the restoration of British colonial rule. Those who were responsible for long-term policy in Malaya were as eager to bring back stringent press regulations as they were to reintroduce the registration of societies. The Straits Settlements Ordinance referred to above, a war measure used in the crackdown on radicals before the Japanese invasion, was reimposed with the resumption of civil government on 1 April 1946.

The ordinance required publishers in Singapore to obtain a special permit or licence to print a newspaper (which could be refused), in addition to registering the press and paper. In the peninsula as well, press regulations were given more teeth and permission could be refused at any stage, from the setting up of a printing press to the publication of a specific newspaper.[118] However, the censors did not refuse permission to every publication of a political or nationalist nature. The conservative, but political, Penang daily, *Warta Negara*, was praised for being 'excellently balanced' and incurred no censorship. *Semboyan Baharu*, a radical Penang weekly, was also permitted to continue despite its publisher's membership of the PKMM and the $500 the publication received from the CPM. This decision may have reflected a careful balancing – on the one hand, the willingness to apply censorship where deemed necessary, and on the other, an evaluation of the journal's potential impact:

[118] For example, the application of one Wu Kherk of Kuantan to start a printing press was denied in April 1946. The grounds were 'that Wu Kherk was not a suitable person to be given a licence', given his connections with the local Communist Party of Malaya. His appeal, argued on the basis of British justice and the fact that no charges had been made against him, was rejected without comment the following month. MU 521/46.

> This journal is critical of the Sultans and the British.... [B]ecause of its criticism of the Sultans and its affinity with the MCP, its influence with Malays is not considered to be great.[119]

Nevertheless, all publications were now subject to scrutiny and suspension at the government's pleasure. Thereafter, the permitted parameters of legitimate political discourse would again be defined explicitly in the interests of imperial preservation.

*

This chapter has argued that in the 1930s and 1940s, those invested in traditionalism as a way of surviving British colonial rule experienced a succession of challenges to their position. Education, urbanisation (limited though it was) and growing awareness of the size and strength of the Chinese community in Malaya before the war produced urgent criticism of Malay backwardness and calls for more education and more representation in the administration of the states. Many of these calls came from members of the aristocracy whose bureaucratic positions made them the embodiment of progress in the Malay community. At the same time, traditionalistic prohibitions on political activity muffled critiques of colonial rule and the Malay ruling class itself. Despite these pressures for change, the British and most of the ruling class worked to preserve a mutually beneficial construction of traditional Malay society. There matters stood as long as the colonial order favoured tradition and rewarded the coordinated efforts of the two segments of the ruling class.

When colonial order broke down, the interests of rulers and chiefs began to diverge. Under the Japanese occupation, Malay bureaucrats experienced both opportunities and dangers from which they had been shielded under British rule. The Malay rulers' experience was less ambiguous; deprived of the allowances and material accoutrements which defined their ceremonial status, the rulers ceased to represent the Malay nature of their polities. Deprived of British protection from Japanese indignities, the rulers were truly glad to welcome the colonial power back to Malaya. But both rulers and chiefs quickly discovered that the old order had not truly returned. The British investigated all highly placed Malays on suspicion of collaboration and, in the face of calamitous Malay–Chinese violence precipitated by the waning of Japanese power, revealed the end of their prewar pro-Malay policies.

---

[119] Extract from Malayan Security Service, Penang, 15 May 1946. MU 521/46, vol. II.

Recognising that nationalist aspirations could no longer be simply suppressed, the colonial power also experimented with loosening controls over 'moderate' political activity and expression. As discussed in the next chapter, this new policy opened a floodgate of criticism against the Malay ruling class. But it also exposed the British Military Administration to an escalating challenge from communist-organised labour and a critical left-wing press. Unable to control the public discourse through its own propaganda alone, the British government reintroduced restrictive legislation controlling association, labour and the press. Despite the experiment with liberal policies, the apparatus for the coercive restoration of the old order had been in place from the beginning of reoccupation. It was reactivated at the end of military rule, was deployed selectively for two years, and would later be fully engaged with the counterinsurgency against the CPM beginning in June 1948. This study turns now to the public discourse of the years 1945 to 1947, which operated within the parameters of imperial preservation described above, parameters which gave the ruling class renewed hope of establishing hegemony over postwar Malay society.

Chapter Five

Aristocratic Ascendancy and the Use of Tradition

The interruption of British colonial power in 1942 abruptly suspended the articulation of traditionalistic Malay culture. The loss of colonial protection, the conditions of Japanese occupation and the new legitimacy of nationalism combined to prevent a simple restoration of that culture after the war. One of the most significant changes was that 'politics' was no longer the preserve of Malay royalty, an elite arena for wringing concessions from the colonial power. Postwar politics was an activity which took new forms – no longer merely bureaucratic, but violent, massive and theatrical. The new politics, an activity which would define the Malays' standing in the postwar world, will be discussed in detail in the next chapter. The connection this new politics had with the politics of the Malay past and with colonial traditionalism is the focus of this chapter.

There were many novel things about postwar politics, the newest being the construction of a new participant, 'the Malay people'. Yet the dominant actors were still those belonging to the ruling class, giving postwar politics, for all its novelty, a strong thread of continuity with the precolonial past: the removal of British backing for rulers would allow chiefs to rebound, acknowledging the rulers' status while competing with them for access to wealth and power. Yet this element of continuity, when examined, also reveals the ongoing significance of colonial constructs of Malay tradition.

Before the war, the use of both rulers and chiefs by the colonial administration had served to legitimise and stabilise colonial rule, but at the same time created rifts within the ruling class. The imperial glorification of the sultans and their heavy investment in tradition set royalty apart from aristocracy, which sought qualifications in the competing idiom of good government. From the rulers' perspective, the elaboration of the ceremonial raja was an outgrowth of past tradition and of benefit to them personally in the new colonial order. To the chiefs, the process was disinheriting, for despite their eventual compensation in federal and state bureaucracies, a gulf in status, wealth and meaning was created. Colonial rule stratified the Malay ruling class and the competition that reemerged was between groups positioned very differently vis-à-vis the challenges of the postwar period.

Political and ethnic violence from the middle of 1945 was the first challenge. It was followed shortly by postwar constitutional changes which aimed to centralise political power in Kuala Lumpur and create a common Malayan Union citizenship, simultaneously erasing the rulers' sovereign status, the chiefs' source of power in state bureaucracies and Malay special privilege as a whole. Finally, a radical nationalist movement, nurtured by the occupation, now organised and published its views with fewer restrictions than in the prewar period. I will argue here that an important aspect of the aristocratic elite's response to these threats was the manipulation of ideas of tradition and progress to create a late, and eventually, postcolonial political arena which retained a privileged place for itself. The inefficacy of traditional leadership in the period from 1942 to 1945 had problematised Malay tradition, bringing the question of its relevance in a changing world to the point of crisis. As the bureaucrats had undoubtedly performed better during the war than the ceremonial rulers, this crisis gave the aristocracy an opening to emphasise its own qualifications to lead Malays into the future. At the same time, the threat of Malay radicalism encouraged this elite not to destroy the legitimacy of tradition altogether, but to create yet another version of tradition in which it could assert its power over its rivals. With the focus of public discourse on the status of the Malay rulers and the formal loss of their sovereignty, the preservation of tradition was linked to the very survival of the Malays in the modern world. And the Malay aristocracy was able to exploit its good government credentials to gain control over the meaning and utility of the Malay rulers from the British.

In the following pages, I first review the Malayan Union proposals and the course of the political contest between mobilised Malays and the British government. I then examine in more detail the postwar discourse through which the Malay rulers were reinvented for the postcolonial nation. This discussion focuses on the manipulation of certain concepts – protection, progress and loyalty – which took place in a series of overlapping discourses in the Malay and English press.

The Malayan Union Struggle

During the war, British planners in London took advantage of what was considered to be a clean slate to draft proposals for a centralised colonial state with a common citizenship. Eager to eliminate the administrative inefficiencies of the prewar structures, the British were also under considerable pressure from the United States to move towards self-government and eventual independence for their colonial possessions. The Malayan Union proposals were meant to solve both problems. By replacing indirect rule with centralised British control, Malaya could quickly be returned to economic profitability. Politically, the creation of a common citizenship was meant to open up government positions to the Chinese, in recognition of their economic contribution and resistance against the Japanese, and to create a 'Malayan' public to take the place of the prewar Malay, Chinese and Indian publics with their varying levels of political consciousness and geographical orientations. It was this new Malayan identity which the government hoped would find expression in the postwar atmosphere of relaxed political and press control, and which it hoped to prepare for eventual self-government through the granting of Malayan Union citizenship. In order to establish the new constitutional arrangement, the British quickly signed new treaties with the Malay rulers of the peninsular states, in which the rulers ceded jurisdiction to the British crown, and in January 1946 made the Malayan Union proposals public.

These two fundamental changes – Chinese citizenship and the loss of the rulers' sovereignty – were quickly perceived by Malays to constitute major threats to their community and became the rallying points of the anti-Union campaign that eventually succeeded in reversing British policy. As the instigation for the first mass political movement by Malays and for the founding of Malaysia's future ruling party, the United Malays National Organisation (UMNO), the anti-Malayan Union campaign has earned a place as the central 'struggle' of postwar Malay nationalism, both in popular conception and in the academic literature.[1] From the perspective of prewar critiques of the plural society, however, this judgement is questionable. Far

[1] Two academic studies which make the present work possible are James de Vere Allen, *The Malayan Union*, New Haven: Yale University Southeast Asian Studies, 1967 and A.J. Stockwell, *British Policy and Malay Politics During the Malayan Union Experiment, 1945–46*, Kuala Lumpur: Malaysian Branch of the Royal Asiatic Society, Monograph no. 8, 1979. Another treatment is Albert Lau, *The Malayan Union Controversy, 1942–1948*, Singapore: Oxford University Press, 1991. The rulers' position under the Malayan Union is also discussed in Ariffin Omar, *Bangsa Melayu: Malay Concepts of Democracy and Community, 1945–1950*, Kuala Lumpur: Oxford University Press, 1993 and Simon C. Smith, *British Relations with the Malay Rulers from Decentralization to Malayan Independence, 1930–1957*, Kuala Lumpur: Oxford University Press, 1995.

from turning back the challenge of foreign demands for representation, the Malay leadership eventually agreed to limited Chinese and Indian citizenship rights under the subsequent Federation of Malaya Agreement and even broader rights when the federation achieved independence in 1957. The Malay mobilisation did succeed in restoring the sovereignty of the Malay rulers, however, and that is the reason the struggle is accorded such stature in the national mythology. It provided the arena in which modern Malay political practices were defined and political leadership over the postcolonial nation won. This involved ideological struggle within the Malay community which was far more significant to the future of the country than the brief victory over British constitutional proposals.

The remainder of this section provides a brief chronology of the Malayan Union crisis, from the first months of the British reoccupation to the inauguration of the Federation of Malaya. The period from September to December 1945 was one of uncertainty for the Malay ruling class, consolidation for the colonial regime and opportunity for Malay nationalists. The latter formed the Partai Kebangsaan Melayu Malaya (PKMM, Malay Nationalist Party of Malaya) in October in Ipoh, Perak. While it did not immediately achieve a national presence, it began organising in several states and published newspapers in both English and Malay. Meanwhile the British envoy Sir Harold MacMichael travelled from state to state signing new treaties with the Malay rulers. The public did not yet know that the rulers had signed their sovereign status and that of their states over to the British crown, but they were nevertheless criticised for signing new treaties without consulting 'the people'. During this time rumours about the Malayan Union were circulating, evoking reactions ranging from cautious optimism to outright opposition.

In January 1946 the British government released details of the Malayan Union proposals and the content of the new treaties. The groundswell of Malay opinion against both the rulers and the British increased. In the following two months, prewar elite state-based associations reestablished themselves, and their newspapers (as well as the PKMM's) furiously debated the proper response to the situation. These associations took united action with the Pan-Malaya Malay Congress which met in early March. The congress supported the restoration of the rulers, rejected the Malayan Union proposals and endorsed the widespread political demonstrations that had been occurring in the states since December. The congress, like its successor UMNO (established in May), was an umbrella organisation. At first UMNO included the PKMM and other left-leaning groups, but they were outnumbered by the conservatives, a situation which led to their departure by June. By early 1946 the PKMM had developed enough of a following to concern the British who welcomed the appearance of UMNO, despite its opposition to the Union, as a conservative counterbalance to the nationalist party.

On 1 April the British Military Administration handed over to civilian government – the Malayan Union. The Malay rulers boycotted the Malayan Union installation ceremonies at the urging of the UMNO leader Dato Onn bin Jaafar and Malay opinion was consolidated against the Union. The rulers all renounced the treaties and retired British officials, including Frank Swettenham, mounted an attack in London. The following month, the British MPs L.D. Gammans and David Rees-Williams conducted an informal parliamentary mission and were greeted by huge demonstrations coordinated by UMNO. The governor of the Malayan Union, Sir Edward Gent, one of its architects, had by this time been persuaded that the Union was a mistake. Shortly afterwards, once Gent's opinion had been endorsed by Governor General Malcolm MacDonald, the British government agreed to negotiate with the Malays.

Onn went on a triumphal pan-Malaya tour following the announcement of the Malay victory, but from June to November 1946, while UMNO and the rulers conducted secret negotiations with the British, UMNO suffered a loss of public momentum. This was exploited by the PKMM, as well as by the Chinese and Indian communities. The latter had earlier been indifferent to the Malayan Union because it did not include a timetable for elections or independence; they were now outraged at being locked out of the process of deciding the future of the country. In December 1946 draft constitutional proposals for the Federation of Malaya were published. The federation would restore the rulers' sovereignty, the individuality of the Malay states and Malay special position, while granting limited citizenship to the foreign communities and providing an effective central government.[2] Anti-federation opinion mounted during the following year among nationalist Malays, moderate Chinese and Indians, and the Communist Party of Malaya (CPM). It was during this time that the nationalist Malays, in the umbrella organisation Pusat Tenaga Rakyat (PUTERA), pursued an alliance with the non-Malay left-wing All-Malaya Council for Joint Action (AMCJA). Against UMNO's wishes, the British sought opinions from the country at large, especially the non-Malay communities, through a consultative committee. The AMCJA/PUTERA boycotted the committee and Malays were forbidden by UMNO to give their opinions through this forum, on the grounds

[2] Stockwell, *British Policy and Malay Politics*, p. 92.

that UMNO had already represented their views. Nevertheless, 15 Malay organisations and individuals testified, as well as many non-Malays.

In July 1947 the revised constitutional proposals, substantially the same as the draft proposals, were published. The secret negotiations and long delay had hurt UMNO's credibility and the nationalist groups had gained in popularity. In October the nationalist Malay opposition joined with that of other communities in opposing the federation, an action that culminated in a one-day *hartal* (strike). In February 1948 the Federation of Malaya was inaugurated. The following June, counterinsurgency measures began against the CPM, which had taken its struggle underground. During the so-called Emergency (1948–1960), progressive organisations and publications in all the communities were banned.

Rulers and Chiefs in the Malayan Union Struggle

Rather than reviving the status quo, the end of the occupation and the return of the British to Malaya had only increased the problems of the Malay ruling class. The effect of the Malayan Union on the rulers was most devastating. In order to put the new constitution into effect, the whole basis of British power in Malaya had to be changed legally. Turning its back on indirect rule and the enabling fiction of sovereign Malay states under British protection, the colonial power, through its emissary MacMichael, bluntly demanded 'full power and jurisdiction' in each state. As noted in the previous chapter, the rulers had expressed almost uniform pleasure at seeing the return of the British. The exceptions were those sultans who had been appointed to their positions by the Japanese, through either the death or deposition of their British-appointed predecessors. These rulers were promptly deposed or voluntarily stepped down. All the rulers were made to understand, in interviews immediately following British reoccupation, that their actions during the war would be examined for collaboration and only when the British were satisfied with their conduct would they be confirmed in their positions. MacMichael's mission was, in practice, the final stage of the examination and the rulers were essentially coerced into signing the treaties relinquishing sovereignty to the British crown. There was no room, or time, for negotiation. No opportunity was given them in MacMichael's two- to four-day visits to consult with their suspended state councils, which had the effect of isolating the rulers from the more legally minded bureaucrats who would certainly have raised constitutional objections. They all signed. The returning British administration, following the new policy devised in London, considered the rulers symbolic, archaic and, although partly British creations, now inconvenient and dispensable.

The rulers' compliance with the new treaties elicited an unprecedented level of public criticism, which is discussed in some detail below. MacMichael's journey through the Malay courts in late 1945 was publicly followed and the acquiescence of the rulers presumed, though the contents of the treaties were still secret. Nevertheless, the citizenship provisions of the Malayan Union had been hinted at as early as July, and the rulers' presumed agreement to them began to elicit public criticism in December. When the White Paper on the Malayan Union was published on 22 January 1946, it became known that the rulers had also agreed to transfer sovereignty of their states to the British crown. Very quickly, the outrage expressed in all sections of the Malay press demonstrated that the prewar barrier protecting the rulers from criticism would not be reinstated. The British and Malays alike professed shock at the vehemence of feeling that was expressed and the moment has justifiably been remembered as an important one in modern Malay history. It should, however, be clear by now that it was not, as it seemed, a purely traditional taboo that fell. Indeed, precolonial society could not have imagined a 'letter to the editor'. The articulation of criticism must be understood as arising, in the first instance, from the changes in Malay society outlined in chapter four, and more immediately, from the failure of British authority which left the traditional rulers to their fate.

The Malayan Union threatened the bureaucratic elite as well, in ways that corresponded exactly to the dual basis of their authority in Malay society. First, the prospect of a centralised administration and competition from non-Malay citizens threatened the bureaucrats' vested interests in the state and federal bureaucracies.[3] Chinese political violence was already immediately endangering; now the Chinese threatened to pose a long-term political challenge to the Malay elite as well. Second, the downgrading of the rulers would deprive the aristocracy of the legitimising power of traditionalism. This was a serious blow at precisely the moment a rival leadership, radical and nationalist, was emerging. Japanese toleration of Malay nationalist rhetoric and sponsorship of anticolonial organisations had given birth to postwar party politics. Before the Malay ruling class had found its political bearings in the postwar arena, elements of the old Kesatuan Melayu Muda (KMM, Young Malays Union) had reassembled themselves into the PKMM. By December 1945 the PKMM had already held a national congress.

---

[3] *Ibid.*, pp. 80–84.

Of these two threats to the bureaucratic elite, an expanded citizenship was the more direct danger. In fact, it was arguably of more importance to Malay society as a whole and what the anti-Malayan Union struggle was actually about.[4] Yet much more was written in Malay newspapers about the attack on traditional leadership. This was because the threat posed by Chinese and Indian immigrants was seemingly clear and unproblematic, having been the centre of public discourse throughout the 1930s. Nearly everyone in Malay society, whether peasant, labourer or bureaucrat, agreed on that threat. The leadership issue, however, was far from transparent and could represent different things depending on one's class and political status. The British action signalled a change in the way traditional authority would be constituted. It also released the Malay rulers from the meaning they had embodied in the imperial hierarchy – short-sighted though this was in terms of colonial restoration – and thus freed them to acquire new meaning in Malay society. As such it presented an opportunity to whoever could gain control of both the rulers and the discourse surrounding their evolving meaning. It was in this context that the potential cleavages within the Malay ruling class were finally actualised.

Before the war, the Malay bureaucratic elite had participated in a coherent body of tradition. The ruling class was kept whole by commonality of experience and interest. The overlap in experience occurred mainly in the realm of ascriptive status and privilege, but also in the realm of bureaucracy, when, for example, a ruler served in the Malay administrative service before being elevated to the sultanate.[5] It was also in the interest of the two segments of the ruling class to cooperate in order to win concessions from the colonial system and to maintain their status in Malay society at the expense of both peasants and a slowly growing urban class. Potential cleavages remained latent, but their potential was visible in the tension between tradition, or the legitimation conferred by the past and progress, or the utility of bureaucratic competence in the modern world. Before the war, the bureaucrats were completely routed by the legitimacy the British vested in royalty as a symbol of a purportedly unchanging and conservative society. Neither could the bureaucracy's lifestyle, as emblematic of progress, rival that of the rulers. The accoutrements of the Malay royalty – steamships, motor cars and golf – were supremely modern; it was their unassailable place in society, used for colonial purposes, which had become archaic.

4 Interview with A. Samad Ismail. See also *Pelita Malaya*, 26 April 1946.

5 Tuanku Abdul Rahman of Negeri Sembilan, for example, who would become the first king (Yang di-Pertuan Agong) of independent Malaya, was a district officer in the 1920s and 1930s.

During the Malayan Union crisis, the bureaucratised aristocracy exploited this archaism to manipulate tradition to its advantage. For the first time, Malay traditionalists differentiated between vital and harmful tradition. In this new articulation, only the restoration of the rulers to their traditional (i.e. prewar) status could guarantee the continued existence of the *bangsa Melayu* (Malay race). This formulation also meant, though, that Malays could not survive in the modern world without tradition, specifically one which privileged certain members of society over others. The aristocratic defence of the rulers' status should be understood essentially as a new round of traditionalism aimed at preserving the ruling class as a whole, rather than as an anticolonial or nationalist response.

The bureaucratic elite found at the same time, however, that it could differentiate itself from the rulers on the basis of modernity and progress. To further this end, its press organs, *Majlis* and *Warta Negara*, characterised 'blind loyalty' as a harmful tradition, one out of step with modern ideals. They participated in, even led, the widespread criticism of the rulers' behaviour. For a short time, discourse in nationalist and conservative papers was indistinguishable on this topic. Radical papers even cited *Majlis* editorials on the rulers, showing that the bureaucratic elite played an important role in validating this violation of tradition. The radical and conservative papers would part, however, when the conservatives successfully labelled further violations as traitorous.

In the following sections, I discuss the bureaucratic elite, its actions and its press organs, as the author at the centre of political discourse, because its recasting of tradition has proved to be a vital component of postwar Malay politics. (Even then, it will be clear that ideas expressed in the radical press, also discussed here, provided much of the tension necessary to this achievement.) But the audience addressed was not constant. The focus of discourse changed as the intended audience shifted among the British authorities, the rulers themselves and a newly constructed Malay political public. Arguments meant to resonate with a British audience mainly sought to reassert the terms of the original treaties and emphasise the idea of protection, while the struggle for supremacy between rulers and aristocracy, as well as the aristocracy's effort to legitimise itself to the general public, revolved around conceptions of progress, loyalty and the people.

The Crisis of Protection

It was crucial to the conservative agenda that the violation represented by overt criticism of the rulers be justified by appeal to another tradition

– the idea that the rulers owed their subjects protection and had failed them. The aristocrats' appropriation of the role of protector, on the basis of this purported failure, was first analysed by Chandra Muzaffar.[6] The appropriation was an important step in the legitimation of the aristocrats as modern political leaders in the eyes of both the British and the Malay public. In this section, I argue that the tradition of protection, by 1945, in fact owed its relevance almost entirely to colonial traditionalism and that it was its very embeddedness in the colonial relationship that made it useful for the bureaucratic elite.

In his discussion of protection and loyalty in Malay society, Chandra Muzaffar argues that in precolonial society, 'the Sultans were seen as the ultimate protectors' and that in the colonial period, the British successfully projected an image of themselves as 'assisting in the protection of the community'. According to Chandra, when the rulers appeared to have 'failed to protect the position of the Malays' by signing the MacMichael treaties in 1945, the bureaucratic elite was able to gain predominance 'as protectors in the feudal tradition'.[7] While this account rightly interprets postwar bureaucratic ascendancy as an appropriation of tradition, I believe it incorrectly traces the lineage of protection. The protection that the aristocracy claimed to provide during the Malayan Union crisis did not derive from classical tradition, but rather from that version of Malay tradition which served colonial power.

One does encounter in classical literature the occasional royal injunction to 'protect the *rakyat* [subjects]'.[8] But by all accounts, the dominant terms of the ruler–ruled discourse were loyalty and treason, justice and injustice. Chandra himself, in his discussion of the Melaka period, focuses exclusively on loyalty, and the pact he discusses in the *Sejarah Melayu* between ruler and subject does not even mention protection.[9] Even more telling, perhaps, are Malay proverbs, the only window we have on what ordinary Malay peasants may have thought. These sayings reflect not a positive feeling of loyalty, but merely the unopposable power of the ruling class – 'whoever

6 Chandra Muzaffar, *Protector? An Analysis of the Concept and Practice of Loyalty in Leader-led Relationships within Malay Society*, Penang: Aliran, 1979.

7 *Ibid.*, pp. 62–63.

8 *Misa Melayu*, cited in Barbara Watson Andaya, 'The nature of the state in eighteenth century Perak', in Anthony Reid and Lance Castles, eds, *Pre-Colonial State Systems in Southeast Asia*, Kuala Lumpur: Malaysian Branch of the Royal Asiatic Society, Monograph no. 6, 1975, p. 23.

9 Chandra, *Protector?*, pp. 1–32, especially 3–4.

may be raja, my hand goes up to my forehead all the same'[10] – and the danger it posed to ordinary people – 'when elephants fight, the mousedeer dies in the middle'.[11]

In fact, the idea of protection had always been more relevant as a link between 'international' relations and a ruler's position within Malay society. Gaining the protection of a larger, outside power had a long precedent in Malay history. Before the British, the protecting powers were China and Siam. In the fifth and sixth centuries, Malay rajas became vassals of China, participating in the tribute trade in order 'to amass wealth as a means of asserting their authority in the fragmented and restless Malay society'.[12] This was true even of Melaka at a time when 'submission to China was valued in South East Asia because it implied equality among the South East Asian rulers' and helped preserve Melaka's independence from Java.[13] The fact of such vassalage was often obscured, as in the *Sejarah Melayu*, but real nonetheless:

> The compiler of the *Sejarah Melayu*, referring to Malacca in the fifteenth century, was embarrassed by the notion that the Sultans were subordinate to China and was at pains to disprove it. Nevertheless, formal admission of vassal status, because of the great rewards from the China trade, was part of Malay history.[14]

The terms of such a relationship, though formally that of suzerain and vassal, accommodated some flexibility in practice. For example, early in the fifteenth century, the Chinese emperor was powerful and actually offered protection to Melaka. At other times, the tribute was offered simply as a pretext to gain the economic advantage of trade. With a less remote suzerain, the terms required more delicate manipulation. The triennial gift of *bunga mas dan perak* (gold and silver flowers) from the northern Malay states to Siam was variously interpreted as a sign of vassalage or friendship. According to the *Merong Mahawangsa* (Kedah Annals), the *bunga mas* was a gift, sent voluntarily to secure the protection of a more powerful, but essentially equal, fellow monarch.[15] The Siamese view, explained to Henry

---

[10] *Ibid.*, pp. 18–20.

[11] Jomo Kwame Sundaram, *A Question of Class: Capital, the State, and Uneven Development in Malaya*, New York: Monthly Review Press, 1988, pp. 31–32, 32n77.

[12] O.W. Wolters, *The Fall of Srivijaya in Malay History*, Kuala Lumpur: Oxford University Press, 1970, p. 37.

[13] *Ibid.*, p. 155.

[14] *Ibid.*, p. 40.

[15] James Low, trans., *Merong Mahawangsa* (The Keddah Annals), Bangkok: The American Presbyterian Mission Press, 1908, pp. 253–55.

Burney in 1826, interpreted the same components – *bunga mas*, protection, good relations – as required tribute and Siamese kindness.[16] The vassal's interpretation was not mere wishful thinking; Malay monarchs preserved their sovereignty in important ways. One of these was avoiding the trip to Bangkok to be confirmed in office and do personal obeisance before the Siamese monarch. Such summonses were evaded by feigning sickness or sending a royal representative. Other evasions were variously successful, depending on the waxing and waning of Siamese power.

By the eighteenth century European powers were participating in this system, which ordered not only interstate and trade relations but also affected ruling class rivalries within states. In Perak, for example, the ruler's alliance with the Dutch East India Company, to whom he granted a tin monopoly, allowed him to concentrate economic and political power vis-à-vis his chiefs.[17] Less successfully, Malay states like Kedah began to appeal to the protection of a third party – the British – to counter Siamese demands.

It is useful at this point to summarise the status of 'protection' in the Malay world on the eve of British intervention on the peninsula. In accordance with traditional Southeast Asian politics, protection from outside powers had often been actively sought by rival factions to strengthen their internal position. In a situation where the suzerain's power was constantly expanding and contracting, vassalage, whether sought or imposed, could be a flexible condition. Protecting powers included other Malay rulers, Chinese, Siamese and Europeans. Although many of these powers were culturally foreign, their relationship with Malay political authority was often incorporated into Malay cultural expression, serving to domesticate the relationship. The presence of Siamese royalty as brother monarchs in Kedah's *Merong Mahawangsa*, for example, both legitimises Siam's domination and the Malay ruler's acquiescence and defines the relationship in Malay terms, providing criteria for rebellion if necessary.[18] Can this experience be taken as a model for the way Malay rulers sought to deal with the British? Like the Siamese, the British were militarily dominant and could not be ignored, but they were potentially useful as allies, i.e. protectors, against Siamese encroachment. In fact, the rulers of both Kelantan (1822) and Terengganu

---

16 Burney was the military secretary in Penang who negotiated the Anglo–Siamese Treaty of 1826 which recognised Siamese suzerainty over Kedah and British protection over Perak and Selangor. Henry Burney, *The Burney Papers*, Farnborough: Gregg International Publishers, 1971, repr. of 1910–1913 ed., p. 227.

17 Andaya, 'Nature of the state', p. 26.

18 Low, *Merong Mahawangsa*, pp. 253–55.

(1869) tried to gain the formal protection of Britain years before they were transferred, without consultation, from Siamese to British control.[19]

Over the course of the nineteenth century, however, there was a qualitative change in the nature of protectorate relationships. Administrative modernisation made the Siamese presence constant and more intrusive, while Britain pursued increasingly defined relationships through treaties. These treaties grounded British power in protectorate agreements with sovereign rulers – the enabling fiction of indirect rule. The extent of British power, which remade the face of much of the Malay peninsula economically and demographically, is evident and in striking contrast with earlier protectorates. Yet despite the tightening of the terms of protection, Malay monarchs retained the presumption of sovereignty. This was illustrated most dramatically in Sultan Abu Bakar's independent relationship with Queen Victoria and his successful legal argument in 1894 that, as an independent sovereign, he could not be sued in British courts.[20] More generally, the Unfederated Malay States used rulers' sovereignty to delay the posting of British residents and to resist incorporation into the FMS. Even in the federated states, where colonial power was strongest, the Malay ruling class found some manoeuvring room in the manipulation of British commitment to the concepts of protection and indirect rule. This can be seen most clearly in the maintenance of what was construed as traditional Malay society. Thus, because it enabled the ruling class to perpetuate privilege and wring concessions from the British, the idea of protection retained relevance before the war.

The biggest change in the experience of protection in the colonial period was the growing relevance of the idea within Malay society. It is not surprising that one aspect of traditionalism should have been the arrogation by the ruler of the status of protector. The most powerful justifications for authority in this period came from the colonial power, which described itself as a protectorate. And colonial rule itself introduced new elements into the Malay world from which Malays saw themselves in need of protection, notably the unprecedented scale of immigration. There was, then, in addition to the conventional idea of protection from outside attack, a new aspect – the protection of Malay society as a whole from the changes occurring around them. The apotheosis of the rulers was a manifestation of

---

19 Barbara Watson Andaya and Leonard Y. Andaya, *A History of Malaysia*, London: Macmillan, 1982, pp. 117, 121–22.

20 Rupert Emerson, *Malaysia: A Study in Direct and Indirect Rule*, New York: Macmillan, 1937, pp. 199–202.

this protection, as was the reservation of government service positions to the Malays. The rulers were not, in fact, protectors, but protected.

During the 1930s awareness of their disadvantaged status vis-à-vis immigrants became widespread in educated Malay society, and the contradiction between the British as protectors of the Malays and as constructors of the plural society became unavoidable. Ishak Haji Muhammad, a Malay administrative dropout, began to develop a critique of British protection which called attention to Malay royalty's role in the charade:

> The British, who steer the administration of the Malay States, have placed them under the protection of a flimsy yellow silk umbrella. When it rains, they get soaked, and when the sun beats down, they shrivel up in the heat.[21]

At the same time, less iconoclastic thinkers continued to press the British to honour the terms of the agreement. Abdul Rahim Kajai is best remembered for honing distinctions within Malay society between *Melayu jati* (true Malays) and those of Arab and Indian descent. Here he reminds immigrant Asians and the British that the colonial power is obligated only to the Malays:

> If they're still dissatisfied, the government can inform these foreigners that the 'protection' of the Malays isn't like the protection of the deer in the forest by the game warden, who sees to it that the deer isn't killed by hunters but allows it to be preyed upon by other enemies such as the tiger.[22]

The experience of Japanese invasion and occupation, ethnic violence and British reoccupation with plans for Malayan citizenship wiped out any illusions that Malay society was under effective protection, by the British or by the rulers. The British had, in the first instance, failed to provide the most basic kind of protection, forcing them eventually to dismiss accusations of large-scale fifth column activity on the part of the Malay peasantry:

> It should be remembered that their attitude, as typical peasants and landowners who had been discouraged as a matter of policy from warlike activity over a long period, was largely influenced by the fact that, as the British withdrew and could offer no protection they had to make the best

21 The yellow silk umbrella is a symbol of Malay royalty. *Warta Ahad*, 28 November 1937, quoted in Abdul Latiff Abu Bakar, *Ishak Haji Muhammad: Penulis dan Ahli Politik Sehingga 1948*, Kuala Lumpur: University of Malaya Press, 1977, p. 62.

22 *Majlis*, 4 January 1932, quoted in William R. Roff, *The Origins of Malay Nationalism*, Kuala Lumpur: University of Malaya Press, 1980, p. 171.

> of a bad job with the Japanese. It could not be expected that they would actively fight the Japanese once the British had withdrawn.[23]

Mountbatten himself acknowledged that the withdrawal of British protection had an effect on 'the confidence of the people in the might and justice of the British Empire'.[24]

Indeed, after the occupation, all sectors of the Malay press openly criticised the British, sometimes linking their failure in 1942, the vulnerability of Malays to Chinese attack, and the effect the Malayan Union was expected to have. The PKMM organ *Suara Rakyat* declared British failure a betrayal, while the nationalist *Seruan Rakyat* angrily demanded that the British protect the rights of the Malays in their own country in order to preserve the peace.[25] The conservative press now, too, took a jaundiced view of protection, treating the idea sarcastically – 'this peninsula has been "protected" by the British for seventy years' – and questioning the granting of equal rights to recently arrived immigrants who offended and looked down on the Malays – 'Is this the kind of justice the Malays and Malay states get from British protection?'[26]

But this proclamation of British failure by the conservative press did not lead it to discard the idea of protection. Instead, attention was drawn to the nature of the original treaties, with their emphasis on sovereignty and protection, in denouncing the new constitutional order. It was, according to conservatives, still necessary for Malays to be under the protection of the British until they developed the ability to govern themselves,[27] an argument which handed control over the pace of Malay progress back to the British and tended to equate protection of the Malays with protection of the rulers.[28] What accounted for this appeal to the norms by which the colonial power

---

[23] Ashley Gibson Report, 1945. BMA/PR 1/6.

[24] Vice-Admiral Earl Mountbatten of Burma, *Post Surrender Tasks: Section E of the Report to the Combined Chiefs of Staff by the Supreme Allied Commander South East Asia, 1943–1945*, London: Her Majesty's Stationery Office, 1969, appendix K: Extracts from a directive by the supreme allied commander.

[25] *Suara Rakyat*, 16 January 1946; *Seruan Rakyat*, 23 December 1945.

[26] *Majlis*, 27 November 1945.

[27] *Majlis*, 24 October 1946.

[28] A letter to the editor appearing 3 January 1946 in *Seruan Rakyat*, an organ of the Selangor branch of the PKMM, which broke from the national organisation because of the latter's support for the Malayan Union, asked: 'Will it [the Malayan Union] protect the rights of the Malays who are the indigenous people of Malaya or will it do just the opposite? Will it give full powers to the Sultans and Malay masses or to the other side?'

had originally justified its authority? Given its experience under colonial protection before the war, it is easy to conclude that the ruling class was asking for the return of its own protected status within Malay society. But it was also a way of alerting the British that as a class it would remain loyal, as well as a means of stating the terms of reconciliation. After the war, ruling class ambitions for English education and administrative postings were overtaken by the advent of revolutionary politics, within Malaya (Chinese communists and some Malays) as well as in the wider region (Indonesia and Vietnam). After an initial period of complacency regarding Malay capacity for revolution, the British took the threat very seriously. But, surprised and distrustful of the aristocracy's unprecedented mobilisation of the peasantry against the Malayan Union and confused by the outpouring of opinion in the Malay press, the British did not immediately recognise their natural allies in the conservative 'nationalists'.[29] The appeal to protection was an appeal to the dominant discourse of prewar colonialism, in which the British might recognise their allies. As suggested by James Scott, 'for anything less than completely revolutionary ends the terrain of dominant discourse is the only plausible arena of struggle'.[30] Avoid revolution, this appeal said, by restoring us to leadership and finally taking seriously our aspirations.

For the Malay rulers, the protection of a powerful outsider had been a historically valid alliance which allowed them to further their position and wealth in the Malay world. Unfortunately for them, British imperialism changed the international context and the Malay world itself, rendering their accommodations suspect, something that suddenly became visible in the signing of the new treaties. The rulers' purported status as protectors of Malay society, derived as it was from colonial protection of their own position, was irrevocably destroyed. In postwar discourse, the idea of protection itself was no longer applied to their actions; *penaung* (protector) and *naungan* (protection) were used only in relation to the British. Bitter condemnation of the rulers, in both the nationalist and conservative press, was based instead on the notion of accountability – a fledging idea that had been suppressed before the war. Because of what the rulers had done, editorialists wrote, they had shown they could not be relied on; they had let

29 'It is difficult even for experienced officers fully to gauge the effects of the war and Japanese occupation on the Malays, both individually and as a race', MSS PIJ, no. 1, 30 April 1946.

30 James C. Scott, *Domination and the Arts of Resistance: Hidden Transcripts*, New Haven: Yale University Press, 1990, p. 103.

the people down.[31] Their actions were likened to selling their states (*menjual negerinya*) and for that their powers should be suspended (*dipecat*).[32] Worst of all, according to one letter writer, was that the posture assumed by the rulers showed the world the weakness of the Malay community, which extended even up to their sultans:

> Our esteemed rulers apparently haven't got the spirit to defend their own true rights. Rather, when the slightest bit of pressure is applied, our esteemed rulers retreat.[33]

Soon the idea that the rulers had signed under duress and coercion began to gain credence, as the rulers defended themselves and details of the MacMichael mission became public.[34] One letter writer from Johor even suggested that the rulers had no choice but to sign because they were obligated, by treaty, to take British advice.[35] But despite this amelioration of the judgement of betrayal, the position and meaning of the rulers in Malay society could not return to the status quo and was henceforth open to acquiring new meaning, as will be discussed further below. In fact, shifting the blame from Malay rulers to British overlords, claiming that the sultans were deceived,[36] only served to reveal the colonial underpinnings of the traditional Malay raja. The rulers had not been toppled from their status of protectors. They had been exposed as British creatures.

Tradition versus Progress

The aristocracy, then, did not usurp the role of protector from the rulers. Instead, it appropriated the role of protecting the rulers, and the Malay tradition they represented, from British efforts to destroy them with the Malayan Union. The aristocracy's credentials for protecting tradition came from its administrative experience. Just as they had assumed district officer positions during the war, aristocrats were ready to fill roles after the war that the British no longer could or would perform. As the Malays most associated with progress, they were able to move comfortably in the highest levels of the plural society created by the British and were qualified to

[31] *Majlis*, 12 December 1945 and 23 January 1946.

[32] *Seruan Rakyat*, 11 December 1945.

[33] *Seruan Rakyat*, 3 January 1946.

[34] For examples, see *Majlis*, 12 December 1945 and 26 February 1946; *Utusan Melayu*, 24 January 1946. BMA/PR 3/7/Vol. 1.

[35] *Straits Times*, 2 March 1946.

[36] *Majlis*, 21 February 1946.

safeguard Malay interests there. Yet, on these very grounds of progress, the aristocrats now faced competition from those who would sweep away the traditional world altogether. The radical nationalist press attacked traditional privilege and challenged the aristocracy's very claim to represent progress. This tension between the claims of tradition and progress was resolved (and ruling class privilege safeguarded) by successfully linking the preservation of tradition to the Malays' survival in the modern world. In the process, the Malay rulers would come to be seen as guarantors of Malay interests in the contemporary nation.[37]

Since the Kaum Muda introduced the idea early in the century, Malay backwardness and its antithesis, progress, had been at the centre of a discourse of self-criticism. Because calls for progress usually focused on cultural goals such as education and the development of the Malay language, they did not violate the political taboo. After the war, some still thought along those lines, like 'Melayu' from Johor, who wrote to *The Straits Times* disavowing any wish for constitutional reform or self-government, demanding instead 'education on a far greater scale than Malaya has hitherto known'.[38] For more Malays, though, the time for overtly political progress was felt to have arrived and that belief lent new urgency to old debates. The quality as well as quantity of Malay education was now scrutinised; political progress could not be made as long as colonial education equipped Malays to become only 'coolies and messengers'.[39] Most of all, political progress meant unity; Malays needed to overcome their division into separate states with separate rulers so they could achieve progress.[40]

A broadening conception of progress placed Malays explicitly in an international realm of sovereign nation states. This view had been encouraged by both Allied war propaganda touting democracy and self-determination, and Japanese propaganda criticising Western imperialism. *Warta Negara* argued that the first Pan-Malaya Malay Congress was proof that Malays were now politically aware; it linked the Malays to 'the awareness of communities all over Asia which now asserted their humanity ... wanted to hold power in their respective states and would no longer be

[37] See, for instance, Chandra, *Protector?*, pp. 64–66; Tan Liok Ee, *The Rhetoric of Bangsa and Minzu: Community and Nation in Tension, The Malay Peninsula 1900–1955*, Clayton, Victoria: Monash University, Centre of Southeast Asian Studies, 1988.

[38] *Straits Times*, 22 January 1946.

[39] Letter to *Seruan Rakyat*, 8 January 1946.

[40] *Utusan Melayu*, 24 October 1946. BMA/PR 3/5.

deceived by colonialists or Western Imperialism'.[41] The Allies-promoted idea that the world consisted of nations which should each enjoy rights of self-determination was used specifically in arguing against the Malayan Union to a British (and international) audience, and thus often appeared in the English press. 'A Kelantan Malay' wrote to *The Straits Times* on the occasion of a large anti-Malayan Union demonstration:

> [The Malays] have arrived at that stage of political development where they will not stand idly by when their interests and integrity are at stake. *Like other peoples*, the Malays have a right to exist in the land which has been undisputedly theirs.[42]

Opponents of the Malayan Union immediately perceived themselves to be acting not only on a national but on an international stage. The rulers had long ago perfected the art of jumping over the heads of local authorities and appealing to London.[43] Now various Malay organisations took up a new weapon – the telegram – and printed copies of their messages in the pages of the local press. One protester was K.M. Sultan Maraicayar, editor of the *Islamic Voice of Malaya*, a Penang English-language monthly with a circulation of 3,000. Maraicayar cabled President Harry S. Truman, 'in the name of the Atlantic Charter and Abraham Lincoln', as well as the secretary general and other high officials of the United Nations, basing his appeal on democracy, human rights, the sanctity of treaties and the 'rights of small nations'. Finally, in February 1946 he cabled both the British prime minister and the secretary of state for the colonies:

> Malays downright opposed against Malayan Union. Sultans bound by sacred treaties with Britain. Voice of Malays to be heard not flouted. Consult Malays before action against them. Long live the king of England. Editor IVM.[44]

Telegrams along these lines were sent by many Malay groups to the British, United States and United Nations governments, and the English press covered the Malays' protest on these terms. *The Straits Times* quoted *Utusan Melayu*'s editorial denouncing the Malayan Union as violating the principle

---

41 *Warta Negara*, 2 March 1946, quoted in Ahmad bin Masjidin, 'Malayan Union dari kaca matt *Warta Negara*', in Khoo Kay Kim, ed., *Sejarah Masyarakat Melayu Moden*, Kuala Lumpur: Jabatan Sejarah, Universiti Malaya, 1984, p. 201.

42 *Straits Times*, 23 February 1946. Emphasis added.

43 Especially during the Selangor succession dispute in the mid-1930s. See Allen, *Malayan Union*, p. 7.

44 BMA/ADM 8/64.

of self-determination. It also printed the text of telegrams sent to the British government by conservative Malay organisations and the rulers. These letters argued against the Malayan Union treaties on the basis of Malay sovereignty, public opinion and the principle of representative government, and were read publicly during the British parliamentary debate on the subject.[45] Malays made direct contributions to this discourse in the English papers, one writer accusing the British of interfering in the rights of small nations.[46]

It may well be argued that this was simply a tactical appeal to the dominant discourse, in this case international rather than colonial. It is true that the majority of these arguments appeared in the English press, but there were many in the Malay press as well. Papers like *Warta Negara* and *Majlis* printed the texts of the telegrams. *Pelita Malaya* attacked the Malayan Union for being undemocratic and *Seruan Rakyat* said it violated the Atlantic Charter.[47] If the Malayan Union were established, according to one editorial, not only the Malays, but the principles of justice championed by the United Nations, would suffer.[48] International principles did become more problematic for Malays when they were not being used as a stick to beat the British. Democracy, for instance, carried the uncomfortable implication of voting rights for Chinese and Indian residents. Despite such limitations, however, the pull of progress was irresistible. The rest of the world was on the move – not just the West, but neighbouring countries of Asia as well. If Malays hesitated they would be left behind again, this time in an atmosphere which might be fatal.

Neither could the rhetoric of international principle be wholly contained to the anti-British struggle. When the rulers fell, it was not hard to see who would rise, rhetorically at least, to fill the breach. The new primacy of 'the people' in relation to the rulers thus can be read as an implementation of progress occasioned by the Malayan Union crisis. *Rakyat Melayu jelata* (the Malay masses or common Malays) were now regarded as paramount in *tanah Melayu* (the Malay states, literally Malay land):

> For the treaties to be valid, they would first have to be agreed to by the Malay masses, because this country is the property of the Malay people together with the Sultans.[49]

---

45 *Straits Times*, 25 January, 5 February and 15 March 1946.

46 *Straits Times*, 25 March 1946.

47 *Pelita Malaya*, 25 May 1946 and *Seruan Rakyat*, 6 November 1946.

48 *Warta Negara*, 12 March 1946. BMA/PR 3/6/Pt. 3.

49 *Seruan Rakyat*, 1 January 1946.

The contention that the treaties were invalid without the people's agreement was a common one.[50] *Majlis* argued that secret treaties with the rulers, signed without consulting the people, were directly opposed to democracy, the ostensible principle of postwar British rule.[51] Eventually, the rulers themselves began to respond cautiously to this new rhetoric, the Sultan of Pahang, for example, telling *The Straits Times*, 'I am one of the people and, therefore, for the people'.[52] In this the Malay rulers were repeating the experience of their fellow European monarchs, who had learned to identify with 'their' people over the course of the previous century.[53]

Disgust with the rulers' capitulation and the new currency of ideas like democracy and rights resulted in a temporary and superficial consensus between the conservative and radical press. Both *Majlis* and *Utusan Melayu*, for example, endorsed the view that the people's rights over their country and destiny were not dependent on the rulers; the people's rights could not be cancelled because of the rulers' misdeeds.[54] Likewise, the articulation of a new relationship between raja and *rakyat* (subjects, now people) was to be found throughout the political spectrum. *Seruan Rakyat* instructed the rulers not to ignore the wishes of the people, while *Majlis* demanded that they 'join with the people with one voice to demand the rights of the Malays'.[55] According to Ariffin Omar's analysis, ruler and ruled were turned upside down when *daulat*, the ruler's 'divine attribute', was linked to *rakyat*, with a new meaning which approached 'power'. A classic proverb had proclaimed the centrality of a raja to the life of the people; it was now inverted: 'If there are not *rakyat*, there will be no raja, but if there is no raja, the *rakyat* can become raja'.[56] Ariffin explains that *daulat rakyat* (the power of the people) was interpreted by conservatives to mean that the rulers 'should reign with the consensus of the majority'. Radicals, however, embraced *kedaulatan rakyat* (the people's sovereignty) or democracy. This

[50] *Seruan Rakyat*, 4 February 1946; *Warta Negara*, 2 and 3 January 1946. BMA/PR 3/7/Vol. 1.

[51] *Majlis*, 26 January 1946.

[52] *Straits Times*, 21 February 1946.

[53] Eric Hobsbawm, 'Mass-producing traditions: Europe, 1870–1914', in Eric Hobsbawm and Terence Ranger, eds, *The Invention of Tradition*, Cambridge: Cambridge University Press, 1983, p. 282.

[54] See, for example, *Majlis*, 14 May 1946; *Utusan Melayu*, 28 January 1946. BMA/PR 3/7/Vol. 11; *Warta Negara*, 2 and 7 January 1946. BMA/PR 3/7/Vol. 1.

[55] *Seruan Rakyat*, 23 December 1945; *Majlis*, 21 February 1946.

[56] *Majlis*, 6 February 1946, cited in Ariffin, *Bangsa Melayu*, pp. 175–76. He also argues that the interests of the *bangsa* (race) came to take precedence over those of the ruler, pp. 50–53.

formulation 'which prevailed in East Sumatra would leave the rulers out of the scheme of government' and threatened to open participation to non-Malays.[57] This is where the consensus on Malay political progress broke down, for it threatened the legitimacy and position of the bureaucratic elite along with that of the rulers.

Not surprisingly, criticism of 'ancient constituted authority' threatened to wash over from the rulers onto the rest of the ruling class. Even before the Malayan Union controversy reached a critical stage, letters appeared in both the English and Malay press attacking entrenched ruling class interests. 'Annoyed' wrote to *The Straits Times* from Terengganu complaining that 90 per cent of the posts that came open in the state were filled by Terengganu-born

> descendants of either the royal family or the 'big men'. Does this mean that non-Trengganu Malays who have slaved for over fifteen years in this State are not fit for such posts or is it because they are not the sons of the soil or are not offspring of the 'big men'?[58]

A supporter of the PKMM in Selangor, writing to *Seruan Rakyat* about the need for higher education to achieve self-government, made it clear that class privilege was no longer acceptable:

> And don't reserve the seats of higher education for the state aristocracies [*orang-orang bangsawan negeri*] only. Help those of our community who are poor but worthy to become educated.[59]

These sentiments came from urban educated Malays, that small but growing group whose frustration with elite privilege could now be expressed openly. A far larger group, just as unhappy but for different reasons, was the rural Malay peasantry. It was widely reported at the time that rural Malays were disillusioned by the inefficacy of their traditional leaders during the ethnic violence that followed the occupation (and that continued well into 1946). Previous studies of this period have therefore taken into account the very real threat the aristocracy felt from Malay and Indonesian revolutionary groups and charismatic religious leadership operating at the village level.[60]

In understanding the ability of the aristocracy to deflect revolutionary threats, however, insufficient attention has been paid to a struggle between the goals of progress and the resurgence of tradition which can be found in

---

57 Ariffin, *Bangsa Melayu*, pp. 176–77.

58 *Straits Times*, 14 January 1946.

59 *Seruan Rakyat*, 23 November 1946.

60 See especially Stockwell, *British Policy and Malay Politics*, chs. 7 and 8.

the suppressed discourse of Malays who favoured the Malayan Union. The eventual unanimity of opposition and subsequent celebration of its result has obscured the fact that the unity of Malays was not an inevitability, but a highly contested process. It is, of course, generally recognised that the PKMM initially favoured the Malayan Union, but this stance has been treated as a political misstep quickly corrected when public opinion made itself felt or explained away by ignorance of the full extent of British intentions.[61] While there is truth in both of these claims, the characterisation of a pro-Malayan Union stance as a political mistake out of step with the zeitgeist only endorses the hegemonic view and does not help us understand how that view came to predominate. It also obscures the early widespread advocacy of a modern, unified administration, as well as the fact that pro-Malayan Union (and anti-UMNO) sympathies only seemed to disappear; they were simply transformed into anti-federation sentiment.

It was the logic of progress that led some initially to favour the Malayan Union. Early *Utusan Melayu* editorials explicitly linked backwardness with the special privileges given to the Malays, arguing that Malays must reject those privileges in order to catch up with the other races:

> The termination of the war prompts the Malays of Malaya to ponder seriously over their future in this country. The backwardness of the Malays is attributed to several causes, of which the most important are disunity, laziness and lack of ambition. These weaknesses in the Malays have been hindrances in establishing their status in their own country.
>
> In the past the Malays have had many privileges from the Government as they were considered the 'sons of the soil', but it will be degrading to receive such favours in the future. We have seen in the past the futility of the preferences given to Malays. No attempt was made to improve their conditions, but instead they deteriorated. The wealth acquired by them was uselessly spent in luxuries.
>
> Let us at least in the future endeavour to improve ourselves, after the sufferings of these three and a half years under the Japanese. There is going to be keen competition in the future, and we must fight on undefeated. We should correct our ways of thinking and lay the foundations for our future prosperity, and catch up with the other races in the postwar world.[62]

In 'this new struggle for progress', the Malay rulers were called on to lead their people forward. A few days later, *Utusan Melayu* welcomed the

---

[61] See, for example, Firdaus Haji Abdullah, *Radical Malay Politics: Its Origins and Early Development*, Petaling Jaya: Pelanduk Publications, 1985, p. 86.

[62] *Utusan Melayu*, 6 October 1945. BMA/COM/61.

'Malay Union', blaming backwardness on provincial divisions and declaring Malayan citizenship to be in line with democratic principles.[63]

This early optimism soon gave way to fear of alien power and the shock of the rulers' betrayal. Conservative papers like *Majlis* and *Warta Negara* – mouthpieces of the bureaucratic elite – threatened to cut the rulers down with progressive ideas, noting that civilised, democratic nations do not give rulers absolute power and supporting the democratic election of sultans.[64] The radical papers went much further. *Pelita Malaya* asked its readers to look at what was happening around Asia, pointing especially to the revolution in Sumatra, where power was being transferred from the rulers to the people, and suggesting that there was no need for rulers in the modern world.[65] Neither did that paper, a PKMM mouthpiece edited by Ishak Haji Muhammad, back down immediately from its support for the Malayan Union, arguing that to oppose it would mean returning to a system which privileged the few over the many.[66] Despite the increasing criticism and isolation which forced the party finally to back away from the Malayan Union,[67] the paper continued to advocate change. It argued that those who opposed reform possessed no aspirations for their people or country[68] and specifically accused high-ranking Malays of opposing the Union in order to save their salaries.[69]

The vigorous populist arguments of the PKMM were countered by conservatives in two ways. The first was to brand the radicals insufficiently Malay, traitors to the *bangsa Melayu* (Malay race), whose very survival was threatened by the Malayan Union. The PKMM's self-proclaimed internationalism, by which it pursued class alliance with the CPM, was used against it. The Partai Kebangsaan Melayu Malaya, the *Seruan Rakyat* accused, was a tool of the other races (*perkakas bangsa lain*).[70]

The conservatives' second line of defence was the rehabilitation or recasting of tradition. The Malayan Union was perceived as a threat to *bangsa Melayu* politically because it rendered Malays a mere *kaum*

---

63 *Utusan Melayu*, 13 October 1946, BMA/COM/61, and 22 October 1946, BMA/PR 3/5.

64 *Warta Negara*, 3 January 1946, BMA/PR 3/7/Vol. 1; *Majlis*, 18 January 1946.

65 *Pelita Malaya*, 11 April 1946.

66 *Pelita Malaya*, 22 March 1946.

67 *Pelita Malaya*, 1 and 3 April 1946.

68 *Pelita Malaya*, 9 April 1946.

69 *Pelita Malaya*, 30 April 1946.

70 *Seruan Rakyat*, 11 December 1946. The use of the epithet 'traitor' against political enemies will be discussed further in the next chapter.

(community or ethnic group) in their own country. Through democratic citizenship rights for immigrants, the validity of the Malay political community was denied. Malays had traditionally recognised that polity, their *kerajaan*, by looking to their rulers. This understanding had not substantially changed with indirect colonial rule, which was facilitated by the apotheosis of the Malay rulers. The destruction of these rulers – the one institution linking Malays to the precolonial past – was therefore easily understood to mean the destruction of the Malays, just as the rulers' preservation could easily mean the reassertion of the Malay polity in the face of Malayan Union. The very visible defeat of the rulers at a time of great Malay vulnerability transformed them into cultural icons; their survival or demise became the embodiment of the Malays' fate in the modern world.[71] This transformation of meaning needed little manipulation by royal apologists, though editorialists were quick to praise those rulers who repudiated the treaties. All educated or even well-travelled Malays could see that places which ceased to have a ruler – Singapore, Penang, Province Wellesley, Melaka – ceased to be Malay places.[72] To the extent, then, that the rulers came to symbolise the Malays, anti-ruler sentiment was a self-limiting exercise, better understood as arising from the self-criticism of the 1930s than as having revolutionary potential. The aristocracy would gain considerable leverage from the exercise, but it was a political dead end for the radicals. Accused of acting in the interest of other races and of attacking the embodiment of the Malays, their rhetoric of progress was twisted into treachery. They had to abandon the Malayan Union and the class levelling of Malay society it might have brought. Meanwhile, royal patronage at conservative political events conferred traditional legitimacy on conservative politicians.[73]

If the central meaning of the royal tradition had transformed itself with little effort (except perhaps from MacMichael), it still remained to articulate that meaning politically and to elaborate the ritual. Could this process have played out as a revival of precolonial ruling class relations? Could the rulers have staged a comeback of real power based on their new postwar meaning? It was unlikely. The context of their transformation, while not revolutionary, was still determined more by the ethos of progress than privilege. Tradition now had value insofar as it safeguarded the interests of the Malays in

---

[71] *Majlis*, 13 April 1946.

[72] A letter to *Utusan Melayu* specifically linked the loss of royalty in these places to the loss of Malay privilege. 27 October 1945, BMA/PR 3/5.

[73] Ariffin Omar points out the importance of this patronage in *Bangsa Melayu*, pp. 99–100.

the modern world. The aristocrats, through their own involvement with the colonial state and their successful marshalling of opinion against the Malayan Union, were in a stronger position than the rulers to mediate between tradition and progress.

Loyalty

The arena of mediation was to be the concept of loyalty and the threat that the Malay people would withdraw their support from the rulers. The conservatives had successfully quietened those who would dispense with traditional authority, but they had not reined in the rulers themselves, some of whom had not yet grasped the new conventions. It was in this context that the Malay tradition of unconditional loyalty began to be openly criticised as out of date.[74] A letter written to *Seruan Rakyat* early in 1946 demonstrates a new examination of loyalty in light of colonial history:

> Malays are loyal to their rulers, but ... these signatures will plant the seeds of Malay resistance against the Sultans, who did not consult the people. Malays are always loyal [*ta'at setia*] to their rulers, but will not be loyal like in ancient times, like we have heard in the story of Sultan Mahmud Shah of Melaka.... Sultan Husin Shah signed a treaty surrendering Temasek (Singapore) to Mr. Raffles because that ruler acted on his own.[75]

February 1946 saw an abortive aristocratic movement to overthrow the Sultan of Johor, based on his violation of the Johor constitution which forbade him from surrendering the state to a foreign power. This episode has been analysed by Ariffin Omar, who discusses the unprecedented nature of a charge of treason (*derhaka*) against a ruler.[76] In understanding the value of tradition to the aristocracy, however, it is just as significant that Onn bin Jaafar stopped the movement in its tracks. More will be said about Onn in the next chapter. It shall suffice here to note his genealogy: Encik Long (Abdullah bin Tok Mohamed Tahir) was *menteri* to Temenggung Ibrahim during the opening up of the state to Chinese planters and until his death in 1863. This post became *menteri besar* during Abu Bakar's reign. Long's nephew, Datuk Ja'far bin Haji Mohamed (d. 1919) held the post, as did three of Ja'far's sons, including Onn, who was raised in the royal household. It is not enough, therefore, to say that Onn remained a royalist. Onn came

---

74 Letter from 'Regular Reader' to *The Straits Times* reporting a conversation with 'a few educated Malay friends', 5 April 1946.

75 *Seruan Rakyat*, 9 February 1946.

76 Ariffin, *Bangsa Melayu*, pp. 53–54.

from a line that assisted in the rather unique invention that was the Johor sultanate and proved to have a sharp understanding of its potential value in modern political life.

As the end of the BMA and the date of the new government's inauguration approached, the Malay Congress brought together delegations from over 40 organisations under the leadership of Onn. It successfully presented a picture of Malay unity, political mobilisation and grassroots opposition to the Malayan Union, and would later be transformed into the second postwar national Malay political party, the United Malays National Organisation. For months, newspapers reported unprecedented political activity as tens of thousands demonstrated against the Malayan Union. Despite the pressure, the colonial government adhered to its 1 April deadline for the installation of Edward Gent as the new governor of the Malayan Union. The inauguration was to be marked with appropriate ceremonial, including the attendance, in full ceremonial dress, of the Malay rulers.

However, Onn and his party were also determined to fight on. An emergency meeting of the Malay Congress, led by Onn, called for a total Malay boycott of the Malayan Union – the installation ceremonies as well as the governor's advisory council. It was especially important that the Malay rulers not legitimise the new scheme by attending the installation, although what the British called their 'innate politeness' seemed to guarantee their attendance.[77] This problem was discussed in the Malay press – what would the Malays do if their new-found unity and political resolve were betrayed by their rulers? Onn visited the rulers the day before the ceremony at the Station Hotel in Kuala Lumpur, where they had gathered in anticipation of attending. He requested them not to do so, with the assurance that, 'All Malay subjects of all Malay States … submit their affection [and] reaffirm their loyalty and allegiance'.[78] The protestation of loyalty barely concealed the threat, which Onn also made explicit in the press: 'If the rajas attend … those rajas will be overthrown (*dibuang*) immediately by the people'.[79]

When Onn visited again the next morning, the rulers were dressed and ready to leave for the ceremony, accompanied by a high British official, the new chief secretary of the Malayan Union. Inside that room, a struggle ensued for the allegiance of the rulers. Outside on the street was a tense crowd of Malays, many wearing a white headband of mourning to commemorate the death of the Malay birthright represented by the

[77] *Straits Times*, 3 April 1946.
[78] *Straits Times*, 4 April 1946.
[79] *Majlis*, 2 April 1946.

Malayan Union. Onn convinced the rulers to go one by one to the window and acknowledge the cheers of the crowd, a moving but also threatening experience for the rulers, at least one of whom wept. Back inside, they all signed a letter to the governor explaining that their absence meant no disrespect, but they could not attend the ceremony.[80] As a body they had capitulated to Onn as representative of the people, and were rewarded in the following days and weeks with protestations of loyalty in editorials, on posters and in public demonstrations.

A New Tradition: Malay Rulers as Icons of the Malay Nation

The culmination of the discourse of loyalty was more than just an aristocratic victory over royalty. More importantly, it was a transformation in the position of the rulers which pictured and reflected the emergence of a Malay nation in several ways.

First, the rulers from all states were present (the only exception being the Sultan of Johor who was out of the country). Previously, only the rulers of the Federated Malay States had gathered publicly as a group. These appearances were made, for example, at the conference of rulers or at federal council meetings. The rulers of the Unfederated Malay States had successfully resisted incorporation into a federation, and had so avoided such command performances. Yet now they were all seen together, the effect of which was to wipe out the difference between the Federated and Unfederated States in public perception, as it already was in legality.

Second, despite the anomaly of their nearly unanimous presence, the rulers were, in fact, gathered together to do a very usual thing – to validate and participate in a British construct, in this case the Malayan Union. Turning against the British, no matter how politely, effectively severed their meaning from the colonial context. They were henceforth in service to the postcolonial future. In turning against the British as a group, they offered one of the first concrete manifestations of what that future would look like – the joining together of Malay states, each retaining its distinct identity through royal leadership.

Third, the rulers were seen together in Kuala Lumpur, previously the capital of the Federated Malay States, now the putative Malayan Union capital, but fast becoming a national capital. Before the first Congress meeting the previous month, there had been talk of meeting in Melaka, a

---

[80] Allen, *Malayan Union*, describes this scene on p. 42.

city of historic importance to Malay political life. But Kuala Lumpur had been chosen instead for its greater facilities. After the successful Congress and this dramatic showdown over the installation ceremony, there was no more talk of returning to Melaka. The colonial centre had been effectively appropriated as the Malay capital.

Fourth, the Malay rulers acquired a new public posture when they acknowledged the primacy of the people by changing their plans. The rulers were forced (through aristocratic mediation) to do the people's bidding and were also forced to accept the approval of the people for their action. One hundred years earlier, Malay rajas had rarely been seen by large groups of subjects. Colonial rule gradually transformed the nature of their visibility. On 1 April 1946 they took the final step in becoming monarchs for public consumption.

Finally, Malay royalty presented itself before a group represented as 'the Malay people'. They were cheered by a crowd of Malays – not Malays in their home state cheering their own ruler, but a crowd of Malays in the capital city mobilised for political action. In that moment and in the public debate over the role of the sultans, the rulers were rendered interchangeable on the national level. Malay newspapers reported events all over the peninsula, referring to the rulers in the plural and holding them all to the same standards. In a related way, 'the Malays', as a national entity, were taking precedence over Selangor Malay, Perak Malay, etc. People asked, what do the Malays want, what behaviour do *the Malays* owe their *rulers* and vice versa. This process had, of course, started before the war, in the debate over Malay identity in the 1930s. But prewar changes took place slowly and unevenly, while the transformation of 1945–1946 occurred on a self-consciously national scale, simultaneously, in print.

Ironically, it could be said that Malay royalty itself had been the first to display pan-Malay proclivities, ignoring as long as possible Anglo–Dutch–Siamese borders in favour of Malay-defined spheres of activity like the old Johor-Riau empire. Indeed, the traditional *kerajaan* did not depend on a state at all, but on a ruler. It was colonialism which increasingly domesticated the rulers, more and more successfully restricting them to influence within their 'own' states. The rulers' transformation at the Station Hotel restored something of the floating, place-free quality of Malay kingship. This newly restored interchangeability was a value transferred to the states themselves. States could fit into a federated nation, any ruler could now be cheered by Malays from any state, and the rulers could one day take turns being paramount ruler or king. At the rulers' conference of 1903, Sultan Idris had referred to a Malay proverb which held that 'there cannot be two masters in one vessel: neither can there be four Rulers in one country'.[81] The new tradition proved Sultan Idris wrong again.

The political struggle over the Malayan Union had transformed the Malay rulers into symbols of the nation, both constructing and helping Malays to picture their future. But the rulers also became icons of traditional Malay culture, or rather a new rendering of tradition which facilitated aristocratic ascendancy in postwar politics. Icons, being invented symbols, have no intrinsic value beyond that ascribed to them. The rulers were, in a sense, invented by colonialism, and then reinvented by Onn and the furious public debate over their behaviour. In 1946 their continued existence, role and meaning were no longer self-evident, even though their representation of tradition was accepted. The ambivalence shown towards them was the ambivalence of the Malays towards their invented tradition, with all its disadvantages in a changing world. The swiftness with which the rulers capitulated in the face of British pressure – after all the indignities of the occupation – made it impossible for Malays to ignore the dual meaning their rulers had come to embody: British creatures and symbols of Malay weakness. In short, the rulers had become problematic. The aristocracy provided a traditional resolution, with modern political advantage. The iconic monarchies were retained, now to guarantee that *tanah Melayu* would remain a Malay land. But real power was passed to those who would bring the Malays progress. In Malay history, when a hero was called for, someone like Hang Tuah, an aristocrat had won the battle for his sultan. So did the aristocracy save the rulers in 1946.

*

This chapter has interpreted the Malayan Union crisis as an opportunity for the resurgence of aristocratic power at the expense of both Malay rulers and Malay radicals. The general outpouring of criticism against the rulers threatened to engulf the aristocrats as well, thus activating the latent division in ruling class interests which had been developing during prewar colonial rule. In the dangerous political climate of 1945 and 1946, aristocratic politicians asserted their claim to modern leadership by distinguishing themselves from the erring rulers and by taking control of the evolving meaning of Malay tradition. The conservative press presided over the revelation that the Malay rulers were creatures of the British rather than protectors of Malay society, thus deposing both those 'protectors'

[81] *Annual Report*, Pahang, 1897. CO 437/2.

in favour of the conservative political leaders. Mass mobilisation and a relentless editorial drive in the conservative press also defeated the minority view that the Malayan Union, by sweeping away the old leadership, might actually benefit the Malays. Finally, having secured the position of the rulers at the head of society, the aristocrats, led most ably by Onn bin Jaafar, then secured the obedience of the rulers to UMNO's policy by updating the Malay tradition of loyalty. This rehabilitation of tradition left the Malay sultans as iconic rulers whose survival was crucial to the fate of the modern Malay nation and rendered UMNO, their protectors, as the embodiment of progress. In a subtle resolution of the old contradiction between preservation and progress, aristocratic power was preserved. UMNO's hegemony, however, was still not secure. The end of UMNO's mass mobilisation, which was coincident with the beginning of closed-door negotiations with the British, left UMNO vulnerable to the continuing activity of the Malay nationalists. In the next chapter, I turn to the construction of the new political discourse and aristocratic efforts to master the language of nationalism.

Chapter Six

Politics and Nationalism

The struggle for aristocratic ascendancy within the ruling class was paralleled by the traditional elite's struggle to dominate the emerging political discourse of the wider society through its political party, the United Malays National Organisation (UMNO). In this endeavour, the conservatives faced a radical nationalist movement which specifically targeted traditional leadership and colonial rule as twin evils endangering Malay society. Emboldened and nurtured by the Japanese occupation, and encouraged by the Indonesian struggle against the Dutch, Malay nationalists took advantage of the weakness of the restored colonial state to disseminate their views, organise and recruit for membership in the immediate postwar period. As discussed in chapter four, the British Military Administration (BMA) policy afforded a window of opportunity for this activity and subsequent policy was to encourage what the British considered legitimate nationalism among the Malays. Once UMNO had emerged as the spokesman of that acceptable nationalism, suppression of radical formulations would proceed apace. Malay radicalism, along with Chinese and Indian, was defeated in the wholesale suppression of progressive politics which commenced in mid-1948 with the counterinsurgency movement known as 'the Emergency' (1948–1960).

Contemporary and current left-wing critics of UMNO's dominance in Malay politics have pointed to British intervention as an important factor in UMNO's victory.[1] While this approach recognises UMNO's weakness in the years from 1946 to 1948, it fails to acknowledge an important process of which British complicity was only a part. What is overlooked is the significant gap between UMNO as established – champion of the Malays in the fight against the Malayan Union – and UMNO's development of a

[1] See, for example, Ahmad Boestamam, *Datuk Onn Yang Saya Kenal*, Kuala Lumpur: Adabi, 1979 and Syed Husin Ali, *The Malays: Their Problems and Future*, Kuala Lumpur: Heinemann Asia, 1981.

credible nationalist persona. In the two years of its existence before the Emergency eliminated left-wing parties, conservative politicians learned to appropriate the powerful tools of nationalist symbolism and practice that their radical competition often pioneered. In this chapter, therefore, I do not attempt to assess the relative strength of opposing political forces, nor to show that a different outcome was possible or probable had the British not protected UMNO and suppressed the left.[2] Instead, I show how conservative politicians constructed an ideological hegemony, casting UMNO as the mainstream party of Malay nationalism, an ideology which aided in UMNO's long-term victory over progressive forces.

The traditional elite had both advantages and disadvantages in this endeavour. In its favour was the power of tradition, its success in gaining control over the meaning of the Malay rulers and the growing complicity of British officials in its project. Working against it was the momentum of change and movement gripping Malay society. More specifically, a Malay political public was emerging precisely in reaction to the colonial milieu which was the basis of elite power. The shape of that emerging political public was a national public, that is, one which was bound, sooner or later, to embrace anticolonialism and demand access to political power in a modern nation. In this dynamic atmosphere, mastery over the language and symbolism of nationalism was necessary for the elite to maintain its relevance.

In the following section, I discuss how prewar Malay public discourse was transformed into a political discourse by 1945. I then examine four important ways in which political nationalism was practised from 1945 to 1948 and how a conservative UMNO appropriated those forms to its own political practice.

The Development of a National Political Public

Throughout the prewar period, Malay public discourse was constructing the basis of a Malay national public. Newspapers like *Saudara* and *Warta Malaya*, though published in the Straits Settlements (Penang and Singapore respectively), were sold and read all over the peninsula, as shown in

---

[2] This argument is criticised in Roger Kershaw, 'Difficult synthesis: recent trends in Malay political sociology and history', *Southeast Asian Journal of Social Science* vol. 16, no. 1, 1988, p. 156n19. Here Kershaw questions Syed Husin Ali's view that British action kept a 'natural historical development' from fruition. Kershaw argues that 'a few years of British suppression should not have held up [Malay left-wing parties'] progress once democratic elections were introduced'.

their correspondence columns.[3] A central concern of journalists was the definition of the Malay community. The Arab-Malay Muslims who published *Al-Imam* had referred to all Muslims of the peninsula as 'our people'.[4] By the 1930s, in opposition to years of Arab-Malay and Indian-Malay (Jawi Peranakan) dominance, Malay public discourse began to refine that definition of community, moving from a religiously-based conception of the *umat* (which made no distinction between Malays and other Muslims) to a secular and ethnic conception of genuine Malays (*Melayu jati*). Yet even as the community was narrowing in this regard, there were, by the late 1930s, several attempts to broaden its definition beyond state-based limitations. Two pan-Malay conferences were held in 1939 and 1940 to bring together the similarly oriented state associations for common purpose. But despite much time spend debating the definition of 'Malay' and discussing the need for 'national' endeavour, at neither meeting could the associations agree to form a unified national body.[5] The associations' mainly aristocratic memberships would not risk alienating their British and royal benefactors.

It is somewhat fitting, in retrospect, that this dead end occurred on the eve of the Japanese occupation. For all that Malay public discourse had done to create a national public, it seemed nationalism could go no further without politics. By disrupting the colonial, traditionalist milieu and substituting Japanese goals and practices, the occupation accomplished two things: it gave legitimacy to the national conception of Malay society and introduced new forms of social organisation and action in order to further that conception. Examples of these will be touched on below in relation to the new political practices of UMNO and the nationalist groups. But first the phenomenon of 'politics' itself requires attention.

It is striking not only that Malays engaged in politics after the colonial restoration, but that their newspapers constantly reminded them of the significance of what they were doing. According to *Seruan Rakyat*, Malays were 'quiet, patient, and gracious ... they have never gone on strike, never even marched, let alone revolted'. But now they 'know how to oppose and how to march'.[6] *Majlis* commented on the change in Malays' attitude, that

---

3 Zulkipli bin Mahmud, *Warta Malaya: Penyambung Lidah Bangsa Melayu, 1930–1941*, Bangi: Jabatan Sejarah, Universiti Kebangsaan Malaysia, 1979, pp. 107–8.

4 William R. Roff, *The Origins of Malay Nationalism*, Kuala Lumpur: University of Malaya Press, 1980, p. 56.

5 *Ibid.*, pp. 242–47. Cheah Boon Kheng reproduces the minutes of the second meeting in *Tokoh-Tokoh Tempatan dan Dokumen-Dokumen dalam Sejarah Malaysia*, Penang: Universiti Sains Malaysia, 1982.

6 *Seruan Rakyat*, 20 December 1945.

they 'no longer dread politics but are taking a vigorous part in them', and attributed it to the Malayan Union proposals and the successful Pan-Malaya Malay Congress of March 1946.[7] It was clear, according to *Warta Negara*, that the '*tidak apa*' (never mind) attitude was gone.[8] There even appeared on the market a *Kamus Politik* (Political Dictionary) of 68 pages, costing one dollar.[9]

The political taboo had been broken, and in radical publications the change in attitude was analysed in just those terms:

> Before the war, it was difficult for us to start a political movement. At that time, politics was like a ghost in the view of the public. At that time, politics was forbidden [*haram*] – there was no use trying to start a political movement then, just mentioning the word 'politics' was forbidden. But now after the war, not only has the ghost vanished, but politics is permitted [*halal*] and demanded as well by the public and also by the authorities. Therefore, what are we waiting for or are we still afraid?[10]

An interesting note of uncertainty is present in that question. For the most part, however, the political activity of the Malays was encouraged and celebrated in phrases which often employed the metaphor of awakening: 'Malay masses: Be aware! Wake up!'[11]

As with the rhetoric of progress discussed in the previous chapter, this unanimous celebration of Malay political activity actually concealed different attitudes and intentions. Politics itself was not simply the affirmation and assertion of the Malays as a people, but a new way of ordering society which represented danger to some and opportunity to others. In order to understand the orientation of conservatives and radicals to this new activity, it helps to recognise three important characteristics of the new politics.

First, everyone in Malay society was, at least theoretically, a political participant. Where prewar politics existed in a circumscribed ruling class arena, postwar politics was mass politics. It was no longer restricted by class: 'It is not just the state aristocracies who may participate in Politics like before. Farmers can participate provided they are worthy'.[12] Nor was it restricted by age or gender, as newspapers commonly pointed out the

---

7 *Majlis*, 23 March 1946.

8 *Warta Negara*, 20 April 1946. BMA/PR 3/6/Pt. IV.

9 MU 11703/47.

10 *Seruan Rakyat*, 2 February 1946. A longer analysis along the same lines can be found in *Kenchana*, no. 3, March 1947, under the title 'Melayu berjuang' (Malays Struggle).

11 *Pelita Malaya*, 4 April 1946.

12 Letter to *Seruan Rakyat*, 11 November 1945.

presence at demonstrations of Malay men, women and children. In fact, the participation of women was the exemplar of the new politics. While making no claims about the effect of political participation on the status of women per se,[13] it is nonetheless clear that their entrance into public life was considered highly significant, both by Malays and by British observers gauging the extent of opposition to the Malayan Union.[14] In Malay papers, the participation of women – at demonstrations and in forming associations – was encouraged and celebrated as a specific indication of Malay progress.[15] Women's political activity was exemplary in one other sense. While the British thought they were witnessing novel behaviour precipitated entirely by the Malayan Union proposals, Malay women's entrance into public life had actually begun during the occupation. Labour service, welfare associations, economic production, education, rallies and public lectures were among the activities encouraged and required by the Japanese regime.[16] As with political speech, associational barriers fell which could not easily be reerected. The new forms of activity could not be unlearned, but would be deployed and mobilised by political leadership.

Second, the primary purpose of politics as articulated in both the radical and conservative press was to safeguard Malay rights which were being

---

[13] Lenore Manderson argues that 'despite the participation of women in politics, the role of women did not change in essence but rather drew its inspiration and its mode of operation from tradition'. *Women, Politics, and Change: The Kaum Ibu UMNO, Malaysia, 1945–1972*, Kuala Lumpur: Oxford University Press, 1980, p. 1.

[14] Captain L.D. Gammans, the Conservative MP whose visit was the occasion of massive demonstrations, was particularly impressed by the women's rallies, especially the one led by the consort of the Sultan of Perak. Manderson comments: 'That women led the march does not indicate that they were initiators – it was obviously a successful tactical decision. That they marched separately reflected the general segregation of women on public occasions'. *Ibid.*, p. 49n51. A *Majlis* editorial (4 June 1946) commented on this march and on Gammans' surprise at seeing 5,000 Malay women standing up for their rights. The Singapore English daily *The Straits Times* often commented on the new participation of Malay women in public life. See 'Malay women want active part', 25 March 1946 and 'Malay women in the new Malaya', 5 December 1946.

[15] *Utusan Melayu*, 23 January 1946, BMA/PR 3/7/Vol. 1. News articles and editorial comment on women's political activity were ubiquitous in the dailies. See, for example, *Majlis*, 26 February, 6 March, 13 March and 12 June 1946; and *Warta Negara*, 12 February and 16 March 1946. Longer analyses and pictures of women meeting and protesting can be seen in the Singapore monthly *Kenchana*, May, September, November and December 1947, and on the cover of the February 1948 issue.

[16] Manderson, *Women, Politics, and Change*, pp. 51–52.

threatened by the Chinese (politically and economically) and by the British constitutional proposals.[17] It was implicitly understood, and explicitly stated by radicals, that it was the failure of the ruling classes that made politics both possible and necessary:

> Now the masses have embraced politics in order to defend their rights and keep their race from sinking to oblivion. But the ruling classes are still fragmented and individualistic which continues to invite British intervention in internal affairs.[18]

It was with this understanding that the aristocrats had at first distanced themselves from the rulers, but all Malays understood who 'the ruling classes' comprised. The aristocrats had lost some of the advantage inherent to their position and would have to try to shape politics in their own image in order to regain it.

Third, the new political consciousness was a national consciousness, though it took conservative politicians some time to shift their bearings from the regional (*kenegerian*) to the national (*kebangsaan*). The Partai Kebangsaan Melayu Malaya (PKMM, Malay Nationalist Party of Malaya) was the first Malay organisation to use the political term 'party' in its name. The combination of *partai* and *kebangsaan* proclaimed a new era in which politics was embraced as the medium of nationalism. PKMM rhetoric also made the new relationship quite clear: 'The Malay Nationalist Party is a *National Movement* and so every Malay has the right to come forward … with his views and findings for the upliftment of his Nation'.[19]

UMNO's own name (Pertubuhan Kebangsaan Melayu Bersatu) is instructive in more than one way, pointing at once to a reluctance to embrace the new forms. First is the eschewing of 'party' for the non-political 'organisation' (*pertubuhan*). Second, neither would the name as originally conceived have included 'national'. Onn bin Jaafar suggested that United Malays Organisation, shortened to UMO, would evoke the sound (and presumably the prestige) of the United Nations Organisation, then commonly referred to in the press as the UNO.[20] That Onn sought evocations in English rather than Malay is not merely anomalous.[21] It points

---

[17] Letter to *Seruan Rakyat*, 19 December 1946.

[18] *Suara Saberkas*, April 1946.

[19] *Voice of the People*, 16 November 1945. Emphasis in original. This publication was the bi-monthly English version of the PKMM's official organ, *Suara Rakyat*.

[20] A. Samad Ahmad, *Sejambak Kenangan: Sebuah Autobiografi*, Kuala Lumpur: Dewan Bahasa dan Pustaka, 1981, p. 216.

[21] According to Samad, it was in September 1947 that Onn pronounced 'Amno' for

to the distance between the goals and mindset of the new organisation and those of prewar Malay nationalism, which was intimately linked with the propagation of the Malay language. Further, the analogy of the United Nations, a federation of mutually exclusive sovereign entities, clearly articulated the aristocratic desire for the prewar status quo rather than that of a forward-looking nationalist movement. Nevertheless, Za'aba (Zainal Abidin Ahmad), doyen of Malay letters, managed to insert 'national' into the name (though the United Nations still exerted a powerful pull on the organisational imagination, providing such structural models as the general assembly).[22] The combination of UMNO's *de facto* appropriation of politics from the rulers and its hasty adoption of the national sobriquet seconded the PKMM's political nationalism and brought it tentatively into the political mainstream.

In sum, the prewar development of a national Malay public, which articulated a critical discourse about Malay society and the state, had probably advanced as far as it could without embracing the medium of politics to further its ends. With the Japanese occupation, the rulers' monopoly on politics was broken, leading in the postwar period to a remarkable transformation in Malay attitudes. Mass politics, predicated on the failure of traditional Malay leadership, was now a legitimate activity and linked firmly to nationalism. I now turn to the new forms of political nationalism and their use by contending political forces.

Nationalism and the Practice of Politics

The critical discourse developed by prewar Malay publishing and associational life was unrelated to the production and propagation of traditionalistic Malay culture and aristocratic privilege. From the beginning, newspapers were published by people who were trying to change the status quo, even if their vision was not radically anticolonial. The traditional elite related to those they ruled in either a traditional or colonial/bureaucratic discourse, and usually needed no such novel approach as print. This began to change with the growth of a literate public, and by the 1930s a discourse of backwardness and progress had evolved which engaged the forward-looking of the bureaucratic elite, as well as Islamic and secular critics of colonialism.

UMNO and it stuck, fixing the English, rather than Malay, name in the public mind. *Ibid.*, p. 245.

22 See the speech by the delegate from the Kesatuan Melayu Singapura in Mohammad Yunus Hamidi, *Sejarah Pergerakan Melayu Semenanjung*, Kuala Lumpur: Pustaka Antara, 1961, pp. 38–39.

After the war, when constitutional crisis and ethnic and political violence produced an atmosphere of urgency and political awakening, the outright denunciation of colonialism sanctioned during the occupation became a norm of political expression against which the colonial restoration moved cautiously at first. This greater range of allowed opinion and the encouragement for everyone to practise politics drastically enlarged the arena of public discourse. But all these new participants, most of them illiterate, could not participate in a critical discourse through the 'public use of their reason'. Modern Malay political life was born in the era of mass democracy, in which the manipulation of 'public opinion' replaced the 'critical public' that had conducted a discourse among literate individuals and with the state.[23] In the colonial territories, as in the metropole, democracy and self-determination were catchwords, often no more than catchwords, it is true; but they certainly lent unquestioned legitimacy to any appeal to public opinion.

It was in this context that the colonial state sought to privilege a 'Malayan' public which it could groom for eventual self-government. The Malay elite countered with the reassertion of a Malay public which was suddenly called upon not only to be political but also to demonstrate unified political behaviour and opinion. In contrast to the slow construction and refinement of a Malay public in the first half of the century, the immediate postwar period saw the startlingly quick construction and manipulation of 'public opinion', first mobilised in opposition to the Malayan Union and then in a struggle to define the nationalist mainstream. The way public opinion was constructed can be seen in the different ways Malays participated in politics and in which avenues were encouraged and which cut off. This section examines four such participatory modes, commenting along the way on the extent to which each contributed to a political nationalism and also on how they reflected the ongoing conservative–radical contest for control over that nationalism.

Propaganda and the Press

The Second World War had a profound effect on the way political elites communicated with their populations throughout the world. This was no less true in Japanese-occupied Southeast Asia, where both old elites and rising nationalists learned about participatory (mass) politics and the art

[23] See Jürgen Habermas, *The Structural Transformation of the Public Sphere: An Inquiry into a Category of Bourgeois Society*, Cambridge: MIT Press, 1989, pp. 236–50.

of propaganda through print and oral media.[24] In Malaya, propaganda in service to the Japanese war effort and directed against the British colonial mentality was incessant in public life – poster and essay competitions on 'The Birth of the New Malaya' and 'The Co-Prosperity Sphere', slogans, songs and films hammered home the message 'Asia for the Asians'.[25] As in Indonesia, Malay nationalists were employed in propaganda departments and at newspapers, which were used for essentially the same purpose. Among the prominent Malay political and literary figures so employed were Ahmad Boestamam at *Berita Perak* and the Ipoh propaganda department, A. Samad Ahmad at *Perubuhan Baharu* (the occupation name for *Majlis*) and as a radio announcer, and Ishak Haji Muhammad at *Berita Malai* and *Semangat Asia*.[26]

The British had also been learning to use propaganda during the war and they applied the lessons learned to their reoccupation of Malaya, where they competed most immediately (and unsuccessfully) with rival propaganda of the Communist Party of Malaya (CPM).[27] By 1945, propaganda – inundating a population with political messages in various media in an effort to construct a political consensus – had become not a singular method but a universal medium of political expression, utilised by every political group to construct and mobilise public opinion. For example, Indian nationalists in Singapore circulated pamphlets, leaflets and photographs of the Japanese-sponsored Indian National Army's war memorial, considered subversive

---

[24] See, for example, Anthony Reid, *The Blood of the People: Revolution and the End of Traditional Rule in Northern Sumatra*, Kuala Lumpur: Oxford University Press, 1979, pp. 134–36, on the propaganda value for Sumatran nationalists of Japan's promise of 'independence in the future'; and Benedict Anderson, 'Japan: "The Light of Asia"', in Josef Silverstein, ed., *Southeast Asia in World War II: Four Essays*, New Haven: Yale University Southeast Asia Studies, 1966, p. 21, on 'the dramatisation of politics, the creation of massive rituals of state, the propagation of "ideological" formulas of vague but patriotic content' in Java.

[25] BMA/ADM 9/1; Cheah Boon Kheng, *Red Star Over Malaya: Resistance and Social Conflict During and After the Japanese Occupation of Malaya, 1941–1946*, Singapore: Singapore University Press, 1983, p. 39; Chin Kee Onn, *Malaya Upside Down*, Singapore: Federal Publications, 1976, first pub. 1946, p. 139.

[26] William R. Roff, Introduction to *Carving the Path to the Summit*, by Ahmad Boestamam, trans. William R. Roff, Athens: Ohio University Press, 1979, p. xv; Samad Ahmad, *Sejambak Kenangan*, pp. 168–70; Abdul Latiff Abdul Bakar, *Ishak Haji Muhammad*, Kuala Lumpur: University of Malaya Press, 1977, pp. 27–30.

[27] See 'Guidance on the duties of a public relations officer in the colonies, for the information of British West Indian governments', CO 875/5/15; and G.L. Edwett, 'Colonial propaganda II – aims and policy', CO 875/11/1.

material by the British authorities.[28] The CPM employed trained orators in Penang.[29] Indonesians imported Republican propaganda from Sumatra which was circulated by branches of the Pembantu Indonesia Merdeka (Aid Free Indonesia) all over Malaya. Indonesian propaganda was especially directed at schools, and in some areas Malay schoolchildren were heard singing the Indonesian anthem on their way to the classroom.[30]

Despite this prevalence of propaganda and new thinking in the Colonial Office about government's communication with colonial peoples, there was little substantive publicity about the Malayan Union among the various communities of Malaya before the release of the government's White Paper on 22 January 1946.[31] Despite Mountbatten's repeated requests for such publicity,[32] the Colonial Office cautiously declined, hoping to safeguard the secret treaty negotiations with the sultans. An important attitude was implicit in this approach. Although the Malayan Union would abandon the prewar 'pro-Malay' policy vis-à-vis the Chinese, the British were inclined to remain 'pro-aristocrat' when dealing with the Malays. Unlike the other communities, in which publicity was expected to play a role in shaping political attitudes, Malays were assumed to remain basically apolitical, despite war and occupation. There was never a full-scale Malayan Union publicity campaign aimed at the Malay population. Instead, surprised by the level of opposition being organised by the Malay community, British officials tried to turn opinion in their favour through selective appeals to those who had worked with them before the war. One such appeal was a Malay newsletter, dated 10 February 1946, over the signature of the chief civil affairs officer, H.R. Hone. The two-page 'personal letter' was specifically designed to address Malay opposition to the January White Paper and

28 Weekly Intelligence Review (hereafter, WIR), no. 61 (1945). WO 203/2076.

29 WIR, no. 60 (1945). WO 203/2076.

30 BMA/ADM 9/16; MSS PIJ, no. 6 (1946), no. 7 (1946), no. 11 (1946), no. 16 (1946), and supplement to no. 10 (Indonesian Influences in Malaya, 1947).

31 James de Vere Allen, *The Malayan Union*, New Haven: Yale University Southeast Asian Studies, 1967, p. 14.

32 Mountbatten argued that the Chinese resistance fighters, whose cooperation he was enlisting in the reoccupation, could well consider the British to be in their debt and ask for an equality of status that Chinese had not enjoyed in prewar Malaya, exactly what the Colonial Office was planning to grant. To release details of the postwar policy *after* the Chinese started making their demands, he argued, would be to appear to be granting concessions. To publicise the plans early would give the Chinese a 'concrete' reason to fight for the British return. See Cheah, *Red Star*, pp. 154–56.

was distributed to about 4,000 'leading Malays'.[33] It is clear from the newsletter that the British hoped the Malay leaders would continue acting as intermediaries with the Malay masses:

> I know that you will continue to assist me by seeing that as far as possible your people are told the truth and kept informed of what is being done for them.... Later on we hope radio sets will be available so that people can hear the daily news in Malay. Until then I know I can count on your co-operation in explaining matters to the people.[34]

The newsletter addressed the ill will and fear British policy had evoked by reminding the recipients of their 'experience of British fair dealings in the past' and by appealing to the principles of modernity and democracy:

> [N]o longer will there be different laws and different taxes in each State but slowly and by degrees the laws of Malaya will be the same throughout the country; all the States being united into a Malayan Union. There will be one central government consisting of a Governor with an Executive and a Legislative Council. This is necessary to give the country strength through unity and is in accordance with the development of all countries in the modern world.
>
> In each State, however, there will continue to be a local State Council which will have certain administrative and legislative powers delegated to it by the Central Authority for purposes of local Government. This is necessary in order that the people may take a full share in their administration and it is also in accordance with sound democratic principles.[35]

The overall message of the newsletter was that the Malayan Union held nothing but advantages for the Malay community. There was some dissent from within the civil affairs staff over the wisdom of this approach. One civil affairs officer, reporting on requested feedback to the newsletter, said that he and his local informants found it too 'rose-tinted'. He felt it would be wiser to admit the loss of privileges, but to call it a sacrifice for progress, a challenge to Malays to 'exert themselves'. Instead of simply extolling the benefits of the British presence, he would have pointed out that British protection couldn't last forever, that 'neither world opinion, British policy nor the temper of the peoples of Asia will permit it'. In this view, 'the Malays will have to stand on their own feet in a hard world eventually'; it would be

33 BMA/PR 1/8.

34 'Malay newsletter no. 2'. BMA/ADM 8/64.

35 *Ibid.*

better to start learning now, while the British were present to ensure 'fair play'.[36]

The Malayan Union newsletter was seriously out of synch with Malay public discourse, right down to the assumptions it made about Malay leadership. If the British were at first complacent about the relationship of the Malay masses to the traditional elite, the conservative politicians were not. When UMNO was established in June 1946, two departments were set up immediately to fight the Malayan Union.[37] One of them was a propaganda department, aimed as much at unifying Malay opinion against the Union as at making representations on the international stage.[38] But UMNO's member associations engaged in propaganda much before this, mobilising peasants across the country to rally, march and wear mourning clothes to mark the Union's inauguration.[39]

UMNO's political opponents were just as active and more tenacious. In December 1945 the PKMM began sending speakers on propaganda missions around the country.[40] In July 1946 there were reported to be PKMM speakers in every Malay state calling for independence for Malaya in association with free Indonesia.[41] In 1947 the British particularly noted PKMM propaganda activity in the schools. This was also true of the PKMM's more militant affiliate, Angkatan Pemuda Insaf (API, Movement of Aware Youth, to be discussed further below). A large number of API members were Malay schoolteachers who were spreading propaganda in villages and rural schools.[42] In urban areas, political messages and desired outcomes were often dramatised as entertainment. The Sri Nooran Opera Company staged the play *Berjuang* (Struggle) at a Kuala Lumpur amusement park to raise money for API. The play, directed by Ahmad Boestamam, depicted battles between Dutch and Indonesian soldiers. Another play

---

36 Letter from J. Gullick, CAO, Seremban and Jelebu, to SCAO, Seremban, 9 March 1946. BMA/ADM 8/64.

37 Ishak bin Tadin, 'Dato Onn and Malay Nationalism 1946–51', *Journal of Southeast Asian History*, vol. 1, no. 1, 1960, pp. 65–66.

38 For the latter, note that demonstrators held banners with messages in both English and Malay.

39 Persetiaan Melayu of Kelantan, for example, had a propaganda section by February 1946. British intelligence reports attributed peasant mobilisation and political action to propaganda, and opined peevishly that the uneducated had no idea why they were wearing mourning clothes. BMA/ADM 9/16; MSS PIJ, no. 1 (1946).

40 WIR, no. 62 (1945). WO 203/2076.

41 MSS PIJ, no. 7 (1946).

42 MSS PIJ, no. 2 (1947), no. 13 (1947).

staged in Selangor, *Chinta Sajati* (True Love), showed united Malay, Indian and Chinese youth working for an end to British rule in Malaya.[43] British intelligence observed in 1947 that Malay nationalist propaganda was repetitive, incessant and successful.[44]

The enrichment of political discourse through new modes of expression did not, however, displace newspapers as the most powerful avenue of communication among the literate and even with the mass of Malay society. This was partially because newspapers had a singular ability to bring authoritative news and opinion-making commentary from the centres of political activity to isolated rural areas. The colonial government itself helped overcome delays in communication and transportation by distributing vernacular newspapers to post offices around the country in the early days of the reoccupation.[45] Later, to help compensate for the wartime depletion of textbooks, 'newspapers were provided in many schools', and according to the 1946 Annual Report on Education, 'were particularly in demand by parents who have always been free to make use of school libraries'.[46] As in the schools before textbooks were replenished, so in rural villages, there was no other reading material of an educational or entertaining nature besides the papers. When one newspaper would reach a village tea stall or coffee shop, it was perused by all who could read and was read aloud to those who could not. Because the nature of the times made national politics the concern of all Malays, newspaper articles became topics of discussion for days or weeks.[47]

Although no one newspaper achieved truly national circulation, each of the three major dailies was read beyond its city of publication. *Utusan Melayu*, published in Singapore, was sent with the English *Straits Times* to Kuala Lumpur, where it enjoyed a circulation rivalling that of *Majlis*.[48] *Majlis*

---

43 MSS PIJ, no. 16 (1946), no. 2 (1947).

44 MSS PIJ, no. 8 (1947). It was often noted, however, that communist propaganda, even when printed in *jawi* (modified Arabic script), was quite unsuccessful with Malays. CO 273/675/50822/56/2; PIJ no. 3 (1946), no. 21 (1947).

45 The aim was to provide one newspaper for every 500 people. The papers distributed were *Majlis, Malaya Tribune, Min Sheng Pau* and *Tamil Nesan*. BMA/PR 2/2.

46 MU 3465/47. The 1946 estimates for the Education Department also included $1,000 to purchase Malay newspapers and periodicals for the Sultan Idris Training College, then the only Malay-medium secondary school in British Malaya. BMA/FIN 406/52.

47 Interview with A. Samad Ismail (23 October 1989), who was an editor of *Utusan Melayu* at the time. I am also grateful to Firdaus Haji Abdullah, a scholar of the period, who shared his personal reminiscences on this topic.

48 Interview with A. Samad Ismail.

itself, though past the peak of its influence of the 1930s, had the advantage of being the Malay newspaper chosen for post office distribution and, as the unofficial organ of UMNO through the late 1940s, was probably the paper which most often found its way into school libraries. *Warta Negara*, from Penang, had access to the large population of the neighbouring Malay state of Kedah. Importantly, all three, as well as the smaller dailies and organs of the PKMM, reported events from all over the peninsula, creating a national community for news consumption. When the British emissary Sir Harold MacMichael arrived to conclude new treaties with the Malay sultans, *Utusan Melayu* wrote that 'the Malays will be asked by Sir Harold to give their opinion', inviting that national community to become political.[49] And as discussed in the previous chapter, the newspapers played a crucial role in reconceptualising the Malay rulers in a pan-Malay setting. Clearly, newspaper journalism continued its prewar role of building a national identity. And the proliferation of radical papers began to articulate a political discourse unrestricted by traditionalism.

Nevertheless, Malay newspaper discourse in the late 1940s held an inherent advantage for conservatives seeking to preserve a privileged place in the new national politics. This was because of the way in which a still largely illiterate and residually oral society related to the written word. Amin Sweeney's study on orality and literacy in the Malay world suggests important ways to understand how newspaper editorials on political matters were apprehended by the Malay public in the 1940s. Sweeney argues that societies are not simply oral or literate, but exhibit 'a whole range of tendencies' and that 'not everything that appears in print reflects interiorization of print-based thought'.[50] He points as well to the importance of literary *consumption* along with composition. Scholars focusing on the changes which occur when literature can be written and read – freedom from memorisation, formula and established themes – have assumed that the new reading public demands new themes. Sweeney shows how the Malay case belies that assumption by demonstrating the continuing oral orientation of much modern written composition and its correspondingly aural (as opposed to visual) consumption:

> In the West, the evolution from the oral/aural cultures of the ancient world to the visualist, type-centered, and electronic cultures of modernity spread out over many centuries. In many Third World countries a similar

[49] *Utusan Melayu*, 16 October 1945, cited in Ishak, 'Dato Onn', p. 58.

[50] Amin Sweeney, *A Full Hearing: Orality and Literacy in the Malay World*, Berkeley: University of California Press, 1987, p. 144.

> development has been compressed into little more than a hundred years. In the Malay world, the study of the way new media interact with the old is particularly complex, and the fairly recent introduction of typographic and electronic technologies has caused radical reorganizations of verbalization and thought. Even so, hardly surprisingly, there remains a strong oral orientation. An understanding of the extent and significance of this orality makes it possible to explain much in modern Malaysian and Indonesian society that may appear strange and exotic or simply dull to the Western observer, not merely in the realm of 'literature,' but also in other areas of communications such as news broadcasts, political speeches, propaganda, television dramas, university lectures, and their impact upon their audiences.[51]

Thus even written literature – in this case, newspaper editorials – may be composed with an oral orientation and consumed in such a fashion as well. Court-produced manuscripts were consumed aurally in the Malay world as early as the seventh century CE, a situation in which 'literacy was not a prerequisite for experiencing the written word'.[52] In the 1940s, we know that many, if not most, Malays *listened to* rather than read the newspapers. The connection between these two experiences of written literature can be seen in the function and style of the works, both of which have political ramifications.

Court literature (*hikayat*) had a prescriptive function, aiming through genealogy to legitimise a ruling family and through narrative to reinforce dominant ideas governing relations between ruling and subject classes. According to Sweeney, the way this literature was consumed reinforced the prescriptive mode, as 'the communal (aural) consumption of oral and written composition tended to limit its content to what was acceptable to the community as a whole and/or to those in a position of power'.[53] The style of *hikayat*-writing was followed by Malay newspapers up until about 1907, when English punctuation and phraseology began to appear. The emergence of the editorial as a regular and prominent feature in Malay newspapers, in about 1930, coincided with marked English-language influence on sentence structure and increased clarity of expression.[54] But the prescriptive function of written composition was maintained, in many cases in the short stories which appeared in all Malay newspapers warning about the Chinese and

---

[51] *Ibid.*, p. 14.

[52] *Ibid.*, p. 73.

[53] *Ibid.*, pp. 5–6.

[54] Mohd. Taib Osman, *The Language of the Editorials in Malay Vernacular Newspapers Up to 1941*, Kuala Lumpur: Dewan Bahasa dan Pustaka, 1966, pp. 30–39.

other internal threats to Malay society.[55] By the late 1940s, with politics a newly sanctioned activity and mobilisation essential, editorialists become masters of exhortation, prescribing to Malays how they should be political. *Majlis* editorials in the latter half of 1946, for example, called on Malays many times to donate money to UMNO and support Malay businesses, reminded them to boycott Malayan Union advisory councils, admonished parents to keep their children in school and asked for donations for the poor. Aside from these special appeals were the everyday calls to support UMNO's policy on the Malayan Union, occasionally accompanied by Onn's draconian warning that 'any Malay person who participates in the Malayan Union will not be acknowledged as a Malay'.[56]

The style of newspaper editorials also reveals certain continuities with older, aurally consumed writings, especially in length, repetition and formula. Editorials were usually laid out on the page in a fashion similar to that of the English papers, that is, in a column running the length of the page, usually on page two. Unlike *The Straits Times*, however, which ran seven columns on a page, Malay papers often ran only two, so that one column consumed half a page. Then, too, editorials quite often ran into the second column and editorial topics were sometimes spread out over two or three days. Sweeney tells us that in manuscript culture, 'the length of telling rather than the content of what is told ... underlines the relative importance of an event or character' and that it is only the transition to visual consumption that shrinks the copiousness of traditional composition.[57] Decorous repetition of one or two main points can well be imagined to have been successful in tea stall readings of editorials.[58] Repetition of one topic over several days' editorials also had a practical function. Perhaps only one out of a week's run of newspapers might reach a particular village. An important message would need to be repeated to be sure it was properly disseminated.

Sweeney further reminds us that the illiterate and residually oral tend to think in formulas, using large schematic 'chunks' of received knowledge

---

[55] Zulkipli, *Warta Malaya*, p. 101.

[56] *Majlis*, 7 August 1946.

[57] Sweeney, *A Full Hearing*, p. 239.

[58] Another work presents the *Majlis* editorials of October 1945 to January 1948 (the BMA and Malayan Union periods) to modern Malay readers. It is highly indicative of the changing style of written Malay that the editorials are summarised, rather than reproduced in their original words and length. The main gist of each editorial is usually captured in one or two short paragraphs. Zakiah Hanum, *Tercabarnya Maruah Bangsa: Satu Himpunan Pemikiran Wartawan Akhbar Majlis 1945–1948*, Kuala Lumpur: Penerbitan Lajmeidakh, 1987.

over and over where the literate person engages in analytical thought. He has observed in this regard that the governments of Malaysia and Indonesia have exploited this tendency 'by deliberately creating formulas, in the form of slogans, mottoes, and catchphrases for adoption by the masses. It might be said that the slogan has become the new proverb'.[59] In fact, it was during the anti-Malayan Union campaign that proverbs themselves first became slogans. The most famous was '*Melayu takkan hilang di dunia*' (Malays will not vanish from the earth), updated from the battle cry of Melaka-era warrior Hang Tuah into a modern political slogan. This sloganising of Hang Tuah utilised tradition as an emotive reinforcement for UMNO's anti-Malayan Union policy. Other formulary features of expression also confirmed received wisdom and worked against the development of new political thinking. The typecasting and stereotyping common to schematic formulation were apparent in the frequent references to 'Si Ah Chong' (standing in for the Chinese) and 'Si Ramasamy' (for the Indians) in *Majlis*. Such stereotyping, always appearing in negative contexts, helped make the PKMM's sporadic efforts at interethnic alliance *a priori* suspect endeavours.

I am suggesting here that the didactic or prescriptive function of newspapers, the persistence of formulary features of expression and the way aural consumption evoked the prescriptive mode of traditional manuscript culture translated into an advantage for political conservatism. The experience of listening to newspaper editorials – especially hearing about Dato X or Raja Y[60] – held an inherent bias towards conventional and conservative political messages. Further, since the bureaucratic elite had successfully transformed itself into something purporting to represent progressive traditionalism, its political messages, transmitted in newspapers that were supported, not suppressed, by the colonial government, had much more credibility than those of younger, mostly non-aristocratic nationalists, who could easily be dismissed as collaborationist (vis-à-vis the Japanese) or communist.

One last note on literacy and the consumption of newspapers concerns the use of *jawi* (modified Arabic script) and *rumi* (romanised script). In the Netherlands East Indies, the universality of Malay as an administrative language led to the predominance of the romanised version. The situation on the peninsula was quite different. In the English language-administered Straits Settlements and Federated Malay States, Malay was quite marginal and its romanisation was of no official concern to the British. In the

---

59 Sweeney, *A Full Hearing*, pp. 141–42, 98.

60 Aristocratic and royal titles.

Unfederated Malay States, Malay was the language of state and it was here as well that the elite had the power to preserve traditional forms, like the use of *jawi*. In neither case were the British hostile to the retention of *jawi*, concerned as they were with preservation, though they did introduce *rumi*, which then became an option for Malays. Education also played a role in preserving *jawi*, as the colonial government's indifferent attitude towards secular Malay education before the war had left a large realm for religious education, which centred around Arabic and Malay in the *jawi* script. In the 1930s and 1940s, then, most literate Malays were literate in *jawi* only, and the use of *rumi* was even controversial. Language organisations and newspapers in the 1930s largely favoured the retention of *jawi* for purposes of purity and quality of language (essentially preferring to borrow from Arabic rather than English), and proponents of *rumi* were sometimes called 'traitors' to the Malay race.[61]

By the late 1940s, however, the tide was beginning to turn. As Sweeney points out, there was 'a limit beyond which *Jawi* could not keep pace with the development of modern Malay'.[62] There was, too, a general momentum favouring progress, which proponents of *rumi* successfully tapped.[63] By 1947 *Majalah Guru*, the influential magazine of the Malay teachers' association, which was itself published in *jawi*, ran an article entitled, '*Jawi* Script and *Rumi* Script are the Malays' Scripts'.[64] Finally, the writers' organisation, Angkatan Sasterawan '50 (1950 Literary Generation) pronounced a few years later in favour of *rumi*, assuring Malays that choosing the romanised script for its many advantages did not mean abandoning Islam.[65] Nevertheless,

61 Zulkipli, *Warta Malaya*, p. 99.

62 Sweeney, *A Full Hearing*, p. 86.

63 A letter from a reader in Penang to *Seruan Rakyat*, a *rumi* paper, extolled the progress made by Turkey under the influence of Kamal Ataturk, who switched to a romanised script. Indonesia was cited as well, as a place where everyone – Europeans, Chinese, Arabs and Indians – could read Malay newspapers and magazines. To those Malays who wondered if they really wanted the other races to read and know their thoughts, the letter writer answered, 'They must! [*Mesti!*] Misunderstanding always leads to social discord'. *Seruan Rakyat*, 8 November 1945. A Sumatran reader of *Kenchana*, a *rumi* monthly published in Singapore, praised the journal's script, saying that it helped Indonesians and the Malay world in general to follow the struggle of Malays to achieve independence. *Kenchana*, no. 5, May 1947.

64 *Majalah Guru*, no. 3, June 1947.

65 'Memorandum mengenai tulisan rumi untuk bahasa melayu', March 1954 in Angkatan Sasterawan '50, *Memoranda: Kumpulan Tulisan Angkatan Sasterawan '50 Dengan Lampiran Rumusan Kongres Bahasa dan Persuratan Melayu Ketiga*, Kuala Lumpur: Oxford University Press, 1962, pp. 14–30.

rumi readership in the late 1940s was very small and publication in *jawi* was still the way to reach the greatest number of readers. It is striking then that conservative publications consistently utilised *jawi*, while progressive newspapers and journals were often printed in *rumi*. The bureaucratic elite which formed the core membership of UMNO were the Malays most likely to know English, and party documents show them to have been comfortable in both *jawi* and *rumi*.[66] Yet the publications associated with the conservative party showed political acuity in making themselves accessible to the greatest number of Malay readers. The more progressive periodicals which published in *rumi*, *Seruan Rakyat* and *Kenchana*, for example, limited their readership among peninsular Malays while seeking, in the case of the latter, to bridge a Malay and Sumatran audience.

A Modern Hero: Onn bin Jaafar as National Leader

The bureaucratic elite and its contribution to the progress of the Malays in the modern world had been a subject of public discourse before the war. It was articulated as a problem of leadership and was discussed by the elite itself in the context of the Malay associations established in the late 1930s. According to the president of the Selangor Malay Association, 'We all lack leaders who can lead us to national salvation. It is with the view to seeking leaders for the future that this Association is founded today'.[67] In a manner consistent with the goals and experience of this elite, higher education in English was seen as the medium through which such leadership would emerge. After the war, the terms of this discourse in the conservative press had not changed much, though now the problem was more urgent. The lack of 'true leaders' was blamed for the Malays' restricted access to the prosperity of the country.[68] Editorials called for the well educated, especially government servants, not to shrink from duty to their country and not to be afraid to get involved in politics, arguing that if they did not the future of the Malays would be grim.[69] Those who were highly placed in society came in for particular censure. Mohammad Yunus Hamidi, editor of *Majlis* and

---

66 Party documents were typed in *rumi*. Letters from private individuals to UMNO officials were written in English, *rumi* and *jawi*. Minutes on the correspondence were written in *rumi* and English. See examples in UMNO/SG 12/1946 and 74/1946.

67 Tengku Ismail, inaugural speech of the Selangor Malay Association, *Majlis*, 23 November 1938, cited in Radin Soenarno, 'Malay nationalism, 1900–1945', *Journal of Southeast Asian History*, vol. 1, no. 1, 1960, p. 25.

68 Letter to *Seruan Rakyat*, 8 January 1946.

69 *Majlis*, 6 April 1946.

secretary of the Selangor Malay Association, was quoted in *Seruan Rakyat* attributing the backwardness of the Malays to the 'unworthiness' of their leaders, from *penghulus* to sultans.[70] As the conservative prewar associations reestablished themselves, however, and the anti-Malayan Union campaign progressed, there were positive examples to extol and specific courses of action to recommend. Malays were urged to unite behind the Malay Congress, soon to become UMNO, and those who risked 'their ranks, their posts and even their lives' to oppose the colonial power were praised as worthy national leaders.[71]

Onn bin Jaafar was quickly singled out for particular mention. From the time he established his Pergerakan Melayu Semenanjung Johor (Peninsular Malay Movement of Johor) in January 1946, Onn was hailed as a leader of extraordinary promise: '[The Movement's] promoter is the national leader long awaited by the public.... He is the leader the nation hoped has for'.[72]

Onn had earlier made a name for himself defusing Malay–Chinese tensions in the Batu Pahat region of Johor where he was district officer in 1945. In that situation he had managed to rein in, while acknowledging the influence of, a local religious cult leader who was preparing to launch an armed attack on a Chinese town.[73] In announcing his new movement, Onn showed similar attention to new forces arising in Malay society, while still bowing in the direction of traditional authority:

> With the permission of the Malay chiefs in the state of Johor, I have formed a new movement which will include within it the entire Malay public in order to guard the rights, interests and safety of the Malays. This movement was started in the villages; it is managed by village people in the interests of village people themselves.[74]

The 'rise' of Onn as the leader of the anti-Malayan Union campaign, and as founder and first president of UMNO, is dealt with in virtually every account of this period. I will not repeat the details here.[75] What needs

---

[70] *Seruan Rakyat*, 18 December 1945.

[71] *Majlis*, 3 May and 30 May 1946.

[72] *Seruan Rakyat*, 10 January 1946.

[73] Cheah, *Red Star*, pp. 225–30.

[74] *Seruan Rakyat*, 10 January 1946.

[75] The English accounts include Allen, *Malayan Union* and A.J. Stockwell, *British Policy and Malay Politics During the Malayan Union Experiment*, 1945–46, Kuala Lumpur: Malaysian Branch of the Royal Asiatic Society, Monograph no. 8, 1979. In Malay, accounts written by participants include Ibrahim Mahmood, *Sejarah Perjuangan Bangsa Melayu*, Kuala Lumpur: Pustaka Antara, 1981 and Mohammad Yunus Hamidi, *Sejarah Pergerakan Politik Melayu Semenanjung*.

to be extracted from these narratives are the two ways Onn's leadership helped shape national political practice. The first was his pivotal role in the reinvention of the rulers, discussed in the previous chapter. Onn was perhaps uniquely qualified to effect this transformation, given his prewar experience as both intimate and opponent of Sultan Ibrahim of Johor. Onn's second influence, of interest here, was his creation, by example, of a new kind of leadership. Onn was the first *national* leader; he transcended state boundaries, constructed political opinion and connected with Malays throughout the peninsula. He did this largely on the strength of oration and his willingness to manipulate the mechanisms of mass politics.

Although the PKMM had speakers touring the states from December 1945, it was the oration of Onn which sent a spark throughout the country, even before he left Johor. The power of this new type of leadership is reflected strongly in the recollection of Onn's political opponent, Ahmad Boestamam, who saw Onn's picture and news about him constantly in the conservative press:

> According to those papers, he held public political meetings, presented the political organisation which he headed, explained its aims and objectives, called the Malay community together, and much more.
>
> Datuk Onn could speak for hours and hours, and his speeches were very spirited, according to reports. He was very good at lifting the spirits of those listening to him talk. The public would be spellbound where they sat listening to his speech, not wanting to leave from beginning to end.
>
> The name of Datuk Onn, it was further reported, was like a magnet to the public. When it was announced that he would speak at a public meeting, it was certain that people would throng to hear him. Thousands of them. Because of this, he was said rarely to have spoken in front of a crowd numbering less than a thousand people....
>
> Datuk Onn's speeches, which never lasted less than one hour, always drew thunderous applause from the audience.[76]

Based on these reports, Ahmad Boestamam wanted to hear Onn speak, but Johor was far from Perak and he had his own responsibilities as a PKMM officer. He finally heard Onn speak at the Malay Congress in early March, to which the PKMM sent a delegation. Ahmad Boestamam's assessment makes it clear that Onn did not disappoint:

> He was not a lecturer ... who put his audience to sleep.... Neither was he simply one who ignited the spirit, an agitator who made the blood boil

[76] Ahmad Boestamam, *Datuk Onn*, pp. 10–11.

> without presenting any new information. On the contrary, lecturer and agitator were both united within him as an orator. That was what was extraordinary about him.[77]

As Ahmad Boestamam describes it, it was Onn's knowledge as much as his charisma which contributed to the powerful consensus he was able to build in those few days, knowledge which he clearly obtained working and socialising at the top of colonial society:

> He could talk for a long time without boring his listeners. And that is what he did throughout the assembly, whenever he had the opportunity. He talked very knowledgeably, giving facts and evidence.
>
> If a doubt arose among the representatives regarding the political situation at that time, the system of government under colonialism, or other such matters, he stepped forward with an explanation. And about those things he indeed knew everything.
>
> In short, let me say that from the time the assembly began he was already regarded as a Malay hero. As the assembly progressed, his stature rose further. As a result, the congress, or at least a large number of the representatives, quickly fell under his influence and were henceforth controlled by him.[78]

Two things are notable about the leadership style evolving here. First is the consensus Onn was able to create on the strength of his character and, increasingly, on the simple fact of his leadership. His unanimous election to the presidency of the Congress, and later UMNO, set a precedent in modern Malay politics for the degree of consensus a leader could demand. His ability to enforce consensus enabled Onn to shape UMNO, in the following years, into a direct membership party over the opposition of several member organisations which strove to retain their distinctive voices.[79] Once completed, this change in turn structurally strengthened the party executive. Onn eventually pushed too far in trying to make UMNO accept non-Malay members, a conflict which ended his association with the party (and his political influence) in 1951. But his style of consensus building survived his fall, leaving power and decision-making in UMNO highly centralised. Onn's

---

[77] *Ibid.*, p. 18.

[78] *Ibid.*, pp. 18–19.

[79] UMNO began life as an umbrella organisation to which about 37 local organisations belonged. In 1947 the local organisations amalgamated so there would be only one UMNO affiliate in each state, but they were still autonomous. It was not until 1949 that UMNO became a direct membership political party with subordinate state branches. Stockwell, *British Policy and Malay Politics*, pp. 118–21.

successor, Tunku Abdul Rahman, the first Malaysian prime minister (1957–1970), exercised power with no interference from UMNO's general assembly, which was required to give a vote of confidence to all the executive's past and future actions.[80] This style of leadership has been exhibited by all subsequent UMNO executives. The longest-serving prime minister, Mahathir Mohamad, for example, though the first non-aristocratic Malay to lead UMNO and the country, carried the centralisation of power to new heights by weakening all rival institutions of government – legislative, judicial and monarchical.

The second innovation Onn pioneered was updating the way aristocratic leadership interacted with the *rakyat*, making bureaucrats into politicians. This he did by going on speaking tours throughout the country beginning in June 1946. Onn attended receptions along the way, 'stressing his now well known and publicised views'.[81] *Majlis* both reported Onn's tours and editorialised about how such visits gave Onn an opportunity to speak with the people and awaken their spirit of struggle. It was also an opportunity, *Majlis* continued, for Onn to pass on important information about national politics.[82] When *Majlis* predicted that many more such invitations would come Onn's way, the newspaper was in essence asking Malay associations to invite Onn to visit. The associations took the hint. In 1947 Onn had more invitations than he could handle, and other senior UMNO officials had to go to local ceremonies in his stead.[83] On the state level, politically-minded aristocrats began to make propaganda tours in emulation of the popular UMNO president.[84] This new style of ruler–ruled interaction was not, however, embraced by all aristocratic leaders. And those who did so understood that they were trying to master the new medium in direct competition with the PKMM. UMNO officials paid careful attention to the impact of propaganda tours by Burhanuddin Al-Helmy, Ahmad Boestamam, Ishak Haji Muhammad and other nationalist leaders.[85]

As time went on, Onn's tours became important more as visual representations of the new Malay leadership and less as opportunities for oratory. The schedule for the last two weeks of April 1947 included 11 major towns and the villages in between, but the number of speeches was

---

80 John Funston, *Malay Politics in Malaysia: A Study of the United Malays National Organization and Party Islam*, Kuala Lumpur: Heinemann, 1980, p. 173.

81 MSS PIJ, no. 5 (1946).

82 *Majlis*, 23 October 1946.

83 UMNO/SG 10/46 (Outstation Visits).

84 For example, Raja Bendahara of Perak went to the Parit area in April 1947, urging Malays there not to get mixed up in the PKMM. MSS PIJ, no. 5 (1947).

85 UMNO/SG 10/46.

diminishing. In the last third of the tour, 'there will be only one or two big gathering[s] where a speech is expected. The rest is in the nature of personal visits and picnics only to give the people a chance to see their leader'. Urging Onn to make the tour, the acting secretary general of UMNO, Zainal Abidin bin Haji Abas, wrote: 'The important thing is that the people want to see you – not necessarily to hear you. They have read all you have said but they have not seen you'.[86]

This emphasis on the visual can also be seen in the large numbers of photographs of Onn sold in Johor.[87] It suggests that the newly politicised traditional leadership had appropriated a function the rulers had performed under colonialism. It was now politicians – especially the popular Onn – who toured the country, symbolically connecting ruler with ruled and simultaneously mapping out the realm – now *tanah Melayu*, not the individual Malay states.

How did this transcendence of the Malay state (*negeri*) come about? It is commonly held that Malay peasants had to overcome state-based loyalties (with some difficulty) in the late colonial period in order to progress to nationalism. Perhaps this has been overstated. If state-based loyalties were so strong, Onn, previously identified only with Johor and Singapore, would not have been so easily accepted as a national leader. The puzzle may be lessened if we recall the colonial inspiration behind the traditionalistic 'ideal' Malay state of the twentieth century and disentangle state identity from the question of leadership.

It was the bureaucratic class which owed its continued stature and influence to the Malay state and this class, rather than the newly literate or the peasants, who were likely to identify and organise at the state level. This supposition is, in fact, borne out by the pattern of political organisation of the 1930s and 1940s. Aristocrats established state-based Malay organisations in the 1930s and reestablished them as openly political organisations in the same format in 1946. The only way this class could conceive of a national organisation at first was as an umbrella group like UMNO, which combined but did not dissolve its constituent member organisations. In contrast, both before and after the Second World War, non-aristocrat-led organisations like the Kesatuan Melayu Muda (KMM) and the PKMM were formed at the national, pan-Malay level. Only then were state branches formed. Even earlier, from the days of *Al-Imam*, reformist ideas were articulated in a geographically inclusive, pan-Malay format.

86 UMNO/SG 10/46.

87 MSS PIJ, no. 3 (1947).

A reexamination of the loyalty owed to Malay leadership similarly downgrades the importance of the *negeri*. Loyalty was ideally owed to the ruler and *kerajaan* referred to the condition of having a ruler, not to a government or a place. An effective ruler could create in a state the circumstances conducive to good living. This is how Abu Bakar of Johor was remembered. Despite his usurpation of the sultanate, for which fellow monarchs despised him, the inhabitants of Johor remembered with pride that he created an independent Islamic state in which Europeans were held to an advisory role.[88] There is no other way to explain why a recent Javanese immigrant, for example, would be loyal to Johor. The colonial 'restoration' of ideal Malay states and the enhanced visibility of rulers in their states may have served to strengthen the link between loyalty to ruler and identification with place.[89] But the visible decline in status and efficacy which the rulers suffered during the occupation may then have uncoupled this pairing of loyalty and identification. After the debacle of the MacMichael treaties, and thanks to the intervention of Onn, one could still be loyal to one's ruler, but choose to *identify* with a more effective and progressive polity and leadership than that represented by the ruler in his state. In the prevailing nationalist climate of postwar Asia, there is no reason at all why a Johor leader, purporting to represent 'the Malays', should not become wildly popular. And insofar as Onn stayed close to the rulers, whether in tension or in support, he successfully rearticulated a Malay leadership with historical resonance. Though both conservatives and radicals spoke of restoring the glory of the Malay past, Onn succeeded in *living* it, a modern-day rendition of Hang Tuah and Hang Jebat rolled into one.[90] Despite the novelty of mass politics, Onn was, as Ahmad Boestamam understood, a Malay hero.

---

[88] Kenelm O.L. Burridge, 'Racial relations in Johore', *Australian Journal of Politics and History*, vol. 2, no. 2, 1957, p. 159.

[89] The most parochial and least well-travelled Malay subjects would have had no knowledge of the increasing uniformity of British Malaya and might easily have assumed the uniqueness of their ruler and state.

[90] Warriors from the Melaka era, Hang Tuah and Hang Jebat have become icons of blind loyalty and murderous rebellion, respectively. In the postwar and independence era, the traditional valorisation of Tuah has sometimes been replaced by the elevation of Jebat to the status of 'national hero', a man before his time. See Kassim Ahmad, *Characterization in Hikayat Hang Tuah*, Kuala Lumpur: Dewan Bahasa dan Pustaka, 1966. For a condemnation of the continuing valorisation of all feudal heroes in contemporary Malaysia, see Shaharuddin b. Maaruf, *Concept of a Hero in Malay Society*, Singapore and Kuala Lumpur: Eastern Universities Press, 1984.

Symbols of Nation

Prewar colonial articulations of place and authority had been premised on the restoration of tradition. Symbols of colonial Malaya were therefore designed to evoke a glorious past, even when they actually introduced entirely new elements, such as the 'Moorish' design of the Sultan of Selangor's palace and the Federal Secretariat buildings. By the late 1930s, even the addition of British iconography – such as statues of British heroes – had long become a familiar part of the representation of British Malaya. These last were to be found, however, in greatest number in the Straits Settlements and fewest in the Unfederated Malay States. The fractured nature of colonial administration, reflecting the priorities of indirect rule and traditionalism, militated against representations of British Malaya per se, and thus against '*tanah Melayu*' as a whole.

After this period of relative stability, the Japanese occupation introduced a time when symbols of power and identity were much more fluid and contested. First, the Japanese, in 'an attempt to erase the last vestiges of British power in Malaya, [removed] the British Imperial coat-of-arms and other foreign heraldic ensigns from the frontages of public buildings and ... British statues (notably that of Raffles in Singapore) from prominent public places'.[91] In addition to the symbols of Japanese culture and power – Nippon-go, bowing and so forth – which replaced those of the British, new possibilities were introduced for representing Malaya as a nation. One outlet for such representation was found in the many contests held by the occupation government, which invited people to use new forms – posters, essays, slogans, oratory – in order to articulate the 'New Malaya'. In such one contest held to create a memorial stamp, the winning design showed farmers superimposed against a map of the Malay archipelago.[92]

The interest in representation of the nation did not cease with the restoration of British colonial power. It was, in fact, reflected in the struggle between the returning British and the newly politicised communities of Malaya. In this aspect of political life, Malay nationalists were, not surprisingly, more innovative than conservative elite politicians. Nationalists had, first of all, been thinking in pan-Malay terms for some time and had gained valuable experience producing nationalist rhetoric and imagery during the occupation. The conservatives, as reflected in the name UMNO, were slower to embrace a nationalism which, in the prevailing international

91 Chin, *Malaya Upside Down*, p. 139.
92 CO 273/669/50744/7.

climate, implied both social revolution and anticolonialism.

The conservatives' relative disinterest in symbolising the nation can be seen in the matter of the national flag. The PKMM acted quickly after its founding to define a national flag which linked Malaya to a glorious past and also to the Indonesian Republic. In proposing a national flag, Ahmad Boestamam acknowledged that every state in Malaya already had a flag, but he attributed those flags' identities and hence their differing designs to their belonging to the individual rulers.[93] He looked askance at anyone actually identifying any more with those flags, smearing them with the tar of 'provincialism' and royal absolutism. To replace all those state flags with a national flag, he argued, was both desirable for the unity of the Malays and easy to accomplish. A new flag did not need to be invented, because the Malays already had a one dating from 'before the year 1511, when the Malays were still a free nation'. This flag was the *merah-putih* (red-and-white), which was also the flag of the Republic of Indonesia.[94] Ahmad Boestamam's logic for adopting the Indonesian flag ran as follows: Malaya 'was not a country by herself' but 'part of the Malay Archipelago along with Java, Sumatra and many other small islands [which now] call themselves Indonesia'. The *merah-putih* had flown over Majapahit (fourteenth-century Java) and was carried by the 'revolutionist' Diponegoro in the nineteenth century. Due to the political awakening of the Indonesian people, the *merah-putih* had now become the national flag of Indonesia. Ahmad Boestamam backed up the Greater Indonesia idea with a local connection as well: 'According to some Historians the Red and White Flag was also the flag of Hang Tuah that great Malay hero of the Melakan Empire and his followers'.

Hang Tuah did indeed prove to be a much more popular justification for adopting the *merah-putih*, even among those who agreed with Ahmad Boestamam that, historically, culturally, linguistically and religiously, Indonesia and Malaya were one and had been artificially separated by the Dutch and the British empires.[95] Others who favoured 'the original white and red flag hoisted by Hang Tuah in Malacca' made no reference at all to Indonesia.[96] It quickly became accepted that the *merah-putih* was the national flag of the Malays. Just as quickly though, letters to newspapers

---

93 This paragraph is based on 'Our national flag', in *Voice of the People*, 16 November 1945. The article also ran, in Malay, in *Seruan Rakyat*, 29 November 1945.

94 The top half of the *merah-putih* is red, the bottom white.

95 Letter to *Seruan Rakyat*, 1 December 1945.

96 Letter from a Kuala Lumpur reader to *Utusan Melayu*, 20 October 1945 (BMA/PR 3/5).

showed that Malays wanted some differentiation on their flag, most commonly calling for a *kris* (dagger) or green crescent, the symbol of Islam, to distinguish the Malays of the peninsula.[97]

Eventually, the question of the flag would provide an excuse for the PKMM to leave UMNO.[98] At the June 1946 meeting in Ipoh (UMNO's second general assembly), delegates decided between four flag designs: one had horizontal stripes of green, white and black, representing fertility, purity and tin (proposed by Onn's Pergerakan Melayu Semenanjung Johor); the *merah-putih* (proposed by the PKMM's Ishak Haji Muhammad, who argued that it was the Malays' historical legacy); the *merah-putih* with a green *kris* in the centre, representing the Malays and Islam (proposed by the Persatuan Melayu Daerah Sabak Bernam); and the *merah-putih* with a green *kris* in a yellow circle, yellow representing the Malay rulers (proposed by the Ikatan Setia Kampung Melayu of Kuala Lumpur). According to a participant, A. Samad Ahmad, the real contest was between the first and the fourth, with the PKMM's choice having little chance of acceptance. The fourth flag was chosen and the PKMM walked out.[99]

Two interesting things have been little noted about this episode. The first is the striking similarity in most of the choices, the extent to which nationalists had, over the preceding six months, defined the discourse on the representation of Malaya. The *merah-putih*, with or without a *kris*, was a powerful reminder of revolutionary Indonesia which Onn's group had specifically avoided. Its popularity as the basis of the Malay flag was a victory of sorts that the nationalists discarded by choosing to withdraw from UMNO on this pretext. The PKMM allowed UMNO to appropriate, and domesticate, the *merah-putih* by treating the flag vote as a defeat.

The second point is also connected to UMNO's appropriation of the *merah-putih*. Ahmad Boestamam and the letter writers cited above were discussing a 'national' flag. What was voted on in June 1946 was the 'UMNO flag', soon to be featured at party flag raisings all over the country.[100] Although there was certainly some blurring between national and party symbols on the part of the PKMM as well, the adoption of a party flag had a distinct effect. Foregrounding the organisation, rather than the nation,

97 Letter to *Seruan Rakyat*, 1 December 1945; letters to *Utusan Malayu*, 23 November and 26 November 1945. The editor pointed out, however, that Islam, as a religion did not connote nationality and that all Malays were not Muslim. BMA/PR 3/7/Vol. 1.

98 It is clear that this issue provided a pretext for leaving what was becoming a very uncomfortable alliance.

99 Samad Ahmad, *Sejambak Kenangan*, pp. 237–40.

100 Onn's outstation visits usually included a flag raising. UMNO/SG 10/46.

allowed conservative politicians to avoid for the moment thorny questions of agenda. If nationalism, and by extension a national flag, had been highlighted, UMNO would have had to answer to a standard then being set by nationalist movements in India, Indonesia, Burma, Vietnam and China – the struggle for independence. Instead, UMNO in effect subordinated the nation and its aspirations to its own vision by attaching the national symbol to the party. It was also the first manifestation of the idea that UMNO was identical with the Malay nation. The following year, when UMNO was working hard to counter PKMM popularity, Onn would say that the UMNO flag represented Malay unity.[101]

The PKMM continued to link Malaya to Indonesia through symbols even after the flag was 'lost' to UMNO. The most important way this was done was through the celebration of Indonesian independence on the seventeenth of each month.[102] Although the anniversaries have been construed as 'any conceivable excuse to hold a mass rally'[103] and attendance fluctuated greatly, they in fact kept the example of Indonesia constantly before the public, an implicit reproach to the pro-British, pro-ruler conservatism of the UMNO movement. The one-year anniversary in August 1946 was celebrated in 'nearly all towns'; PKMM speeches called for Malay unity to fight for freedom and warned that the sultans could not be trusted.[104] The PKMM had other ways of keeping Indonesia before the public. While UMNO held an 'UMNO song competition', the PKMM simply sang 'Indonesia Raya', the Republic's anthem, at official occasions.[105] In the final act of a performance of Malay opera in Kuala Kangsar, Perak, actors dressed as Javanese, Balinese, Sumatran and other Indonesians were joined on stage by an actor and actress representing Malaya; the opera featured Indonesian songs and urged Malays to join the Republic.[106] At a play sponsored by API, the PKMM's militant youth wing, in Singapore, the curtain was painted with a map of Malaya, Java, Sumatra, Bali, Sulawesi and Borneo, with the words '*Indonesia Merdeka*' (Free Indonesia) superimposed.[107] The prestige of the Indonesian revolution put

---

101 MSS PIJ, no. 10 (1947).

102 Indonesian independence was declared on 17 August 1945.

103 Firdaus Haji Abdullah, *Radical Malay Politics: Its Origins and Early Development*, Petaling Jaya: Pelanduk Publications, 1985, p. 92.

104 MSS PIJ, no. 9 (1946). See also BMA/ADM 9/16; PIJ no. 13 (1946) and no. 14 (1947).

105 UMNO/SG 94/46; MSS PIJ no. 5 (1946).

106 MSS PIJ, no. 7 (1947).

107 MSS PIJ no. 9 (1947).

UMNO under considerable pressure and *Majlis* did begin to acknowledge the monthly anniversaries, but a proposal at UMNO's March 1947 general assembly to celebrate Indonesian independence day every year received no support.[108]

In early 1947 an event took place that seemed to prompt UMNO to articulate a response to the PKMM's *Indonesia Raya* (Greater Indonesia) vision of the Malay nation. In February of that year the birthday of the Prophet coincided with the PKMM's monthly observance of Indonesian independence. These events were celebrated in Kuala Lumpur with a procession by the PKMM, API and a Malay labour organisation, after which the Sultan of Selangor spoke on the Prophet and Islam.[109] From this point on, UMNO began using the rulers much more actively to symbolise a politically and religiously conservative vision of the nation. In March the ruler of Perlis paid tribute to the Malay Association of that state, asking Malays to join the association which was affiliated with UMNO and recognised by the rajas.[110] In April UMNO held a ceremony in Selangor at which a new labour section was announced and the sultan recognised UMNO as 'the Malay political body'.[111] Within the next two months, the Sultan of Kelantan raised the UMNO flag before a crowd of 5,000 and the Regent of Johor called on Malays to unite at a flag raising in Mersing at which Onn spoke darkly of upheavals in India and Indonesia.[112] In June UMNO concentrated on building up its youth movement in Johor (established in opposition to API and headed by Onn's son Hussein), which was to be centred on loyalty to the sultan.[113]

Thus UMNO at times appropriated symbols of the nation – as with the flag – and disarmed them of revolutionary potential. At other times it simply emulated nationalist innovations and infused them with traditionalism. In neither case did the conservative formulations overwhelm the opposition, but they were important steps in mastering the language of nationalism and allowed UMNO more and more confidently to assume a nationalist posture.

---

108 The proposal was made by the Persatuan Melayu Selangor 'in order to strengthen and [intensify] feelings of nationalism among all Malays in Tanah Melayu'. UMNO/F 7/47.

109 MSS PIJ, no. 2 (1947).

110 MSS PIJ, no. 4 (1947).

111 MSS PIJ, no. 6 (1947).

112 MSS PIJ, no. 8 (1947) and MSS PIJ no. 10 (1947).

113 MSS PIJ, no. 10 (1947). Sultan Ibrahim returned to Johor from London for the September 1947 UMNO general assembly, at which Hussein Onn led a parade of his youth organisation, which swore allegiance to Islam, the sultan and UMNO. Stockwell, *British Policy and Malay Politics*, p. 99n58.

Gathering in Defence of *Bangsa Melayu*: Demonstrations and Drilling

The single most important political act Malays were asked to perform in the first eight months of the reoccupation was to participate in public demonstrations against the Malayan Union. In fact, political meetings and mass rallies by all the communities signalled to the British the vast changes which had occurred in public life since 1941. When a communist rally drew more than 15,000 people in Singapore in November 1945, intelligence reports remarked that it was the first of its kind held in Malaya.[114] Political meetings presented opportunities to engage in political imagery, as at the PKMM's inaugural congress, which observed a three-minute silence for the Indonesian war dead, and to work out political programmes and tactics.[115] Participants in mass rallies heard speeches, sang anthems and learned slogans which often encapsulated all their knowledge about the political events in which they took part.[116]

Government reaction to this new and pervasive form of political activity, much like its relations with the press, was governed by pragmatism, attempts to aid groups considered friendly, and harassment and eventual suppression of radical gatherings. There was a certain amount of inconsistency during the BMA period. Ahmad Boestamam recalls easily obtaining permission to hold a mass meeting at Jubilee Park in Ipoh to commemorate six months of independent Indonesia.[117] A month earlier, a Pan-Malayan Congress of Indonesians was 'cancelled' by the BMA; the meeting was held despite the ban, and several participants were stopped and searched on their journey home.[118] In one case, a public rally became a private meeting when the first option was disallowed by the government,[119] but organisers did not always heed official pronouncements. In March permission was requested for a PKMM congress and British intelligence noted dryly that preparations were proceeding unworriedly even before permission was obtained.[120]

---

[114] WO 203/2130.

[115] See 'Malaya political climate', no. 6, WO 203/5660 and Firdaus, *Radical Malay Politics*, p. 79, for details of the congress and the eight resolutions passed.

[116] See MSS PIJ, no. 1 (1946), no. 5 (1946) and no. 11 (1947) for examples of the uses of '*Malaya Hak Melayu*' (Malaya for the Malays).

[117] Ahmad Boestamam, *Carving the Path*, p. 34.

[118] BMA/ADM 9/16.

[119] *Ibid.*

[120] *Ibid.*

Government attitudes towards anti-Malayan Union demonstrations were markedly different before and after the inauguration of the civil government. While the Pan-Malaya Malay Congress in early March was allowed, permission for a procession through the streets of Kuala Lumpur was denied. Within a month of his installation as governor, however, Edward Gent had concluded that the Malays should be conciliated[121] and the local British government was thereafter allied with the Malays in convincing the Colonial Office to change course. In late May two British parliamentarians were greeted warmly by Onn's movement with friendly mass demonstrations. The Labour member, David Rees-Williams, later cheerfully acknowledged how the local administration worked against his own government's policy:

> The Europeans were on the side of the Malays almost to a man. This had a curious result. British flags flew everywhere, the very dais from which vitriolic speeches against the British Government were made was draped with the Union Jack and *the British Army helped to marshal the crowds* and to provide transport for the demonstrators.[122]

The Conservative MP, L.D. Gammans, actually spend more time than Rees-Williams travelling the country with Onn and meeting Malays. His progress was especially facilitated by Gent's government, which allowed half-day holidays for schoolchildren and government employees to attend rallies and provided a special plane for the Sultans of Kelantan and Terengganu to fly to the west coast.[123]

Onn reciprocated the government's goodwill, approving Malay participation in the official Victory Day celebrations in June 1946, even though the Malayan Union was not yet defeated.[124] And government officials were invited to public events in connection with UMNO's meetings, beginning with a formal evening meal on the last day of the March congress.[125] Officials were also present at nationalist meetings, but in a surveillance capacity rather than as honoured guests. At one PKMM meeting, the speaker openly asked the participants not to fear the note-taking police in their midst.[126]

---

[121] See Stockwell, *British Policy and Malay Politics*, pp. 87–89.

[122] D.R. Rees-Williams, foreword to E.E. Dodd, *The New Malaya*, London: Fabian Publications, 1946, p. 4. Emphasis added.

[123] MU 1212/46.

[124] *Majlis*, 8 June 1946.

[125] Mohammad Yunus Hamidi, *Sejarah Pergerakan Politik*, pp. 106–8.

[126] MSS PIJ, no. 4 (1947).

Even before the government lent political and logistical assistance, mobilisation for demonstrations was impressive. Just as important was the consistent coverage given these political events in Malay papers throughout the peninsula: 3,000 farmers rallying at Tanjong Karong (Selangor), reported by Majlis, *Seruan Rakyat* and *Utusan Melayu*;[127] 10,000 Kelantan Malays protesting against MacMichael, reported in the Kuala Lumpur papers;[128] 3,000 in Perlis;[129] 2,000 in Alor Setar (Kedah);[130] 1,000 at the Abu Bakar Mosque (the anti-Sultan Ibrahim meeting in Johor);[131] 3,500 in Rembau (Negeri Sembilan) with petitions for the government;[132] 2,000 outside the palace in Kuala Kangsar (Perak) to express loyalty to the ruler.[133]

The demonstrations, and the coverage, reached a peak with the visit of Gammans and Rees-Williams, who were met by thousands of Malays at every stop, proving to the British government in London that 'Malaya has undoubtedly become acutely politically conscious overnight'.[134] Only days after the visit ended, Gent made known to the rulers Britain's willingness to deal and, ironically, that success stopped political momentum in its tracks. For the political process now returned to closed room dealings between the British and the Malay ruling class; suddenly mass politics became awkward and inconvenient for those trying to put the Anglo–Malay relationship back together.[135] The long months of negotiation stretched from June to November, after which draft constitutional proposals were published in December 1946. The British then insisted on consultation with the other communities, amendments were considered by the original working committee and the revised constitutional proposals were published in July 1947. The Federation of Malaya Agreement would not be signed by the rulers (superseding the MacMichael treaties) until January 1948 and the

---

127 *Majlis*, 13 December 1945; *Seruan Rakyat*, 15 December 1945; *Utusan Melayu*, 18 December 1945. BMA/PR 3/7/Vol. 1.

128 *Majlis*, 12 December 1945; *Seruan Rakyat*, 20 December 1945.

129 *Suara Rakyat*, 3 January 1946. BMA/PR 3/7/Vol. 1.

130 *Warta Negara*, 2 February 1946. BMA/PR 3/6/Pt. II.

131 *Majlis*, 4 February 1946.

132 *Majlis*, 7 February 1946.

133 *Majlis*, 10 April 1946.

134 Gammans' press statement in Kuala Lumpur, 25 May 1946. Cited in Stockwell, *British Policy and Malay Politics*, p. 89n12.

135 UMNO preconditions for negotiation barred any Malay representatives except those of UMNO and the rulers. Ishak, 'Dato Onn', p. 65. Certain of the rulers went a step further. After the British signalled willingness to guarantee the rulers' positions, some of them tried to discard mass politics and shake off UMNO's control. Stockwell, *British Policy and Malay Politics*, p. 99.

Federation inaugurated on 1 February.[136]

From the moment negotiations began, conservative Malay politics – the political movement centred solely on the issue of Malayan Union – was in a 'state of suspense', waiting for results from London.[137] Yet it was not so easy for Onn and the other leaders of UMNO to dampen the anti-British feelings that had been stirred up by the political campaign. According to Stockwell, 'when Malay leaders softened their attitude in order to negotiate with the British, they endangered their standing within their own community, and the stability of the Malay united front grew more precarious as the constitutional talks proceeded'.[138] Malay nationalist politics – fractured though it was in ideology – stepped in to fill the vacuum. In August 1946 British intelligence noted:

> Little has been heard from UMNO, which still claims the allegiance of the majority of Malays. The leaders have doubtless deemed it inexpedient to initiate any new policy whilst negotiations between government and Malay representatives are in progress. There is evidence, however, that the lack of news of a definite progress and the opportunity this gives to more extreme elements to gain a hearing is already giving rise to serious misgivings.... The extremist elements most feared by UMNO are of course represented in the Malay Nationalist Party. Efforts to enhance its prestige and extend its influence continue unabated by the party amid some success.[139]

Despite indications that UMNO had no pressing agenda beyond the dismantling of the Malayan Union, it was forced by the challenge of PKMM efforts to continue to gather the public and make political representations before it. Thus UMNO replaced mass demonstrations with the political events discussed above – flag raisings, speeches by Onn and appearances by the rulers which reinforced the solidarity of the Malay ruling class on the stage of mass politics. For the next two years, UMNO–PKMM rivalry was played out through public meetings as well as in press debates. The waxing and waning of the parties' relative strengths was watched carefully by the colonial power and judged by attendance figures and the 'draw' of different speakers. In October 1946, for example, it was noted that the PKMM anniversary celebration in Kuala Lumpur drew 500 participants, while that in Singapore had only 200 and the meeting in Kedah 'flopped' with only 15

[136] For a fuller account of the negotiations, see Stockwell, *British Policy and Malay Politics*, pp. 89–94.

[137] MSS PIJ, no. 3 and no. 4 (1946).

[138] Stockwell, *British Policy and Malay Politics*, p. 97.

[139] WO 203/6436.

in attendance.[140] The following month, PKMM mass meetings ranged in size from 50 (in Pahang) to 1,000 (in Penang and Taiping).[141] Speeches at PKMM rallies during this time called for the federation then being negotiated to include Singapore and to be centrally governed through democratically elected councils. It was, even to government observers, a message with 'a certain realism and definite appeal to emergent Malay nationalism'.[142] As time went on, the PKMM's moderate tone towards the Malay rulers, adopted for the sake of the united front against the Union, was dropped and anti-ruler rhetoric increased. Anti-imperialist and pro-independence themes predominated, as speakers pointed to the example of Indonesia and the universal principles embodied in the Atlantic Charter.[143]

Competition between the two parties intensified in early 1947, when the PKMM had the published federation proposals to criticise. The federation was condemned by their speakers on two different grounds. On the one hand, it was portrayed as being no different from the prewar constitutional arrangement, specifically in its privileging of ruling class, state-based politics. On the other hand, 'Malaya for the Malays', a slogan familiar from the anti-Union demonstrations, was now used against a federation which included citizenship rights for the alien races.[144] UMNO's defence of the federation, as articulated by Onn, was that it provided for each state to have its own constitution, chief minister and state secretary, as only Johor had had before the war.[145] It was difficult enough for Onn to sell this Anglo–Malay agreement to the UMNO general assembly, where some delegates wanted to resume confrontation with the British.[146] It was an even harder sell on the tour circuit, for the federation agreement had no nationalist appeal. It essentially offered well-qualified Malays (i.e. the English-educated elite) more positions in government administration; it said nothing to about self-government or independence. To compensate for this shortcoming, UMNO speakers called attention to other things: the spectre of Chinese control which the federation agreement was said to have averted; the need for greater educational opportunities which would prepare Malays for self-government; the restoration of the sultans to their rights courtesy of UMNO;

140 MSS PIJ, no. 13 (1946).
141 MSS PIJ, no. 14 (1946).
142 WO 203/6435.
143 See MSS PIJ, no. 6 (1946) to no. 4 (1947).
144 MSS PIJ, no. 3 and no. 4 (1947).
145 MSS PIJ, no. 14 (1947).
146 Stockwell, *British Policy and Malay Politics*, p. 100.

and the need to avoid violence in pursuit of independence.[147]

The PKMM had the more compelling political rhetoric – nationalism – but UMNO had been able to harness the rulers to a vision of Malay security and gradual advance which appealed to those who did not feel compelled to pursue independence with Indonesia or in alliance with left-wing Chinese. Neither party was able, as a consequence, to gain a clear advantage in membership or support. Throughout 1947, in fact, there was considerable evidence of great volatility in interest in the two parties, as reflected in widely shifting attendance at political meetings and intense competition for followers. In one instance, during Ishak Haji Muhammad's tour of the northern states, he and a companion were assaulted, while the local UMNO affiliate held an anti-PKMM demonstration of 2,000 people.[148]

If the opposing parties had reached something of a draw in their pursuit of followers using speeches, meetings and rallies, UMNO was less able to compete with another kind of political gathering. This was revolutionary militarism as exemplified by armed and uniformed drilling. During the prewar period, a Malay military tradition had not been rearticulated within colonial structures of authority as the monarchy had been. The British had suppressed Malay military prowess in response to aristocratic rebellions against their authority which continued sporadically into the 1890s. In the first decades of the twentieth century, other factors made Malay military skills irrelevant to colonial rule: the localisation of each ruler's influence to his own state and British-imposed pacification of ruling class relations and relations with Siam.[149] Further, British Malaya fell within the larger plural society of the British empire, in which Sikhs were designated as the military caste. The first resident of Perak, for example, had called for a force of sepoys to back up his own Sikh guards shortly before his assassination by Malay chiefs in 1874.[150] Later that state had a ceremonial troop of Indian cavalry, the First Battalion Perak Sikhs, who accompanied Sultan Idris when he travelled in his carriage.[151] The unfederated state of Johor did have a Malay

---

147 MSS PIJ, no. 3 and no. 8 (1947).

148 MSS PIJ, no. 3 (1947).

149 Benedict Anderson refers to this 'pacification' of external relations from the perspective of the Thai (Siamese) military from the mid-nineteenth century. 'Studies of the Thai state: The state of Thai studies', in Eliezer B. Ayal, ed., *The Study of Thailand*, Athens: Ohio University Center for International Studies, 1978, pp. 202–3.

150 R.J. Wilkinson, *A History of the Peninsular Malays*, Singapore: Kelly and Walsh, 1923, p. 136.

151 J.M. Gullick, *Rulers and Residents: Influence and Power in the Malay States, 1870–1920*, Singapore: Oxford University Press, 1992, p. 235.

force, under European officers, which grew to a strength of 576 in 1915, but its function was mainly ceremonial.[152] Eventually Malays would be heavily employed in police work; however, no links were forged, conscious or otherwise, to an earlier martial tradition. According to Gullick, 'in the early years of colonial rule the police force was an alien institution, whose Malay personnel were recruited from outside the State, often from Melaka'.[153] This was no doubt because, as noted by Wilkinson about Perak in the 1870s, 'a corporal and his police in a Malay village were so many rivals to the local headman'.[154]

The active military forces of twentieth-century British Malaya were the Malay States Guides (1896–1919), a non-Malay body meant to quell disturbances such as arose in Kelantan in 1915,[155] and a battalion of the Burma Rifles, on loan from India. By the 1930s Malay military prowess, which had so impressed (and harassed) Europeans into the nineteenth century, seemed completely lost. This fact was a continuing point of dissatisfaction for the ruling class, which grew tired of being considered effete. In response to 20 years of Malay urging, the 1st Experimental Company, Malay Regiment, consisting of 25 men, was established in 1933.[156] It was experimental in that it had to prove to naysayers that the 'individualistic Malay' could submit willingly to military discipline and become an efficient soldier. This it had proved by 1935, when it became a permanent force. Yet despite popularity (judging from the number of applicants), loyalty (many of the recruits came from 'leading Malay families')[157] and unquestioned success in achieving high military standards, the Malay Regiment did not entirely succeed in recreating a Malay martial tradition within the context of colonial rule. There was, to be sure, a Malay component to the culture of the regiment – dress uniforms in the 'national costume' and compulsory Friday mosque attendance – but the substance of military training was entirely British. All commands were delivered in English, due to 'the inherent difficulty of translating British military terms and phrases', and 'the squad was trained and brought up on the lines of a

---

[152] *Ibid.*, p. 129n105.

[153] *Ibid.*, p. 258n34.

[154] Wilkinson, *Peninsular Malays*, p. 129.

[155] Gullick, *Rulers and Residents*, p. 130n115.

[156] See Dol Ramli, *History of the Malay Regiment, 1933–1942*, Singapore: Regimental Committee of the Royal Malay Regiment, 1963, pp. 6–19, for the background to the establishment of the Malay Regiment.

[157] *Ibid.*, pp. 21–22.

British infantry unit down to the traditional army way of instruction – much profanity on the parade ground and no ill-feeling afterwards'.[158]

But the Malay Regiment's greatest limitations were in function and size. Although it received superlative praise from British military and civilian observers throughout the 1930s, that praise was always for its ceremonial functions – good drill, smartness of attire, performance on parade.[159] Neither was the regiment large enough to make a difference in the defence of the country. Despite urging by the Malay press and numerous applications from all over the peninsula, the regiment had only reached the size of one battalion by 1941 and was in the midst of expansion when the Japanese invasion began. A postwar assessment commended the 'young and untried soldiers' for their efforts in the 1941–1942 campaign,[160] but clearly the Malay Regiment, like the other Asian-manned regular and volunteer forces, was underestimated and/or distrusted by the colonial government until the situation had become hopeless.[161] The Malay Regiment ended up helping British forces to withdraw and for this several Malay officers were executed by the Japanese.[162]

The failure by the British to take full advantage of Malay willingness to fight for sultan and empire thus left militarism available for revolutionary symbolism, as was developed by the Japanese during the occupation and continued by radical nationalists afterwards. During the occupation, the large-scale mobilisation of young Malay men created 'a new elite, a military elite, exposed to intense training and exhortation to patriotic sacrifice'.[163] The

---

[158] *Ibid.*, pp. 27, 30, 39.

[159] *Ibid.*, pp. 28, 33.

[160] A.E. Percival's foreword to Mubin Sheppard, *The Malay Regiment, 1933–1947*, Kuala Lumpur: Department of Public Relations, Malay Peninsula, 1947.

[161] Virginia Thompson, *Post-Mortem on Malaya*, New York: Macmillan, 1943, pp. 250–54. See also James Ongkili, *Nation-Building in Malaysia, 1946–1974*, Singapore: Oxford University Press, 1985, pp. 23–24, on British failure to mobilise Malay forces during the Japanese invasion.

[162] Dol Ramli, *Malay Regiment*, pp. 103–5. After the war, the regiment's problems continued. There was an abortive attempt, in connection with the Malayan Union, to open the ranks to non-Malays. In late 1946 *Majlis* complained that the Malay Regiment did not have enough Malay officers (29 November 1946). As late as 1950 the regiment was still recruiting from Britain in sufficient numbers to prompt the publication of pamphlets for the 'newcomer to the Regiment [to] obtain … an elementary knowledge of … the History, Customs, Beliefs, Superstition and Religion of the Malay'. N. Staniforth, comp., *Papers on Malay Subjects. The Malay Regiment*, Port Dickson: Malay Regiment, 1950.

[163] This discussion is based on Cheah, *Red Star*, pp. 33–36.

Heiho, a mostly Malay auxiliary force, and the Giyu Gun, a Malay regular army under the command of the KMM leader Ibrahim Yaacob, were used frequently against the communist guerrillas. Recruits received military training in the use of anti-aircraft guns and artillery. Both organisations were very popular among less well-educated Malays; in its first five months, the Giyu Gun recruited 2,000 men. Malays lives were touched by other quasi-military organisations as well. The 'semi-military'[164] Malay Police Officers' Training School in Singapore had, by early 1944, graduated over 1,800 students and, in late 1944, a women's auxiliary to the Heiho was established. Beyond the fact that thousands of Malays were influenced directly by military institutions was the general militarisation of society, as reflected especially in the ubiquity of uniforms:

> Everywhere could be seen uniforms, military caps and badges of all shapes, colours, sizes and designs. Government servants, Kaisha clerks, Kumiai employees, factory or foundry hands, Police trainees, trade-school students, Normal school students, Youth Training Corps, and even departmental coolies and lorry-drivers sported their distinctive caps and badges.[165]

Physical drill and the singing of patriotic and martial songs were also common in these civilian and educational settings.[166]

Militarism and its attendant attitudes of physical fitness, sacrifice and commitment to the motherland appealed to emergent nationalism, and it is thus not surprising that it was the nationalist groups, not UMNO, which replicated the spirit and organisation which had been learned under the Japanese.[167] API had been founded in February 1946 to take part in the PKMM's celebration of six months of Indonesian independence. In the recalled conversation of Ahmad Boestamam (its leader) and the Perak PKMM leader Abdul Rahman Rahim, we see the new organisation, like an emergent butterfly, shedding its Japanese cocoon:

> 'How can we get the young people together? And if we can get them together, where's the time for us to train them to drill properly?'

---

[164] Chin, *Malaya Upside Down*, p. 142.

[165] *Ibid.*, p. 143.

[166] *Ibid.*, pp. 136–37.

[167] This was true in the other ethnic communities as well. The San Min Chu Yi Youth Corps was a Kuomintang affiliate whose members in Penang and Singapore were organised in regiments. Ex-Indian National Army cadres on the estates formed militia concerned with social and religious reform. T.N. Harper, 'The politics of disease and disorder in post-war Malaya', *Journal of Southeast Asian Studies*, vol. 21, no. 1, 1990, pp. 104, 108.

'If that's the situation it's difficult for sure, but we can look for youths who are already good at drilling. Those with skills of this sort are not so scarce because they were trained during the Japanese time'.

'But they were trained Japanese fashion. We don't want to use Japanese when we give orders during the parade'.

'The training's the same, whether in Japanese or any other language. The present Indonesian Independence Army, aren't most of them youths who had Japanese training? How come they're given orders in Indonesian?'

'Because Indonesians have translated the language of command from Japanese into Indonesian. It only remains to match them up. And that's easy'.

'And we can do that, for sure. What's more, commands in Indonesian are widely known here. Why can't we just use those orders?'[168]

API recruitment literature made clear that patriotism demanded change: 'API is open to courageous and confident young men desirous of reforms and ready to make sacrifices in order to achieve those reforms'.[169] Its rhetoric was openly hostile to both the ruling class and the British. Ustaz Yunos, API's secretary, condemned the sultans and the *kathis* (state Islamic officials) for being 'paid creatures of the British Government', and other API members were heard saying '*apuskan perentah Inggeris*' (abolish English rule).[170] Its aims were: '(1) to unite all awakened youths under one organisation; (2) to strengthen the fighting front for the nation and the motherland; (3) to give training in politics – both physical and spiritual – to its youths in order that they may be able to lead whenever required; (4) to rebuild Malaya in accordance with genuine democratic principles and people's sovereignty; (5) to obtain the right of representation in the Government of Malaya'.[171] These aims, according to API, would be pursued by force, if necessary; API's battle cry was '*merdeka dengan darah*' (freedom through blood) and its emblem was a black clenched fist on a red background.[172]

Within two months of its founding, API's influence was spreading quickly, and by the end of 1946 the colonial government attributed to it over 2,500 members, its strongest states being Perak, Melaka and Pahang. Ahmad Boestamam claimed 10,000 members in March 1947. That figure was probably high, but the government did admit that both the PKMM

168 Ahmad Boestamam, *Carving the Path*, p. 35.

169 *Pelita Malaya*, 30 April 1946. BMA/PR 3/6/Pt. IV; see also meeting announcement in *Semboyan Baharu*, 8 May 1946.

170 MSS PIJ, no. 3 and no. 4 (1947).

171 *Testament Politik A.P.I.*, cited in Firdaus, *Radical Malay Politics*, p. 99.

172 Ahmad Boestamam, *Carving the Path*, p. 45.

and API were successfully infiltrating the police and Malay Regiment, and that API gained 900 new members in May 1947 alone.[173] In February there had been well-attended parades in several cities to mark API's one-year anniversary, and British handling of the parade in Kuala Kangsar highlights what was to the colonial regime the most unsettling aspect of API's political practice – uniformed drilling. From their first meeting in February 1946, the youth group had worn rudimentary uniforms, a white shirt and trousers and a red-and-white armband with the name API written on it.[174] Thereafter they always appeared in uniform, for example, at PKMM mass meetings or when conducting military training in public.[175] For the Kuala Kangsar meeting, leaders put out the call for all API members in Perak to flood 'the feudal town' (seat of the sultanate) in uniform. The British, fearing an outright ban on the event would simply be ignored, instead threatened all owners of commercial buses and trucks with loss of licence if they provided transport to anyone in uniform on the day in question. According to Ahmad Boestamam, the obstacle was circumvented quite easily – API members travelled the day before or marched in from nearby towns.[176]

It was in response to API's popularity that UMNO-affiliated youth movements were established. These did not reflect the conservative politicians' original attitude towards youth. At the Malay Congress and at many anti-Union demonstrations, young children held signs imploring parents to save their future.[177] The message seemed to be that adults were responsible for shaping the future, and the only way youth should manifest itself was as a helpless child. UMNO had to counter API's mobilisation of youth, however, and it did so by emulation. The British government noted with approval that UMNO had increased its efforts 'by adopting methods hitherto used by the opposition, i.e., the use of religious institutions, religious anniversaries, flag flying, appeal to youth and the wearing of uniforms', but also observed that the opposition had stepped up its own activities, resulting in little change in the proportional strength of the PKMM and UMNO.[178] At this point, when API was seen marching with *parang* (the knives responsible for many Chinese deaths in 1945) and had

---

[173] MSS PIJ, no. 16 (1946); no. 3 and no. 8 (1947).

[174] Ahmad Boestamam, *Carving the Path*, pp. 36–37.

[175] MSS PIJ, no. 13 and no. 15 (1946).

[176] Ahmad Boestamam, *Carving the Path*, pp. 93–94.

[177] According to *Warta Negara*, schoolchildren at an Alor Setar demonstration held banners reading, 'Oh, fathers and mothers, preserve our rights until we grow up'. BMA/PR 3/6/Pt. II.

[178] MSS PIJ, no. 3 (1947).

just embarked on a new round of propaganda, the colonial government went on the offensive. In March 1947 Ahmad Boestamam was arrested on sedition charges in connection with his *Testament Politik A.P.I.*, and uniforms, drilling and the uncontrolled collection of money were banned. For a short time, API drilling and recruiting slowed down, as Burhanuddin Al-Helmy, the less militant president of the PKMM, advised API members to obey the laws and avoid wearing uniforms, carrying weapons and using the word *darah* (blood). By April, however, soon after Ahmad Boestamam's conviction, API training and recruiting had resumed, and new branches were opened in Singapore and Terengganu.[179]

The government, in the meantime, was turning a blind eye to the uniforms worn by UMNO-affiliated youth movements. (A typical uniform closely resembled those worn by API – white shirts and trousers, black caps and UMNO badges.) In Perlis, just after the banning, a youth group greeted the ruler in uniform, drawing no comment from the intelligence officer who recorded the event. A few months later, Hussein Onn told his group in Johor to wear white trousers and shirts and black caps, saying that the government would not regard this as a uniform.[180] In actual fact, the government did not bother to enforce the ban on uniforms. Instead, with the reintroduction of societies' registration, API itself was banned, on 17 July 1947, the first postwar organisation to be suppressed in this manner. The API ban, the societies' ordinance and the sedition enactment were all protested against by a coalition of left-wing groups, and the increasingly repressive atmosphere was challenged in progressive journals like *Kenchana*.[181] A month after the banning, the government estimated that API membership was down to an enthusiastic core of 3,000–4,000, but that large numbers of ex-members were interested in continuing the movement.[182]

Meanwhile, Hussein Onn resigned from his government job to devote himself full-time to the Pemuda Pergerakan Melayu Semenanjung (and later the amalgamated UMNO Youth). He devised a military salute, a prescribed greeting – '*Assalam Alaikum Hidup Melayu – Wa Alaikum Salam Hidup Melayu*' – and a dress uniform consisting of formal Malay ceremonial dress and the UMNO badge.[183] This appropriation of the trappings of militaristic

---

179 MSS PIJ, no. 3 to no. 6 (1947).

180 MSS PIJ, no. 4, no. 9 (1947).

181 MSS PIJ, no. 14 (1947); 'Dimana letaknya democracy "Kedaulatan Rakyat"', *Kenchana*, August 1947.

182 MSS PIJ, no. 13 and no. 14 (1947).

183 MSS PIJ, no. 10 (1947).

nationalism did not flourish, however, until the rivalry of 'the real thing' was quite stamped out.[184] The declaration of the Emergency in June 1948 finally accomplished that, and only then did UMNO Youth grow in influence and membership.

*

This chapter has examined the ways in which UMNO attempted to maintain its popularity after achieving ascendancy within the ruling class. In an atmosphere of political nationalism, the rearticulation of tradition alone could not secure aristocratic hegemony in Malay society. The linking of nationalism with mass politics, which began during the Japanese period, demanded innovation on the part of conservatives that was supplied largely by the political acuity of Onn bin Jaafar and the selective appropriation of nationalist political practice. Onn's genius was to update a classic figure – the Malay hero – for modern political practice and even impressed his enemies. UMNO more slowly learned the importance of symbols and uniforms to represent the nation visually and conceptually to its followers, but having adopted these practices, successfully attached their meaning not only to the nation but also to the party. Finally, in shaping the emerging political arena to fit its agenda, UMNO benefited, probably unknowingly, from an inherent bias towards traditionalism in the way Malays produced and consumed newspaper editorials, the daily currency of political nationalism. It was this variety of strategies, all occurring within the context of increasing support from the colonial government, that left UMNO poised for triumph on the eve of Emergency. In the epilogue, I show how once UMNO had developed these nationalist credentials, it engaged in a final round of traditionalism to secure its position as the only legitimate voice of the Malays.

---

[184] See Stockwell, *British Policy and Malay Politics*, pp. 126–28, for Hussein Onn's difficulties in the early years.

CHAPTER SEVEN

Epilogue

'Hidup Melayu' is a national slogan not political.[1]

Depoliticising Nationalism

Despite its growing mastery over the new forms of political practice - propaganda, popular leadership, symbolism, public gatherings - UMNO was unable to gain decisive victory over the nationalists in the political arena. This was because political nationalism made certain demands that UMNO was unable to appropriate, namely the restructuring of traditional society along egalitarian lines and independence from British colonialism. The first demand was implicit in the practice of politics in a democratic era, the second an inevitability since the Japanese shattered the colonial world. The Malay aristocrats who led the campaign against the Malayan Union by uniting their state organisations into a national body learned the forms of mass politics and the language of nationalism, but their interests still lay in a traditionalist formulation of Malay culture and, for the time being, in the protection of the colonial state. Salvation would come in disarming the political practice of nationalism: dampening political debate and updating traditional ideas of loyalty, treason and sovereignty. The result was a dominant narrative of struggle which cast UMNO as hero and Malayan Union as villain, a narrative which marginalised from mainstream Malay nationalism progressive demands for social change and independence.

Early in the postwar period, during the universal celebration of the Malays' politicisation, newspapers called for all Malays to voice their political views and applauded the widening debate. *Seruan Rakyat*, at the

---

1 Letter from Hussein Onn, head of UMNO's youth affiliate, to the secretary general of UMNO, distinguishing UMNO activism from revolutionary politics. *Hidup Melayu* (long live the Malays) was UMNO's official slogan, adopted during the anti-Malayan Union campaign. UMNO/SG 126/1947.

time still favouring the PKMM, expressed support for the reestablishment of the conservative Malay associations, saying the more voices the better.[2] A month later, after it had broken with the PKMM over its stance on the Malayan Union, the paper still editorialised in favour of a multiplicity of political views:

> In a self-governing country, there are bound to be several parties because the people are free to think for themselves. In view of the coming changes, Malaya is going through the same stage. The mushroom growth of unions and parties should not cause concern, because they all aim at the betterment of the people and the country.[3]

Majlis as well called for debate as a political tool, issuing in January 1946 an early call for a conference of organisations at which the problems of the Malays and proposals for their future could be 'freely discussed'.[4] In August of that year *Majlis* proposed a new magazine to be called 'U.M.N.O.', which would feature essays on politics written by the public.[5] A final example is provided by *Kenchana*, in which pictures and text featured congresses of both conservative and progressive parties, a celebration of politics regardless of views.[6]

At the same time, however, another idea was growing which would prove much stronger. This was the idea that unity was necessary for Malay political progress. While couched in modern political terminology, the idea had historical resonance. It invoked a glorious past when the Malay world was unified under the leadership of Melaka. The suggestion that the unity of the Malays even at that time was deficient made contemporary calls all the more urgent:

> If the Malays had been united before the Portuguese came, Melaka would not have come under Portuguese rule for Java would certainly have come to her assistance against the outsiders. If united, the sale of Singapore and Pinang and the treaties inviting British advice would never have happened.[7]

In the more recent past, it was argued, lack of unity was responsible for the Malays falling behind, a variation on the pervasive critique of Malay backwardness.[8]

---

2 *Seruan Rakyat*, 3 November 1945.
3 *Seruan Rakyat*, 14 December 1945.
4 *Majlis*, 5 January 1946.
5 *Majlis*, 6 August 1946.
6 *Kenchana*, nos. 2/3, February 1948.
7 *Majlis*, 7 March 1946.
8 *Majlis*, 18 February 1946.

The political benefits of this line of reasoning are fairly obvious – a party successfully claiming to unify the Malays could gain enormous advantage. But the unity argument was not used exclusively along conservative–progressive battle lines. Early in the anti-Union campaign, before political postures had hardened, all Malay newspapers called for unity behind Onn bin Jaafar's party, citing the need to coordinate the many organisations' activities, to assert the Malays as equals with the other nations of the world and to present a united front against the Malayan Union.[9] Soon, however, the conservative papers *Majlis* and *Warta Negara* began to emphasise the dangers of disunity in order to isolate the PKMM's ambivalent stance on Union. *Majlis* especially engaged in a debate with the papers of the PKMM, accusing that party of undermining the unity of the Malays by opposing UMNO.[10] According to Yunus Hamidi, editor of *Majlis*:

> It's good to have all kinds of Malay organisations, from labour to independence movements, even to communist movements, as long as they can all unite on the problems of the nation.[11]

Before the PKMM withdrew from UMNO, its official organ, *Pelita Malaya*, countered that it was the conservative editorialists themselves who were causing disunity and that there were only minor differences between UMNO's and the PKMM's position.[12] They also tried to popularise alternate visions of unity, such as the unity of labour or the unity of all races against colonialism.[13] But *Majlis* overwhelmed these efforts with a constant barrage of editorials identifying UMNO with Malay unity and victory over the Malayan Union. By newspapers and through Onn's speeches, flag raisings and use of the rulers, UMNO was presented as the most viable, if not the only, national body of the Malays.[14] This ideological formulation was fairly believable in the first half of 1946, when UMNO's prestige was at its highest. Once mass mobilisation had ended, however, unity became more elusive and was increasingly achieved by stifling debate. Within UMNO, the executive

---

9 *Utusan Melayu*, 26 November 1945; *Suara Rakyat*, January 16, 1946; *Warta Negara*, January 28, 1946. BMA/PR 3/7/Vol. 1.

10 *Majlis*, 8 March 1946 and 14 May 1946.

11 Quoted in *Seruan Rakyat*, 18 December 1945.

12 *Pelita Malaya*, 14 May 1946.

13 *Pelita Malaya*, 20 and 27 May 1946. BMA/PR 3/6/Pt. IV.

14 In this period, UMNO's main membership strength was in the states of Johor and Perak. Both UMNO and the PKMM claimed about 100,000 members; in neither case were all the membership fees paid up.

began to vet suggested topics of discussion before general assemblies met.[15] In January 1947 an UMNO leader commented about the upcoming general assembly vote on the draft federation proposals:

> If this is done without any debate, well and good. If at all there is going to be any debate it should be in close session for we would not like our ill-wishers to know that there is even the hint of division or disunity among ourselves UMNO members.[16]

Prescriptions for unity were now used to silence opposition both within and outside of UMNO, and political debate, once celebrated as a sign of the Malays' vitality and progress, was now condemned as dangerously divisive.

Disavowing political activity or identity became a signal to the colonial power that a publication or organisation was non-threatening. In June 1946 the president of the Kesatuan Melayu Muda, Alor Gajah, Melaka, sought permission to publish *Pemuda*, a new magazine for youth with the aim of defending society, the fatherland and religion through social, not political, activity. In contrast to the immediate postwar attitude celebrating the birth of political activism, increasingly only nationalist publications professed to be political. Conservative papers applying for permission to publish either claimed outright to be non-political or simply included a list of proposed topics – 'True story. Education and Religion. Advice on economy and business. Good and sound thinking advice. General News' – from which politics was pointedly absent.[17] It was in this spirit of disavowing politics that Hussein Onn protested against a government order banning political youth organisations from the schools, an order which greatly harmed the already struggling UMNO youth groups. Correctly assuming that the ban's true target was 'a certain Pemuda organisation which has revolutionary and militant objects' (API), Hussein outlined why the UMNO-affiliated groups should be allowed to operate:

---

15 See item no. 20 in UMNO/SG 45/46, which is a list of proposals made by member organisations from July to September 1946. Beside each proposal is a notation in English, such as 'Debate', 'Unnecessary to debate' and 'This should be in the form of a question.... There will be no debate on this.'

16 Letter from Mohamed Ali Rouse, UMNO/SG 1/47, cited in A.J. Stockwell, *British Policy and Malay Politics During the Malayan Union Experiment, 1945–46*, Kuala Lumpur: Malaysian Branch of the Royal Asiatic Society, Monograph no. 8, 1979, p. 100. A. Samad Ahmad recalls this as a critical time. Because enemies were attacking through newspapers and growing in popularity, he says, a large part of the January 1947 meeting was held in secret. *Sejambak Kenangan: Sebuah Autobiografi*, Kuala Lumpur: Dewan Bahasa dan Pustaka, 1981, pp. 240–44.

17 MU 621/46 vol. II.

> These organisations, though political in the general sense, have definite stated objects of their own. They indulge more, if not exclusively, in sports; physical culture; music and dramatic, social and cultural activities; education; thrift; voluntary work of various kind, all of which bring benefits not only to the community and Race but to the members as well. They are not and have never been revolutionary or militant and have not done anything which is detrimental to the peace, security and welfare of the country.

Further in this vein, Hussein protested against the education department's objection to Malay teachers teaching schoolchildren to say *Hidup Melayu* (long live the Malays). According to Hussein, UMNO's slogan was 'a national slogan not political'.[18]

Dampening political debate in favour of unity and cultural activities had the effect of elevating 'Malayness' to a suprapolitical position. Put another way: nation trumped politics. Nativistic and seemingly non-ideological, any activity which was 'political in the general sense', but which was strictly about culture or improvement of the race, was compared favourably to a contentious politics which drew on 'foreign' ideologies like democracy or communism. The uncritical emphasis on Malayness also allowed aristocrats to introduce into modern politics ideas and practices they presented as intrinsically Malay, but which critics then and now call 'feudal' – namely, updated conceptions of deference, loyalty and treason which were used to further the creation of a nationalist mainstream identical with UMNO policy.[19] In short, conservative politicians sought to redefine postwar Malay

---

[18] Hussein Onn to secretary general, UMNO, 25 July 1947. UMNO/SG 126/47. (English original.)

[19] These practices have persisted into the post-independence era and have prompted a number of sociological studies by academic critics of UMNO. See Syed Husin Ali, 'Patterns of rural leadership in Malaya', *Journal of the Malaysian Branch of the Royal Asiatic Society*, vol. 41, no. 1, 1968; Syed Hussein Alatas, 'Feudalism in Malaysian society: a study of historical continuity', *Civilisations*, vol. 18, no. 4, 1968, pp. 579–92; A. Kahar Bador, 'Social rank, status-honour and social class consciousness amongst the Malays', in Hans-Dieter Evers, ed., *Modernization in South-East Asia*, Kuala Lumpur: Oxford University Press, 1973, pp. 132–49; Chandra Muzaffar, *Protector? An Analysis of the Concept and Practice of Loyalty in Leader-led Relationships within Malay Society*, Penang: Aliran, 1979, p. 63, where he writes that the Malayan Union period saw 'the emergence of new notions of unquestioning loyalty'; and Shaharuddin Maaruf, *Malay Ideas on Development: From Feudal Lord to Capitalist*, Singapore, Kuala Lumpur: Times Books International, 1988. Shaharuddin skips over Onn's UMNO and its formative influences on Malay politics, attributing what he calls aristocratic or traditionalistic nationalism to Tunku Abdul Rahman (see

politics along traditionalistic lines, prompting this critique from *Semboyan Baharu*:

> The masses have waited and waited for the arrival of the *zaman gemilang* [brilliant era, often used in relation to fifteenth-century Melaka] in the Malay states, but the brilliant era for which the sultans and Dato Onn's Congress strive only aims to return Malaya to a *pemerintahan cara feudalism* [feudalistic government] (in which the people must pay homage and say *daulat tuanku syah alam* [hail, my lord, king on earth]).[20]

Commoner members of UMNO, like the Malay schoolteachers and well-off peasants who constituted the local membership, had difficulty unlearning the habit of deference to aristocratic political leaders. One brave soul wrote to UMNO protesting against aristocratic privilege and control in the Persatuan Melayu Perak, questioning the seemingly sudden nationalism of the ruling classes and demanding that the Malay College Kuala Kangsar be opened to commoners – 'If it's not opened in this manner, then just change the name to Aristocric [sic] Malay College'. Even such a crusader within UMNO opened his handwritten letter with *Tuan* (sir), which was then crossed out and replaced with the more egalitarian *Saudara* (brother).[21] Others within the conservative political movement made no such effort. The *Majlis* correspondent in Ipoh, asking the secretary general of UMNO (Dato' Panglima Bukit Gantang) to pass along news of the organisation for publication, took a tone strikingly at odds with the egalitarian expectations politics had engendered. He used the formal expressions with which commoners traditionally addressed nobility, referring to himself throughout his letter as *hamba dato* (your slave).[22] It was probably not difficult to graft deference to traditional authority onto the new political culture; the

---

especially pp. 116–20). Although Onn did come into conflict with the rulers in a way that the Tunku (from the royal house of Kedah) avoided, the present work demonstrates that ruling class solidarity defined UMNO from the start. When Onn was accused of disloyalty in his final confrontation with the rulers, it was not an anomalous moment. His own weapon was merely being turned against him.

[20] *Semboyan Baharu*, 8 May 1946.

[21] Md. Yusuf bin Ayub to secretary general, UMNO, 15 October 1946. UMNO/SG 12/46. The letter was in Malay with the exception of several English references to the aristocracy and democracy. Otherwise he referred to the ruling class as *bangsawan* (aristocracy) and *raja-raja dan dato-dato* (rajas and datos). An unsigned minute in the file registered this reaction: 'There is a lot of truth in what he says but the way he says it is magnificently rude'.

[22] Abdul Rahman Alyobi to Dato' Panglima Bukit Gantang, 16 July 1946. UMNO/SG 12/46.

prohibition on political activity had been lifted such a short time. When asked for their views on the federation agreement, some Malays 'preferred not to make any comment, as they thought it was a matter for the UMNO to comment'.[23] Onn encouraged such reliance, warning that politics could be interesting, but dangerous, and that a slight mistake could have grave consequences.[24]

To further the impression of Malay unity and to encourage obedience to its leadership, UMNO began to solicit expressions of loyalty from organisations throughout the country, echoing the colonial practice of the loyal toast and telegram. Declarations like this one from the writers at *Warta Negara* were published in friendly newspapers:

> Resolution – That a meeting of the *Warta Negara* writers, which took place on August 31, 1946 in Pulau Pinang, came to the unanimous decision to support the policy of the United Malays National Organisation and to pledge loyalty [*berikrar taat stia*] to its leader, the honorable Dato Onn, to be confident in his leadership, and to be prepared to cooperate with the United Malays National Organisation.[25]

Those who opposed UMNO policy were attacked by Onn and *Majlis* for being disloyal and even their membership in the community was questioned. We have seen the epithet traitor used against the rulers for signing the MacMichael treaties; it would also be used against those who supported the Malayan Union and those who later opposed the Anglo–Malay accommodation resulting in the Federation of Malaya. Onn told a meeting of the Malay Congress in May 1946 to stand firm and united against the Malayan Union. As for those who disagreed: 'Unfortunately, there are people here who look like Malays, but in their hearts they are not Malays'.[26] In a speech in Melaka that same month, he further defined opponents right out of the community, saying that there were no traitors among the two and a half million Malays.[27] This method of enforcing ideological conformity was picked up with alacrity by pro-UMNO newspapers, which called for ostracising and disowning those not in agreement with UMNO. On many occasions Malays were warned not to participate in the Malayan Union in

---

23 News clipping contained in UMNO/SG 125/47.

24 MSS PIJ, no. 14 (1947).

25 Ibrahim Mahmood, editor, *Warta Negara*, to Dato' Panglima Bukit Gantang, secretary general, UMNO, 5 September 1946. UMNO/SG 72/46.

26 *Pelita Malaya*, 14 May 1946.

27 *Warta Negara*, 6 May 1946. BMA/PR 3/6/Pt. IV.

any way or they would 'not be acknowledged as Malay'.[28] Thus, loyalty to UMNO became conflated with loyalty to the nation. In rituals across the peninsula, UMNO youths raised the national-turned-party flag and swore allegiance to Islam, the sultan and UMNO.[29] This formulation subsumed the nation, not even mentioned, to a triumvirate over which UMNO claimed control. In Onn's words, '*UMNO itulah Melayu – Melayu itulah UMNO*' (UMNO is the Malays – the Malays are UMNO).[30]

In 1947, as the federation proposals began to draw criticism from the PKMM and the other ethnic communities, UMNO's opponents were branded tools of the foreigners or, worse, accused of working for the foreigners' benefit to the detriment of the Malays.[31] Onn told an audience in early 1947 that the PKMM belonged to a prewar association (referring to the KMM) which had sold the Malays to the Japanese and that the party therefore could not be trusted. He also claimed that the PKMM could not represent the Malays because it was dependent on the other ethnic communities.[32] This was a reference to the All-Malaya Council of Joint Action (AMCJA) and its Malay associate, Pusat Tenaga Rakyat (PUTERA).[33] These two coalitions worked uneasily together to oppose first the exclusion of all but UMNO and the rulers from the negotiating table, and second the federation agreements. Because the federation itself offered little positive to nationalist aspirations, editorialists for UMNO were forced to rely on negative commentary about the federation's opponents. Developing a political equation in which Malay interests would always, and by definition, be in opposition to those of the other communities, they found the PKMM guilty by association. Malays were told that the PKMM opposed negotiations

---

28 See examples in *Majlis*, 2 April, 22 April, 1 June and 7 August 1946.

29 MSS PIJ, no. 15 (1947).

30 A. Samad Ahmad, *Sejambak Kenangan*, p. 247.

31 In January the following Malay groups rejected the proposals as being against the Atlantic Charter, democracy and the interests of the Malay masses: Lembaga Persatuan Melayu Johor, Joint Association of Malay National Welfare Associations, the PKMM, API, General Labour Union (Malay Section), Electric Workers' Union, Drivers' Union of Kota Bharu. *Straits Times*, 29 January 1947. In *Majlis*, this rhetoric began a year earlier: 'there are certain elements among us who are trying to undermine unity in the interest of other communities'. 8 March 1946.

32 MSS PIJ, no. 1 and no. 5 (1947). Earlier, the PKMM condemned the 'whispering campaign' against it 'to the effect that it is not an independent political organisation' and pointed out that it, unlike UMNO, had 'never stooped to curry favor with imperialism'. *Democrat*, 7 July 1946.

33 UMNO leaders denounced the AMCJA as a 'fake' at a meeting attended by 7,000 in Johor. *Straits Times*, 6 February 1947.

between UMNO, the rulers and the British, and that this dubious stance was shared by the other ethnic groups. They were warned against propaganda urging them to back the PKMM and were told in the same editorial that some Malays had been influenced by propaganda of the foreigners.[34] It was often stressed by conservative editorials and speeches that attacks on UMNO made the Malays weak, disunified and easier for foreigners to take advantage of.[35]

But the federation agreement, which granted limited citizenship rights to domiciled Chinese and Indians and said nothing about elections or a timetable for independence, was similar enough to the Malayan Union to be very vulnerable. The PKMM had only to cry '*merdeka!*' (freedom) to highlight UMNO's greatest weakness and to increase its own support.[36] The contradiction inherent in a nationalist movement which did not seek independence threatened to expose the true relationship between the British and UMNO, which, according the PKMM, 'has merely been dissatisfied with the British rulers for withdrawing from the Malay upper classes the privileges which they had enjoyed prior to the war'.[37] PKMM rhetoric and progressive journals hammered away at this point, saying that the demand for independence was what distinguished the 'left' from UMNO,[38] and that UMNO 'still cling[s] to the belief that British "protection" is good for the Malay people':

> I would like my fellow-countrymen to appreciate this lesson to the full – the lesson that imperialism is anything but benevolent; that to expect sincere protection from the imperialists – whether Dutch, French, British or American – is equivalent to hoping for mercy from a cobra poised to strike; and that British imperialism, in particular, is going all out to safeguard its interests and possessions in this part of the world at all costs.[39]

UMNO leaders had also to keep their own membership's aspirations closely in check. It was not unheard of for letters to UMNO from the public to close

---

34 *Majlis*, 6 December 1946 and 12 December 1946.

35 *Majlis*, 18 December 1946.

36 Interview with A. Samad Ismail.

37 *Democrat*, 7 July 1946.

38 *Kenchana*, no. 3, March 1947 (article entitled 'Melayu berjuang' [Malays struggle]). Other articles with the same theme included 'Kemerdekaan tidak diterima tetapi dituntut' (Independence is not received, but demanded), no. 4, April 1947 and 'Terus berjuang untok kemerdekaan' (Struggle on for independence), no. 5, May 1947.

39 Ahmad Boestamam, quoted in *Democrat*, 7 July 1946.

with *Hidup Melayu-Merdeka*, combining UMNO's own 'long live the Malays' with the PKMM's more militant slogan or for an UMNO youth group to be seen giving the *merdeka* salute.[40] For this reason, UMNO speakers responded to calls for independence with particular venom, waging what Ahmad Boestamam called a war of words (*perang mulut*).[41]

Onn's most prominent argument against immediate independence[42] was that the Malays were not ready to compete against the Chinese – politically or economically – without British protection. Here the articulate, well-educated aristocrat mocked his fellow Malays:

> *Membuat sebatang jarum pun tak tahu, hendak merdeka pula konon.*
> [Can't even produce a single needle, they say they want independence.][43]

He also argued, somewhat ingenuously, that there were no Malays fit to be ministers, representatives or ambassadors.[44] And more and more often, Onn evoked the spectre of Chinese political control, reminding his audience of the ethnic violence of 1945 and arguing that if the British left, the Malays would all be 'trapped by communism'.[45]

But the most important way in which political conservatism deflected calls for independence was to counter contemporary anticolonialism with the older idea of sovereignty. The colonial protectorate, by retaining the nominal sovereignty of the Malay rulers, had left the Malay conception of sovereignty intact. We have seen how the articulation of that idea in colonial society located Malay sovereignty with the greater power of the British empire. The Malayan Union crisis challenged both British and Malay conceptions of sovereignty – the rulers would lose their Western-defined legal jurisdiction in the Malay states as well as their role as guarantor

---

40 UMNO/SG 10/46; MSS PIJ, no. 9 (1947). To give the *merdeka* salute one raised the left fist while shouting *merdeka*. MSS PIJ, no. 10 (1947).

41 Ahmad Boestamam, *Datuk Onn Yang Saya Kenal*, Kuala Lumpur: Adabi, 1979, pp. 24–25.

42 It should be noted that Onn set up something of a straw man. The PKMM demanded immediate steps *towards* independence, including unification of the states, civil liberties, the promotion of democracy and so forth. See Firdaus Haji Abdullah, *Radical Malay Politics: Its Origins and Early Development*, Petaling Jaya: Pelanduk Publications, 1985, p. 79, for the PKMM's eight-point manifesto. Even API, while expanding the political discourse to include militant nationalism, never physically attacked a European or a colonial institution.

43 Ahmad Boestamam, *Datuk Onn*, p. 24.

44 Account of the January 1947 UMNO general assembly in CO 537/2145. A slightly different account is given in A. Abdul Samad, *Sejambak Kenangan*, pp. 240–44.

45 A. Abdul Samad, *Sejambak Kenangan*, pp. 232–33; MSS PIJ, no. 22 (1947).

of the Malay nature of those states. We have also seen how conservative anti-Malayan Union rhetoric focused on the terms of the original treaties between the British and the rulers, emphasising the sovereignty of the Malay states and highlighting the arrogance and presumption the British showed in their postwar plans for Malaya. In countering anti-federation sentiment, UMNO continued to insist upon the sovereignty of the Malay states and their rulers. This strategy gave voice to the feeling of most rural Malays that they lived in a Malay state. To the Malays, rulers were not symbols of sovereignty as the British had thought, but the meaning of sovereignty. Once restored, they guaranteed that the Malay states were again sovereign. Most important to UMNO's contest with the PKMM, the notion of sovereignty within colonial rule thwarted a clear understanding of British imperialism by perpetuating the fiction of a protectorate.

The colonial sovereignty myth was articulated in language which was used to confuse calls for independence. Consider the words of Onn's secretary and biographer on the effects of the Malayan Union:

> The Malay States, known as free and sovereign [*merdeka dan berdaulat*] territories under British protection, had become colonies.[46]

And the use of 'independent' in this editorial:

> The Malay peninsula is not 'British'. There is no doubt whatsoever that the [original] treaties between each Malay State and Great Britain were treaties between two independent states [*negeri yang merdaheka*] and conducted according to international law. The Colonial Office has no right to make a 'plan' for the Malay peninsula.[47]

Defeat of the Malayan Union – and restoration of sovereignty – thus made further demands for independence at once unnecessary and awkward. Unnecessary, because if the Malay states were sovereign, in both the Western and Malay senses, all that was needed was to gain control of the *administration* of the country, to achieve self-government (*berkerajaan sendiri*). Calls for independence were awkward because they pointed to the need for sociopolitical change – the nation that would achieve independence would be different from the states which were already sovereign.

Instead of independence, the traditional elite needed time to consolidate its position in the late colonial state so that, eventually, it could simply

46 Anwar Abdullah, *Dato Onn: Riwayat Hidup*, Petaling Jaya: Pustaka Nusantara, 1971, p. 139.

47 *Seruan Rakyat*, 31 January 1945.

replace the British at the helm. The idea of gradually attaining self-government was one that Onn spoke of often.[48] It was a safe topic that returned political discourse to the familiar terrain of Malay backwardness and the need for more education and administrative positions – the themes of good government the aristocracy had made its own. The idea that the Malay states were sovereign again, thanks to UMNO, also helped Onn to construct a narrative of nationalist struggle – and victory – to displace the PKMM's call to struggle for independence. In his mass meetings around the country, where he often appeared with a ruler and raised the UMNO flag, Onn began to tell a story. He described the birth of UMNO, the boycott of the Malayan Union, how Malays all over the country were mourning for the loss of their birthright. He then told of the visit of Gammans and Rees-Williams, the size of Malay demonstrations and the resulting capitulation by the British. He emphasised UMNO's role in the negotiations and how UMNO was responsible for restoring the rulers to their rights.[49]

This narrative presented aristocrats as nationalists. It positioned UMNO as the hero who protected the Malay *bangsa* against British treachery and Chinese domination. It ignored the Malay nationalists who provided the political language and practices that enabled UMNO to achieve its ends. Neither did it acknowledge that the British granted concessions to UMNO largely out of fear of fuelling that nationalist movement. And it featured the anti-Malayan Union campaign as the centre of the anticolonial struggle – a struggle and victory which left national independence more than a decade away. By positing the struggle as over and the battle as won, it assured the Malays that they could unproblematically assume nationhood. The 'natural' ascension of Malays to nationhood reinforced the 'natural' ascendancy of certain Malays within the nation. Finally, centring this narrative of Malay nationalism on the Malayan Union struggle defeated enemies within the Malay community who questioned UMNO's position in the federation.

This narrative succeeded in winning a dominant place in Malay popular and scholarly historiography. Despite the many thousands who supported the PKMM and other independence-oriented political groups in the late 1940s, and despite a robust print culture which vigorously criticised the slide back into 'feudalism', the victory of the aristocrats' narrative has most commonly been attributed to the conservatism of the Malay public. But on the contrary, the Malay political public that debuted in 1945 was much less inherently conservative than is usually assumed. Indeed, one of the

[48] MSS PIJ, no. 3 (1947).

[49] MSS PIJ, no. 8 and no. 15 (1947).

first things it was asked to do was to threaten to disown the rulers, a feat it performed convincingly. Malay public opinion was, in fact, constructed, shaped and fought over using political tools learned first by nationalists during the Japanese occupation.

The aristocrats, more precisely Onn bin Jaafar, succeeded by doing three things. The first was to adjust quickly to the changing times, to be right behind the nationalists in learning mass politics and to appropriate from them the practice of political nationalism. In this way the aristocrats constructed a nationalist facade for what was, in Onn's time, a reactionary project. Their second success was in reinventing Malay traditions – as they knew them from the colonial period – for the era of mass politics. The rehabilitation of the rulers revived aristocratic legitimacy and the manipulation of ideas like loyalty and treason countered egalitarian impulses inherent to political democracy. Finally, even at the height of the anti-Union campaign, the Malay ruling class cultivated British complicity. Colonial intelligence knew as early as February 1946 that Onn was firmly against independence for the peninsula.[50] Through social meetings (like tea parties and dinners) during the period of political opposition, Anglo–Malay relationships were repaired so that once negotiations began, the relationship between aristocrats and colonial officials was quite operational, if occasionally prickly. The British government backed UMNO from mid-1946 and first used its revived legislative apparatus for repression against enemies of that conservative party. It was not merely this last element, however, but the combination of all three which guaranteed that a conservative political agenda would dominate the Malay political mainstream throughout the late colonial period and into independence. This was Onn's legacy to Malays – the ideological hegemony of the United Malays National Organisation.

Traditionalism, Nationalism and the State in Late- and Postcolonial Malaya

Despite British Malaya's growing uniformity of laws and procedures, outside observers before the war had been struck by how little land and how few people were divided into so many administrative structures.[51] Centralisation

---

50 WO 203/5660.

51 Roughly 50,000 square miles (130,000 square kilometres) inhabited by just over five million people were governed by 10 administrations within the Federated Malay States and Unfederated Malay States alone. See Virginia Thompson, *Post-Mortem on Malaya*, New York: Macmillan, 1943, p. 1.

of the state, such as occurred in Siam in the late nineteenth and early twentieth centuries, was resisted by the indirectly-ruled Malay monarchies and aristocracies in the 1920s and 1930s in the name of local identity and with the backing of 'pro-Malay' traditionalists in the British administration. The same fight was repeated for the same interests, over the Malayan Union, which would additionally have deposed traditional authority. After successfully restoring its position through mass mobilisation, however, the aristocracy, as much as the radical nationalists, realised that the mini-states of the peninsula would not be compatible with a strong Malay position in the future. Unwilling to take an anticolonial position, UMNO therefore compromised by accepting the Federation of Malaya, which preserved the state-based power of the party's leadership, while granting citizenship to a portion of the immigrant communities. In preserving aristocratic privilege in this way, UMNO committed itself to a future nation which conformed to the prewar colonial state.

UMNO's loyalty to the colonial state, which would become a container for different nationalisms, precluded a strictly Malay nation state. It had, therefore, to reject all other visions of the nation, some of which were the product of nationalist efforts to unseat traditional authority. The PKMM actually proposed two alternatives. In the first, the idea of *Melayu Raya* (Greater Malaya), nationalists looked for a future nation state to erase the colonial past. Union with Indonesia would restore the precolonial Malay world as well as establish Malay demographic dominance over the immigrant Chinese.[52] After the colonial restoration in Malaya and the separate fate of Indonesia was clear, the PKMM was part of the AMCJA–PUTERA coalition which produced the People's Constitutional Proposals for Malaya. In what was essentially an attempt to create a nation to fit the existing state, these proposals included a blueprint for a new conception of *bangsa Melayu*, enshrining the hegemony of Malay language and culture, while respecting religious differences.

Both PKMM visions of a nation state proved vulnerable to UMNO's 'foreigner-baiting'. They were, of course, attacked by UMNO because they would have dislodged the Malay elite from its privileged position. But their defeat also highlighted the victory of a traditionalistic Malay polity, the territorially based and politically distinct Malay states that had emerged under colonial rule. The consequences of this victory can be seen

---

[52] See Rustam Sani, 'Melayu raya as a Malay "nation of intent"', in H.M. Dahlan, ed., *The Nascent Malaysian Society: Developments, Trends and Problems*, Kuala Lumpur: Jabatan Antropologi dan Sociologi, Universiti Kebangsaan Malaysia, 1976, pp. 25-38.

in UMNO's stance towards three groups on the cultural and geographical margins of the emerging nation: Eurasians, Orang Asli (aborigines) and the Malays of southern Siam. The left-wing API had signalled its willingness to accept Eurasians, the descendants of Dutch and Portuguese colonists, as Malay. But UMNO clung to a more rigid conception. When the Eurasian associations applied to the Malay rulers to become non-Muslim subjects, UMNO rejected the application, thus confirming the narrow (i.e. Malay only) utility the reinvented rulers would have for the Malaysian future.[53] On the other hand, UMNO was eager to incorporate the Orang Asli into the Malay fold, an effort it pursued through education in combination with Islamisation.[54] In this UMNO can be seen to have inherited the colonial state's posture towards the Orang Asli, who were viewed by both as uncivilised and in need of protection. Finally, the Malays of southern Siam generated a flurry of publicity in the immediate postwar period. They had long been under the control of the Siamese, whose centralising and Thai-icising activities were becoming more and more burdensome. Despite the appeal in restoring the 'original' boundaries of the Malay world and an abundance of sympathy within UMNO for the plight of these Malays, the party leadership kept the issue firmly off the agenda.[55] In these three cases, as well as in the larger challenge of alternative visions of a Malay nation state, UMNO faithfully conformed to the ethnic, cultural and geographical map of British Malaya.

UMNO had to appeal to popular nationalism as its main source of political legitimacy after the Second World War, but its adherence to the forms and priorities of the colonial state would produce an uncomfortable distance (rather than congruence) between nation and state. UMNO's nationalism was reactive, the appropriation of a timely discourse in an effort to preserve ruling class hegemony. It may most accurately be termed 'official nationalism', following Benedict Anderson's description: 'an anticipatory strategy adopted by dominant groups who are threatened with marginalization or exclusion from an emerging nationally-imagined community'.[56] In its use of traditional elements of Malay culture, UMNO's was much like the official nationalism of Siamese elites who utilised

53 UMNO/GA 28/47; MSS PIJ, nos. 20 and 21 (1947).

54 UMNO/SG 74/46. Onn favoured appointing a Malay officer to be responsible for the welfare of the Orang Asli. MSS PIJ, no. 3 (1947).

55 BMA/ADM 9/16; *Majlis*, 7, 12 and 25 February 1946; MSS PIJ, supplement to no. 16 – Political Developments in Siam and their Probable Effect on Malaya, 1947.

56 Benedict Anderson, *Imagined Communities. Reflections on the Origin and Spread of Nationalism*, rev. ed., London and New York: Verso, 1991, p. 101.

monarchy and religion to consolidate their position in society. Official nationalism in Malaya succeeded not because of its own strength or an ability to mobilise popular forces, which it sent home after the Malayan Union demonstrations. (In fact, most aristocrats 'went home' themselves, to jobs in the state administrations.) The colonial state's continuous narrowing of the range of acceptable political activity, combined with UMNO's appropriation and depoliticisation of those nationalist symbols and activities, left little choice but official nationalism by mid-1948.

In 1957, UMNO attained independence within an Alliance coalition with the 'mainstream' parties of other ethnic groups. But did UMNO embrace, let alone achieve, the goals of popular Malay nationalism? Judging by three important criteria, it clearly did not. First, the primacy of Malay language and culture was central to the emergent nationalism of the prewar period. After independence, the Malay language was added to English for (some) official purposes, but did not supplant it. This policy protected the monopoly of the English educated and maintained the foreignness of the state to those literate only in Malay. A second central demand was for improvement in Malay economic status. However, UMNO's class alliance with the Malayan Chinese Association protected existing Chinese economic activities. At the same time, continuing British ownership of important sectors of the economy was preferred to increased Chinese dominance. As a result, economic nationalism against foreign ownership of the economy was moderate in comparison with other Southeast Asian states.[57]

Finally, mobilisation against the Malayan Union had revealed deep Malay discomfort with the construction of a nation which ignored their special connection with *tanah Melayu*. The Malayan Union had denied that contiguity of people and territory. If anyone who called the peninsula 'home' could be called a Malayan, there would be no exclusivity, resulting in an unacceptably porous nation. The Malayan Union, in other words, had put naturalisation before definition. In opposing these blows to an emerging nationality, Malay opposition to the Union rejected the Union's characterisation of the territory: Malaya (as in Federation of Malaya for *Persekutuan Tanah Melayu*) was an acceptable translation of *Melayu*, but the hated Malayan (Who are these so-called Malayans? asked Tunku Abdul Rahman) was not. It also insisted that *tanah Melayu* belonged to the Malays, who alone should be entitled to the modern rights of national citizenship.

---

57 Frank Golay, 'Malaya', in Frank H. Golay, Ralph Anspach, M. Ruth Pfanner and Eliezer B. Ayal, *Underdevelopment and Economic Nationalism in Southeast Asia*, Ithaca: Cornell University Press, 1969, pp. 330–48.

Although that Union was defeated under UMNO's leadership, the victory was pyrrhic. Within five years, over half of Malaya's Chinese and Indian residents were granted citizenship. UMNO's anti-Malayan Union campaign was successful for the bureaucratic elite, who would enjoy a privileged position within a multiethnic federation. But it was unsuccessful for the kind of nationalism it purported to represent – Malaya for the Malays.

As the ruling party, UMNO made few alterations to the inherited state, so the essential relationship of Malay nationalism to that state stagnated as well and continued to be articulated in terms of special privilege and protection. Aristocratic hijacking of the nationalist movement had prevented the logical next step in the development of popular Malay nationalism: a restructuring of society in which all citizens had equal access to the benefits of nationhood. The continued hegemony of the traditional leadership perpetuated the following types of ideas: that few Malays were qualified for leadership positions; that Malays were in danger of being overrun by foreigners in their own land, like the 'Red Indians' of America; and that what Malays continued to need, above all, was protection. The popular Malay nationalism which survived independence was a colonial form, encouraged to look to archaisms like the rulers for validation and satisfaction.

UMNO would remain unresponsive to the nationalism of the mass of Malays until captured by a new generation in the 1970s. Its relationship with the rulers also continued to reflect the transformation wrought by Onn at the Station Hotel in 1946. Because the aristocracy had used the legitimising power of the rulers to deflect radical criticism against itself, it was unable to move as decisively against royal power as it may have wished. And because the status and power of the rulers were the very things at stake in the Malayan Union crisis, the rulers remained centre stage during negotiations to determine the Malayan Union's successor state. The rulers came out of the crisis with veto power over constitutional change and the green light to further elaborate their traditional positions. After Onn, neither power was seriously challenged until Mahathir Mohamad became prime minister. The first non-aristocratic leader of UMNO and the country, Mahathir moved away from traditionalism as a mechanism of power, even as his modernisation of Malay life remained in constant dialogue with it and even though he retained inherited features of it, such as autocratic control over the party. In 1983 and again in 1992 and 1993, Mahathir moved to cut back the rulers' political powers and legal privileges. During both confrontations, Mahathir appealed to the popular nationalism Onn had repressed in 1946. Temporarily lifting the legal ban on criticising the rulers, Mahathir allowed Malaysian newspapers to unleash a barrage of outraged commentary on the personal and financial corruption of Malay royalty. Mahathir also showed how well he understood the dynamic of the 1946 aristocrat–ruler conflict. During the constitutional crisis of 1983, he staged a mass rally at Batu Pahat, Johor, the site of the second Congress meeting at which UMNO was founded, reminding citizens and rulers alike of the inversion of ruler and *rakyat* which began the modern political era.

Glossary of Non-English Terms

akal	reason
apuskan perentah Inggeris	abolish English rule
balai	ceremonial hall
bangsa	race or nation
bangsa Melayu	Malay race or nation
bendahara	chief minister
bergerak	to move
berikrar taat stia	pledge loyalty
berkerajaan sendiri	self-government
bersatu	unity
bunga mas dan perak	gold and silver flowers
campur tangan	intrusive interference, lit. mix hand/arm
darah	blood
daulat	ruler's divine attribute
daulat rakyat	power of the people
daulat tuanku syah alam	hail, my lord, king on earth
derhaka	treason, disloyalty
dipecat	suspended
halal	permitted
hamba	slave or dependent
haram	forbidden
hartal	strike
hikayat	court-generated historical narrative
Indonesia Merdeka	Free Indonesia
'Indonesia Raya'	Indonesia's national anthem, lit. Greater Indonesia
istana	ruler's residence
jawi	modified Arabic script for Malay
kampung	village
kathi	state Islamic official
kaum	group
kebangsaan	national

kedaulatan	sovereignty
kedaulatan rakyat	people's sovereignty
kenegerian	regional
kerah	corvée labour
kerajaan	traditional Malay polity, lit. condition of having a ruler
kesetiaan	loyalty
ketua kampung	village head
ketuanan Melayu	Malay supremacy
Koa Kunrenjo	Japanese leadership training schools
kris	dagger
kuasa	authority given to someone by the ruler
laxamana	chief, sometimes admiral
madrasah	modern Islamic school
manis	graceful
mara	progress
Melayu jati	true Malay
Melayu Raya	Greater Malaya
menghina	insult
menjual negerinya	selling states
menteri	chief
menteri besar	chief minister
merah-putih	red-and-white, the Indonesian national flag
merdeka	free, independent
muafakat	consultation, consensus
mukim	subdistrict
naungan	protection
negeri	state
Nippon-go	Japanese language
orang kaya menteri	senior (rich) chief
parang	knife
pemerintahan cara feudalism	feudalistic government
penaung	protector
penghulu	subdistrict chief, village head
pentadbiran	administration
perang mulut	war of words
percaya	belief
pertubuhan	organisation
peterana	mat of honour
raja muda	heir apparent

rakyat	common people, subject class or (lately) citizens
rakyat jelata	common people, the masses
rantau	outlying area
rumi	romanised Malay
saudara	brother
setia	loyalty
shahbandar	intermediary between traders and a ruler
singgasana	royal dais
songkok	formal rimless hat
tanah Melayu	the Malay states, lit. Malay land
temenggung	state minister
tuan	sir
ulu	upriver
umat	community
undang	territorial chief
yam tuan besar	paramount ruler
zaman gemilang	brilliant era, i.e. fifteenth-century Melaka
zaman mas	golden age

Bibliography

Unpublished Sources

Arkib Negara Malaysia, Kuala Lumpur

BMA/ADM	British Military Administration, Administrative
BMA/DEPT	British Military Administration, Departmental
BMA/SCAO	British Military Administration, Senior Civil Affairs Officer
BMA/PR	British Military Administration, Public Relations Department
BMA/FIN	British Military Administration, Finance
MU	Malayan Union Secretariat
UMNO	UMNO Files

National Archives, Kew, London

CO 273	Colonial Office: Straits Settlements Original Correspondence
CO 437/2	Colonial Office: Pahang Sessional Papers. Annual Reports
CO 469/13	Colonial Office and Successors: Selangor: Government Gazette
CO 537/2145	Malayan Union: Reactions to constitutional proposals: Miscellaneous correspondence
CO 875	Colonial Office: Public Relations Department, later Information Department: Registered Files
CO 882	War and Colonial Department and Colonial Office: Confidential Print Eastern. Straits Settlements
WO 203	War Office: South East Asia Command: Military Headquarters Papers, Second World War. South East Asia Command. Malaya: constitutional policy: relations with Sultans

Rhodes House Library, Oxford

MSS PIJ	Malayan Security Service, Political Intelligence Journal

Published Government Sources

Donnison, F.S.V., *British Military Administration in the Far East, 1943–46*, London: Her Majesty's Stationery Office, 1956.

Malaya, Federation of, Department of Public Relations, 'Political crime in Malaya. Vigilant efforts of police', 4 February 1949.

Mountbatten of Burma, Earl, *Post Surrender Tasks: Section E of the Report to the Combined Chiefs of Staff by the Supreme Allied Commander South East Asia, 1943–1945*, London: Her Majesty's Stationery Office, 1969.

Nathan, J.E., *The Census of British Malaya 1921*, London: Dunstable & Waterford, 1922.

Sheppard, Mubin, *The Malay Regiment, 1933–1947*, Kuala Lumpur: Department of Public Relations, Malay Peninsula, 1947.

Staniforth, N., comp., *Papers on Malay Subjects. The Malay Regiment*, Port Dickson: Malay Regiment, 1950.

Vlieland, C.A., *British Malaya: A Report on the 1931 Census and on Certain Problems of Vital Statistics*, London: Waterlow & Sons, 1932.

Contemporary Newspapers and Periodicals

Democrat (Kuala Lumpur, English)
Kenchana (Singapore, Malay)
Majlis (Kuala Lumpur, Malay)
Malay Mail (Kuala Lumpur, English)
Pelita Malaya (Penang, Malay)
Semboyan Baharu (Penang, Malay)
Seruan Rakyat (Kuala Lumpur, Malay)
Straits Times, The (Singapore, English)
Suara Rakyat (Ipoh, Malay)
Suara Saberkas (Alor Setar, Malay)
Sunday Mail (Kuala Lumpur, English)
Utusan Melayu (Singapore, Malay)
Voice of the People (Ipoh, English)
Warta Ahad (Singapore, Malay)
Warta Negara (Penang, Malay)

Books and Articles

A. Kahar Bador, 'Social rank, status-honour and social class consciousness amongst the Malays', in Hans-Dieter Evers, ed., *Modernization in South-East Asia*, Kuala Lumpur: Oxford University Press, 1973, pp. 132–49.

A. Samad Ahmad, *Sejambak Kenangan: Sebuah Autobiografi*, Kuala Lumpur: Dewan Bahasa dan Pustaka, 1981.

Abdul Latiff Abu Bakar, *Ishak Haji Muhammad: Penulis dan Ahli Politik Sehingga 1948*, Kuala Lumpur: University of Malaya Press, 1977.

Abdul Rahman Hj. Ismail, 'Kewibawaan mutlak raja dan ketaatsetiaan mutlak rakyat kepada raja', *Kajian Malaysia*, vol. 3, no. 1, 1985, pp. 32–57.

Abinales, Patricio N. and Donna J. Amoroso, *State and Society in the Philippines*, Lanham MD: Rowman & Littlefield, 2005.

Adams, Theodore, 'The Malay in Malaya', *Asiatic Review*, vol. 40, no. 141, 1944, pp. 98–100.

Ahmad bin Masjidin, 'Malayan Union dari kaca matt *Warta Negara*', in Khoo Kay Kim, ed., *Sejarah Masyarakat Melayu Moden*, Kuala Lumpur: Jabatan Sejarah, Universiti Malaya, 1984.

Ahmad Boestamam, *Carving the Path to the Summit*, trans. William R. Roff, Athens: Ohio University Press, 1979.

Ahmad Boestamam, *Datuk Onn Yang Saya Kenal*, Kuala Lumpur: Adabi, 1979.

Ahmad Fauzi Abdul Hamid and Muhamad Takiyuddin Ismail, 'The monarchy and party politics in Malaysia in the era of Abdullah Badawi (2003–09): The resurgence of the role of the protector', *Asian Survey*, vol. 52, no. 5, 2012, pp. 924–48.

Ahmad Fauzi Abdul Hamid and Muhamad Takiyuddin Ismail, 'The monarchy in Malaysia: struggling for legitimacy', *Kyoto Review of Southeast Asia*, issue 13, 2013, at: http://kyotoreview.org/issue-13/the-monarchy-in-malaysia-struggling-for-legitimacy/.

Akashi, Yoji, 'Japanese military administration: its formation and evolution in reference to the sultans, the Islamic religion, and the Moslem Malays, 1941–45', *Asian Studies*, vol. 7, no. 1, 1969, pp. 81–110.

Alatas, Syed Hussein, 'Feudalism in Malaysian society: a study of historical continuity', *Civilisations*, vol. 18, no. 4, 1968, pp. 579–92.

Allen, James de Vere, *The Malayan Union*, New Haven: Yale University Southeast Asian Studies, 1967.

Allen, James de Vere, 'The elephant and the mousedeer – a new version: Anglo-Kedah relations, 1905–1915', *Journal of the Malaysian Branch of the Royal Asiatic Society*, vol. 41, no. 1, 1968, pp. 54–94.

Andaya, Barbara Watson, 'The nature of the state in eighteenth century Perak', in Anthony Reid and Lance Castles, eds, *Pre-Colonial State Systems in Southeast Asia*, Kuala Lumpur: Malaysian Branch of the Royal Asiatic Society, Monograph no. 6, 1975, pp. 22–35.

Andaya, Barbara Watson and Leonard Y. Andaya, *A History of Malaysia*, London: Macmillan, 1982.

Anderson, Benedict, 'Japan: "The Light of Asia"', in Josef Silverstein, ed., *Southeast Asia in World War II: Four Essays*, New Haven: Yale University Southeast Asia Studies, 1966, pp. 13–50.

Anderson, Benedict, 'Studies of the Thai state: The state of Thai studies', in Eliezer B. Ayal, ed., *The Study of Thailand*, Athens: Ohio University Center for International Studies, 1978, pp. 193–247.

Anderson, Benedict, *Imagined Communities: Reflections on the Origin and Spread of Nationalism*, rev. ed., London and New York: Verso, 1991.

Angkatan Sasterawan '50, *Memoranda: Kumpulan Tulisan Angkatan Sasterawan '50 Dengan Lampiran Rumusan Kongres Bahasa dan Persuratan Melayu Ketiga*, Kuala Lumpur: Oxford University Press, 1962.

Anwar Abdullah, *Dato Onn: Riwayat Hidup*, Petaling Jaya: Pustaka Nusantara, 1971.

Ariffin Omar, *Bangsa Melayu: Malay Concepts of Democracy and Community, 1945–1950*, Kuala Lumpur: Oxford University Press, 1993.

Buckley, Charles Burton, *An Anecdotal History of Old Times in Singapore 1819–1977*, with introduction by C.M. Turnbull, Singapore: Oxford University Press, 1984, first pub. 1902.

Burney, Henry, *The Burney Papers*, repr., Farnborough: Gregg International Publishers, 1971, repr. of 1910–1913 ed.

Burns, P.L., 'Introduction', in R.J. Wilkinson, ed., *Papers on Malay Subjects*, Kuala Lumpur: Oxford University Press, 1971, pp. 1–10.

Burridge, Kenelm O.L., 'Racial relations in Johore', *Australian Journal of Politics and History*, vol. 2, no. 2, 1957, pp. 151–68.

Butcher, John, *The British in Malaya, 1880–1941: The Social History of a European Community in Colonial Southeast Asia*, Kuala Lumpur: Oxford University Press, 1979.

Cannadine, David, 'The context, performance and meaning of ritual: the British monarchy and the "invention of tradition", c. 1820–1977', in Eric Hobsbawm and Terence Ranger, eds, *The Invention of Tradition*, Cambridge: Cambridge University Press, 1983, pp. 101–64.

Chandra Muzaffar, *Protector? An Analysis of the Concept and Practice of Loyalty in Leader-led Relationships within Malay Society*, Penang: Aliran, 1979.

Chatterjee, Partha, *Nationalist Thought and the Colonial World: A Derivative Discourse*, Minneapolis: University of Minnesota Press, 1986.

Cheah Boon Kheng, 'Some aspects of the interregnum in Malaya', *Journal of Southeast Asian Studies*, vol. 8, no. 1, 1977, pp. 48–74.

Cheah Boon Kheng, 'The social impact of the Japanese occupation of Malaya (1942–1945)', in Alfred W. McCoy, ed., *Southeast Asia Under Japanese Occupation*, New Haven: Yale University Southeast Asia Studies, 1980, pp. 75–103.

Cheah Boon Kheng, *Red Star Over Malaya: Resistance and Social Conflict During and After the Japanese Occupation of Malaya, 1941–1946*, Singapore: Singapore University Press, 1983.

Cheah Boon Kheng, ed., *Tokoh-Tokoh Tempatan dan Dokumen-Dokumen dalam Sejarah Malaysia*, Penang: Universiti Sains Malaysia, 1982.

Chin Kee Onn, *Malaya Upside Down*, Singapore: Federal Publications, 1976, first pub. 1946.

Clifford, Hugh, *Saleh: A Prince of Malaya*, Singapore: Oxford University Press, 1989, first pub. 1926.

Cohn, Bernard S., 'Representing authority in Victorian India', in Eric Hobsbawm and Terence Ranger, eds, *The Invention of Tradition*, Cambridge: Cambridge University Press, 1983, pp. 165–210.

Dodd, E.E., *The New Malaya*, London: Fabian Publications, 1946.

Emerson, Rupert, *Malaysia: A Study in Direct and Indirect Rule*, New York: Macmillan, 1937.

Firdaus Haji Abdullah, *Radical Malay Politics: Its Origins and Early Development*, Petaling Jaya: Pelanduk Publications, 1985.

Fujitani, Takashi, 'Electronic pageantry and Japan's "symbolic emperor"', *Journal of Asian Studies*, vol. 51, no. 4, 1992, pp. 824–50.

Funston, John, *Malay Politics in Malaysia: A Study of the United Malays National Organization and Party Islam*, Kuala Lumpur: Heinemann, 1980.

Gellner, Ernest, *Nations and Nationalism*, Ithaca: Cornell University Press, 1983.

Golay, Frank H., Ralph Anspach, M. Ruth Pfanner and Eliezer B. Ayal, *Underdevelopment and Economic Nationalism in Southeast Asia*, Ithaca: Cornell University Press, 1969.

Gomez, Edmund Terence and Johan Saravanamuttu, eds, *The New Economic Policy in Malaysia: Affirmative Action, Ethnic Inequalities and Social Justice*, Petaling Jaya: Strategic Information and Research Development Centre, 2012.

Gullick, J.M., *Indigenous Political Systems of Western Malaya*, London: University of London, Athlone Press, 1958.

Gullick, J.M., *Malay Society in the Late Nineteenth Century*, Singapore: Oxford University Press, 1989.

Gullick, J.M., *Rulers and Residents: Influence and Power in the Malay States, 1870–1920*, Singapore: Oxford University Press, 1992.

Habermas, Jürgen, *The Structural Transformation of the Public Sphere: An Inquiry into a Category of Bourgeois Society*, Cambridge: MIT Press, 1989.

Harper, T.N., 'The politics of disease and disorder in post-war Malaya', *Journal of Southeast Asian Studies*, vol. 21, no. 1, 1990, pp. 88–113.

Hobsbawm, Eric, 'Introduction: inventing traditions', in Eric Hobsbawm and Terence Ranger, eds, *The Invention of Tradition*, Cambridge: Cambridge University Press, 1983, pp. 1–14.

Hooker, Virginia and Norani Othman, eds, *Malaysia: Islam, Society and Politics*, Singapore: Institute of Southeast Asian Studies, 2003.

Ibrahim Mahmood, *Sejarah Perjuangan Bangsa Melayu*, Kuala Lumpur: Pustaka Antara, 1981

Innes, Emily, *The Chersonese with the Gilding Off*, Kuala Lumpur: Oxford University Press, 1974, first pub. 1885.

Ishak bin Tadin, 'Dato Onn and Malay nationalism, 1946–51', *Journal of Southeast Asian History*, vol. 1, no. 1, 1960, pp. 56–88.

Jomo Kwame Sundaram, *A Question of Class: Capital, the State, and Uneven Development in Malaya*, New York: Monthly Review Press, 1988.

Kahn, Joel S. and Francis Loh Kok Wah, eds, *Fragmented Vision: Culture and Politics in Contemporary Malaysia*, Honolulu: University of Hawaii Press, 1992.

Kassim Ahmad, *Characterization in Hikayat Hang Tuah*, Kuala Lumpur: Dewan Bahasa dan Pustaka, 1966.

Kershaw, Roger, 'Difficult synthesis: recent trends in Malay political sociology and history', *Southeast Asian Journal of Social Science* vol. 16, no. 1, 1988, pp. 134–58.

Kessler, Clive, 'Archaism and modernity', in Joel S. Kahn and Francis Loh Kok Wah, eds, *Fragmented Vision: Culture and Politics in Contemporary Malaysia*, Honolulu: University of Hawaii Press, 1992, pp. 133–57.

Khasnor Johan, *The Emergence of the Modern Malay Administrative Elite*, Singapore: Oxford University Press, 1984.

Khoo Kay Kim, *The Western Malay States, 1850–1873: The Effect of Commercial Development on Malay Politics*, Kuala Lumpur: Oxford University Press, 1972.

Khoo Kay Kim, 'Malay society, 1874–1920s', *Journal of Southeast Asian Studies*, vol. 5, no. 2, 1974, pp. 179–98.

Lau, Albert, *The Malayan Union Controversy, 1942–1948*, Singapore: Oxford University Press, 1991.

Levenson, Joseph R., *Confucian China and its Modern Fate: The Problem of Intellectual Continuity*, London: Routledge and Kegan Paul, 1958.

Loh Fook-Seng, Philip, 'A review of the educational developments in the Federated Malay States to 1939', *Journal of Southeast Asian Studies*, vol. 5, no. 2, 1974, pp. 225–38.

Low, James, trans., *Merong Mahawangsa* (The Keddah Annals), Bangkok: The American Presbyterian Mission Press, 1908, pp. 253–55.

Mahathir Mohamad, *The Malay Dilemma*, Singapore: Times Books International, 1970.

Maier, Hendrik M.J., *In the Center of Authority: The Malay Hikayat Merong Mahawangsa*, Ithaca NY: Cornell University Southeast Asia Program, 1988.

Manderson, Lenore, *Women, Politics, and Change: The Kaum Ibu UMNO, Malaysia, 1945–1972*, Kuala Lumpur: Oxford University Press, 1980.

Marx, Karl and Friedrich Engels, 'Manifesto of the Communist Party', in Eugene Kamenka, ed., *The Portable Karl Marx*, New York: Viking Penguin, 1983, first pub. 1848, pp. 203–41.

McCoy, Alfred W., 'Introduction', in Alfred W. McCoy, ed., *Southeast Asia Under Japanese Occupation*, New Haven: Yale University Southeast Asia Studies, 1980, pp. 1–13.

Milner, A.C., *Kerajaan: Malay Political Culture on the Eve of Colonial Rule*, Tucson: University of Arizona Press, 1982.

Milner, Anthony, *The Invention of Politics in Colonial Malaya: Contesting Nationalism and the Expansion of the Public Sphere*, Cambridge: Cambridge University Press, 1994.

Milner, Anthony, '"Identity monarchy": interrogating heritage for a divided Malaysia', *Southeast Asian Studies*, vol. 1, no. 2, 2012, pp. 191–212.

Mohammad Yunus Hamidi, *Sejarah Pergerakan Melayu Semenanjung*, Kuala Lumpur: Pustaka Antara, 1961.

Mohd. Taib Osman, *The Language of the Editorials in Malay Vernacular Newspapers Up to 1941*, Kuala Lumpur: Dewan Bahasa dan Pustaka, 1966.

Muda Mohd. Taib A. Rahman, 'Pendudukan Jepun di Terengganu', in Khoo Kay Kim, ed., *Sejarah Masyarakat Melayu Moden*, Kuala Lumpur: Jabatan Sejarah, Universiti Malaya, 1984.

Muhamad Ikmal Said, 'Malay nationalism and national identity', in Muhamad Ikmal Said and Zahid Emby, eds, *Malaysia: Critical Perspectives: Essays in Honour of Syed Husin Ali*, Petaling Jaya: Persatuan Sains Sosial Malaysia, 1996, pp. 34–73.

Muhammad Ghazzali, 'Court language and etiquette of the Malays', *Journal of the Malay Branch of the Royal Asiatic Society*, vol. 11, pt. 2, 1933, pp. 273-87.

Ongkili, James, *Nation-Building in Malaysia, 1946–1974*, Singapore: Oxford University Press, 1985.

Parkinson, C. Northcote, *British Intervention in Malaya, 1867–1877*, Kuala Lumpur: University of Malaya Press, 1964.

Ramli, Dol, *History of the Malay Regiment, 1933–1942*, Singapore: Regimental Committee of the Royal Malay Regiment, 1963.

Ranger, Terence, 'The invention of tradition in colonial Africa', in Eric Hobsbawm and Terence Ranger, eds, *The Invention of Tradition*, Cambridge: Cambridge University Press, 1983, pp. 211–62.

Reid, Anthony, *The Blood of the People: Revolution and the End of Traditional Rule in Northern Sumatra*, Kuala Lumpur: Oxford University Press, 1979.

Roff, William R., 'Kaum muda–kaum tua: innovation and reaction amongst the Malays, 1900–1941', in K.G. Treggoning, ed., *Papers on Malayan History*, Singapore: Journal of South-East Asian History, 1962, pp. 162–92.

Roff, William R., *The Origins of Malay Nationalism*, Kuala Lumpur: University of Malaya Press, 1980, first pub. 1967.

Rustam Sani, 'Melayu Raya as a Malay "nation of intent"', in H.M. Dahlan, ed., *The Nascent Malaysian Society: Developments, Trends and Problems*, Bangi: Jabatan Antropologi dan Sociologi, Universiti Kebangsaan Malaysia, 1976, pp. 25–38.

Sadka, Emily, *The Protected Malay States, 1874–1895*, Kuala Lumpur: University of Malaya Press, 1968.

Scott, James C., *Domination and the Arts of Resistance: Hidden Transcripts*, New Haven: Yale University Press, 1990.

Shaharil Talib, *After Its Own Image: The Trengganu Experience, 1881–1941*, Singapore: Oxford University Press, 1984.

Shaharuddin b. Maaruf, *Concept of a Hero in Malay Society*, Singapore and Kuala Lumpur: Eastern Universities Press, 1984.

Shaharuddin Maaruf, *Malay Ideas on Development: From Feudal Lord to Capitalist*, Singapore and Kuala Lumpur: Times Books International, 1988.

Sheppard, Mubin, *Taman Budiman: Memoirs of an Unorthodox Civil Servant*, Kuala Lumpur: Heinemann, 1979.

Smith, Simon C., *British Relations with the Malay Rulers from Decentralization to Malayan Independence, 1930–1957*, Kuala Lumpur: Oxford University Press, 1995.

Soenarno, Radin, 'Malay nationalism, 1900–1945', *Journal of Southeast Asian History*, vol. 1, no. 1, 1960, pp. 1–27.

Stockwell, A.J., *British Policy and Malay Politics During the Malayan Union Experiment, 1945–46*, Kuala Lumpur: Malaysian Branch of the Royal Asiatic Society, Monograph no. 8, 1979.

Sutherland, Heather, 'The taming of the Trengganu elite', in Ruth McVey, ed., *Southeast Asian Transitions: Approaches through Social History*, New Haven: Yale University Press, 1978, pp. 32–85.

Suwannathat-Pian, Kobkua, *Palace, Political Party and Power: A Story of the Socio-Political Development of Malay Kingship*, Singapore: National University of Singapore Press, 2011.

Sweeney, Amin, *Reputations Live On: An Early Malay Autobiography*, Berkeley: University of California Press, 1980.

Sweeney, Amin, *A Full Hearing: Orality and Literacy in the Malay World*, Berkeley: University of California Press, 1987.

Syed Husin Ali, 'Patterns of rural leadership in Malaya', *Journal of the Malaysian Branch of the Royal Asiatic Society*, vol. 41, no. 1, 1968, pp. 95–145.

Syed Husin Ali, *Malay Peasant Society and Leadership*, Kuala Lumpur: Oxford University Press, 1975.

Syed Husin Ali, *The Malays: Their Problems and Future*, Kuala Lumpur: Heinemann Asia, 1981.

Syed Husin Ali, *The Malay Rulers: Regression or Reform?* Petaling Jaya: Strategic Information and Research Development Centre, 2013.

Tan Liok Ee, *The Rhetoric of Bangsa and Minzu: Community and Nation in Tension, The Malay Peninsula 1900–1955*, Clayton, Victoria: Monash University, Centre of Southeast Asian Studies, 1988.

Tan Sooi Beng, *Bangsawan: A Social and Stylistic History of Popular Malay Opera*, Singapore: Oxford University Press, 1993.

Thio, Eunice, *British Policy in the Malay Peninsula, 1880–1910. Vol. 1. The Southern and Central States*, Singapore: University of Malaya Press, 1969.

Thompson, Virginia, *Post-Mortem on Malaya*, New York: Macmillan, 1943.

Thongchai Winichakul, *Siam Mapped: A History of the Geo-Body of a Nation*, Honolulu: University of Hawaii Press, 1994.

Trocki, Carl A., *Prince of Pirates: The Temenggongs and the Development of Johor and Singapore, 1784–1885*, Singapore: Singapore University Press, 1979.

Wan Abdul Kadir, *Budaya Popular Dalam Masyarakat Melayu Bandaran*, Kuala Lumpur: Dewan Bahasa dan Pustaka, 1988.

Wilkinson, R.J., *A History of the Peninsular Malays with Chapters on Perak and Selangor*, 3rd ed., rev., Singapore: Kelly and Walsh, 1923.

Wilkinson, R.J., *Life and Customs: Part One: The Incidents of Malay Life*, Kuala Lumpur: Federated Malay States Government Press, 1925.

Wilkinson, R.J., ed., *Papers on Malay Subjects*, selected and introduced by P.L. Burns, Kuala Lumpur: Oxford University Press, 1971, first pub. c. 1907.

Winstedt, R.O., *A History of Malaya*, Singapore: Malayan Branch of the Royal Asiatic Society, 1935.

Winstedt, R.O., *The Malays: A Cultural History*, 5th ed., London: Routledge and Kegan Paul, 1961, first pub. 1947.

Winstedt, R.O., ed., *Malaya: The Straits Settlements and the Federated and Unfederated Malay States*, London: Constable, 1923.

Wolters, O.W., *The Fall of Srivijaya in Malay History*, Kuala Lumpur: Oxford University Press, 1970.

Zakiah Hanum, *Tercabarnya Maruah Bangsa: Satu Himpunan Pemikiran Wartawan Akhbar Majlis 1945–1948*, Kuala Lumpur: Penerbitan Lajmeidakh, 1987.

Zulkipli bin Mahmud, *Warta Malaya: Penyambung Lidah Bangsa Melayu, 1930–1941*, Bangi: Jabatan Sejarah, Universiti Kebangsaan Malaysia, 1979.

Index